KNOW WHO YOU ARE!

by

LADY WISE

KNOW WHO YOU ARE!

The content of this book is intended to inform, entertain and provoke your thinking. This is not intended as medical advice. That is your choice. It is your life and health in your hands. The intent of the author is only to offer information of a general nature to help you in your quest for emotional and spiritual well-being. Neither the author nor the publisher can be held responsible or liable for any loss or claim arising from the use or the misuse of the content of this book.

EBook ISBN: 978-1-8384275-3-5
Paperback ISBN: 978-1-8384275-2-8

Published by Lady Wise
Typeset by Raspberry Creative Type

KNOW WHO YOU ARE!

by
LADY WISE

Letter of Introduction

Aloha Mahalo,

Welcome to 'Know Who You Are!' as the esoteric book of choice
Where you can relax, read and listen to your own inner voice
Allow me to inspire you with creativity and open your eyes
Together let's expect the unexpected and be informed by the surprise!
On self-development and self-transformation I hope to bring you fun in learning
Mixed with laughter, wisdom, knowledge and joy in a style distinctly discerning
This is all about the discovery of love and your sense of self
As you can live and laugh in joy with active health and wealth
You are never alone on this journey, just ask yourself "What do I feel?"
Keep an open mind to things you don't know that might be real!
What if there are esoteric things bigger than you were ever told?

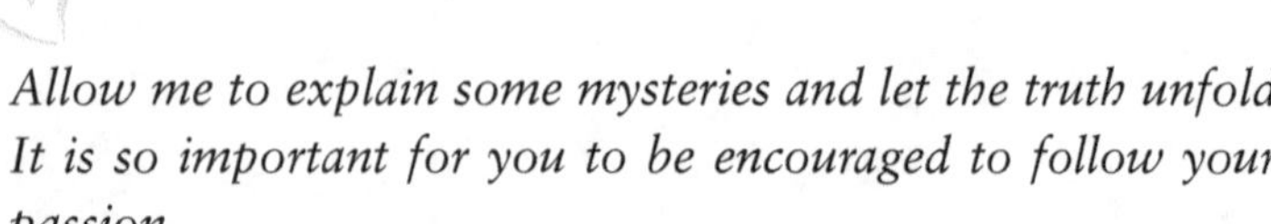

Allow me to explain some mysteries and let the truth unfold
It is so important for you to be encouraged to follow your passion
Especially in this time of the Shift when the currency of compassion is in fashion!
Live your life in happiness from the heart of your being
Never lose sight of heart coherence and the ability of feeling!

Remember, there is no-one like YOU! You are one of a kind with the capability to become one with the mind and the universe. WOW!

Do you know the real power and truth of who you are? Do you realise that everything is changeable? This may come as a surprise or a shock to you, but you do know that you are in charge of your own destiny, don't you? You are the master builder of every nano second of your life. You can choose to have full creative control over everything that you think, say and do! Did you know that when you have the intention, you can enjoy inner peace too? It is time for you to understand with a heightened awareness that you are the only one who can use spiritual logic (much of which is now supported by science) to better understand 'WHO AM I?'

You are the only one who can define you!

Do you wonder why is there so much drama, sorrow, disappointment, pain, hurt and warring on planet earth? There is an explanation for this at this particular time and so do not despair. Hope is at hand. Is it possible that there is a system of love that is so beautiful that it exists only for YOU and is active and waiting for you, with FREE CHOICE, to awaken to its power, to awaken to YOUR power? Perhaps it would only take the willingness to open a door, metaphorically speaking, that once opened, allows the light to pour in and shine in you, in your beautiful, sacred heart? In the passing and the coming and the going of the eternal cycle of birth, death, birth, death, birth, death on this planet, we are each of us so dearly loved by invisible energies. Do you believe that you have the compassion in your heart and mind to be healed and to be free of worry, anxiety, fear and stress?

It takes some soul searching and courage to better understand why many of us are not 'at ease' with our whole being. Today, we have an ageing demographic across the world and among other issues continue to witness the burden of disease. Perhaps, however, you have never looked at this word in a different light before and observed how the word disease is formed: 'dis-ease'. Yes, this is one of the puzzles of life that whenever any of us has any kind of ailment, temporary or permanent, we are effectively out of balance and out of comfort with ourselves. The greatest human need for many is the demand for improved healthcare. Yet, the safest and most efficient health and care system we have wherever we are, provided it is nurtured and treated with tender love and care through "self-love", is remarkably our own human body and our connection to part of our DNA called innate! With an improved understanding of DNA, for example, and a more peaceful and compassionate countenance for which we were born, we can see a better way of doing things and connect with our consciousness that allows us to become healthy, free from dis-ease and even to start youthing.

Only with free thinking and an "open heart" approach to new discoveries will the magnificence of a self-supported medical intuitive body be recognised. So much on this topic is presently being scientifically proven. Kryon, the Magnetic Master and support entity helping in the evolution of

humanity at this time, suggests to us that we can with free will, choose to have soul communication that will enrich our life and our very existence for being alive! Welcome to an enhanced understanding of why we are alive so that we can better understand our life's purpose and have fun!

One of my favourite quotes from OSHO is:-

"

*Life means abundance, richness in
every possible dimension.*

This book is to inform about the present period of time on our planet called The Shift and the beauty of connecting and co-creating with the universe through free choice, to manifest a life of purpose, filled with love, compassion, harmony, kindness, peace, joy, laughter and unlimited abundance. It provides encouragement for you to open up to your real feelings and emotions. It gives hope through self-understanding to let your physical, emotional, mental and spiritual inclinations manifest your abilities to be balanced and to feel inner contentment no matter what nonsense is going on around you and in your life at any time.

It is a good time to reconnect with your own feelings. It is a good time to connect with your emotions. It is a good time to connect with your eternal soul and to the energy of who you are. It is a good time for personal healing. Indeed, there is no better time than NOW. You have wonderful capabilities that are remarkable, some of which are hidden and have not revealed themselves to you yet.

We are in a wonderful position to build the future one step at a time! Understand that there are better ways and new

solutions becoming available in this New Era. There are better ways to build new systems of all kinds across all disciplines. There are better ways to affect societies, governments, economics, politics, industries, financial markets, healthcare and agriculture to name just a few sectors. This is different from how it used to be. Remember that truth is relative to each person's path. This is experienced through intent, compassion and feeling the love of the creative source, God, spirit or by whatever name you choose, deep inside your heart. When you know yourself better, you understand and open up to a purpose in your life. You start to manifest a beautiful life for YOU! You are your own treasure of love, wisdom, joy and light energy. What a gift!

What happens next? You then have the good health and energy to find others who are as peaceful and benevolent as you, without frustration, to start creating the new world with peace on earth as the first goal. It will take time for as humans we are not the most patient of beings! Ha! Ha! You are in the right place at the right time for your highest good, thinking the right things for the right reasons! Embrace the synchronicity of mastery, maturity and wisdom. The centre of the creative source of the universe is providing the supportive, beneficient, loving energy that we all need for developing a beautiful way of love on planet earth. It has already started with the Old Souls and the need for honesty and integrity in all we do. The definition of an Old Soul is one who has lived at least one hundred lifetimes, perhaps even as many as a thousand lifetimes or more, on planet earth. The Old Souls are the futurists, the influential "Wayshowers" of the planet. They (we) are starting to awaken en masse but are often unsure of where to turn to for next steps in life as a way forward. Perhaps I can help?

When my Uncle (in name only) took seriously ill in Australia and was sent home to die with a life expectancy of only a couple of weeks, I felt compelled to write to him from Scotland and tell him of what I had been learning about the puzzle of life. I knew that in this present lifetime, all the knowledge that we choose to learn remains with our eternal soul when we physically die and is picked up again from the Cave of Creation for us to know and use when we are reborn. Every single lifetime builds a library of wisdom. As this lifetime is the most important lifetime ever in the history of planet earth, I wanted to make sure that my Uncle was departing his physical life with the most esoteric knowledge possible, so that he would return and be off to a flying start next time round!

I started to write to him most mornings and evenings and have modified the letters slightly for ease of delivery into 111 letters for you to read. They are of a personal story unfolding between two 'Old Souls' about which I knew would be controversial. Why? Well, my Uncle was a religious teacher and my information would most definitely stretch his current belief system and take him out of his traditional comfort zone! Were these teachings appropriate for a dying gentleman I hear you ask? It was a question that I too asked myself. I did not have much time to make a decision and so I chose to go with my gut feeling. My fast-track deliberation was made easy. My heart urged me to impart what I had learned and accepted as my truth, sweet in the knowledge that in hearing or reading these letters, my Uncle would similarly have the opportunity to either believe it or not! While a human can listen to information and choose not to believe it, the one thing that they cannot do, once it has been given, is to delete it! There is no 'Delete' key! We cannot 'unknow'

something. We can only choose either to act on the enhanced information that we have received or to ignore it. Ha! It is forever remembered at a soul level and our soul is eternal!

Many of you may have noticed that the children being born since 2012 are starting to grow up wiser than we did and often have a remembrance of who they were in a past lifetime. Indeed, one mother has already published a book about her two year old son who remembers that he previously experienced a lifetime as the famous cricket player, Lou Gehrig, and who, in this lifetime, is a remarkable baseball player despite his young age. The remembrance by an individual of their own Akashic records can be used to improve their current life in an enriched way.

Consciousness is starting to evolve. Some people are helping to raise the consciousness of this planet by placing a standing stone in their garden to increase the connection to Gaia (Mother Earth). It can be any size or type that you want it to be. The power of the connection to Gaia comes from your intention when you find your own stone and choose your place for it in your garden. The power of your intention for that stone is greater than the size of the stone that you select. If you decide to contribute to raising the earth's consciousness in this way, know that your choice of a 3cm high stone will be as powerful as someone who chooses a 3 metre high stone. Ha! Do not think your stone must be the equivalent size of one from Stonehenge, for example, for it to be effective. If you live in an apartment or a flat in a city, perhaps you may take great pleasure from placing a smaller standing stone in your window box. Yes, it will make a difference. Everything is entangled. Your standing stone will be in soil that is connected to the window box, connected to the structure of the building in which you live which in turn is

connected to Gaia and the various grids which will be explained to you. Let your light shine bright! Follow your own excitement and have gratitude for all of earth's creations!

Happy reading and enjoy taking time to get to know yourself better with this esoteric guide, "Know Who You Are!"

Thank you in advance for taking the time to nurture YOU with the help of my book! Congratulate yourself that you are alive here on planet earth at this important time! I hope you are beyond excited at the potential for enhancing your own soul journey in this lifetime. Remember to expect the unexpected and make your life count!

Much love, hugs and abundant blessings. Mahalo kokua!

With love and gratitude,

Lady Wise ♡
@LadyWiseWorld
www.ladywiseworld.com

Introduction

Once we understand ourselves better, we can overcome tendencies towards self-doubt, self-deception and the feeling of being taken advantage of by others. Any feelings of self-doubt are only negative energies that can hold us back from being the best version of ourselves. Why would you not want to be the best version of YOURSELF that you can be? This mindset can then be used in all things, personal and business to accelerate your own well-being and performance for ultimate personal satisfaction in whatever way you choose to live your life.

Lady Wise is keen to help seekers in connecting with and knowing their true relationship to their soul, to Source and their overall purpose for being here, through enhanced information, much of which she has received from Lee Carroll and the support entity Kryon, the Magnetic Master, in addition to her own channelled wisdom. The journey of self-development and self-transformation invites you to be patient with yourself as you remember how to reconnect with your inner world in love and with a feeling of harmony in all you do. When you are able to put your attention towards the purpose of bringing good things into your life for your highest good, you are closer to evolving as a balanced

person living in harmony and working with a natural energy that is within each of us.

The excitement in recent years is that there is now proof from specific universities and major institutions that consciousness changes physics. Consciousness must therefore be energy. Who would have thought that we can now both better understand and evidence the proof of the integrated relationship between science and spirituality – the entanglement of science with the soul?

The target audience for whom she has written this book is individuals who are keen to awaken to the truth and ability of who they are. In acknowledgement of this mastery, the individual can focus on what is going on in their life now and use their inner power to manifest their own unique, extraordinary talents to achieve their desires and fulfil their potential. It is an entanglement of spirit with science, of the linear with multi-dimensionality, of love with wisdom. And yes, out of all of this, the way of it is love! Pure love!

"

As a man allows himself to depend increasingly on circumstances outside himself of this physical, mental and spiritual nourishment, never looking within to his own source, he gradually depletes his reserves of energy!
~ Stanza 65 from The Rubaiyat of Omar Khayyam

Be encouraged to tune in to the mastery of the powerful energy that thrives within you, embrace truth and be thrilled by the opportunity to gain a lot in your self-development from this reading experience! The challenge is for you with freewill to nurture yourself and take charge of what you desire! What a gift it is for you to know that you are the creator of your own experience! YOU are able to birth your own unique contribution into this elegant, benevolent and loving universe. Feel inspired! Feel the healing! Feel the power!

There is the demystifying and unveiling of the true story of humanity. It starts with your awareness and intention to honour your sacredness and decide how you personally want to change and evolve as a new human in the New World of truth, integrity, love and compassion. You are your own wonderful system of self-reliance. You are a creating creator! There are no rules! Authors, educators, speakers and teachers can suggest things but in order to stand in your own power with full confidence, you have to feel the essence and energy inside of yourself. Know that you alone must choose and know what is really best for you.

Lady Wise hopes this book is everything you were hoping for and more!

Acknowledgements

Special thanks to Lee Carroll and the support entity Kryon, The Magnetic Master, helping in the evolution of humanity at this time, for giving me permission to share some of their knowledge and wisdom with you as I have come to understand it.

Enjoy listening to free audio channelled through the voice of Lee Carroll from the support entity Kryon available at the Kryon Library: https://www.kryon.com to further enhance your inner guidance system.

Special thanks to Monika Muranyi the author and archivist of Kryon information including the Kryon Glossary and specifically her book entitled 'The Women of Lemuria' as she continues to help in the evolution of humanity at this time.

Special thanks to the sect of the Pleiadians supporting us in the evolution of humanity on earth.

Dedication

This book is dedicated to YOU!
I AM YOU,
YOU ARE ME,
WE ARE ONE TOGETHER!
I AM YOU,
YOU ARE ME,
WE ARE ONE FOREVER!

Contents

LETTER 1

AWAKENING WITH LIGHT!

"

Life has not been created by chance, but instead by
human design
These are some of the many truths being uncovered after
eons of time
The Human Being who was changed here 200,000 years
ago
Is awakening one by one, to be in the know!
~ Lady Wise

Dear Uncle Jim,

The test of this beautiful planet earth is one of energy because everything in the Universe is made up of energy including human beings. Who are you really?

Before I continue may I prepare you for truth? Yes indeed, truth is commonly stranger than fiction at this time. Sometimes the power of truth surprises us in ways that we

1

find difficult to believe because of the conditioning that we have experienced over many lifetimes. May I suggest that you do your best to suspend any disbelief for a moment, switch off your linear mind and lapse into receptivity from the purity of your heart. Feel a subtle shift from linear thinking to simply feeling! Start to feel the truth of who you are from your gut. Your gut feeling is instinctual and never lets you down. Let my poem remind you of the importance of listening to your intuition.

Mr. Gut Feeling

How many times do you go with the flow
And trust your body to be in the know?
Let go logic and let go science
Trust in your inner voice of defiance
That rises up against outer consciousness
And has you challenging the drama and senselessness
Which other people would have you believe
Makes sense of your life when it's not how you please
Know that with every decision you make
There are consequences and actions to take
The choice that you make will reflect on yourself
Your sense of purpose, self esteem and self worth
Hold your head high, cast out fear and doubt
View your reflection and feel good in and out
Pat yourself on the back, breathe in deep and stand tall
When Mr. Gut Feeling's your driver there are no brick walls
To run into each time an issue arises
Only knowhow and genius, disguised as surprises
When others would have you believe their advice
Step back to observe, digest and think twice
Before committing to a wrong decision

Trust Mr. Gut Feeling and your intuition
If your solar plexus stirs and you feel instantly sick
About turn on their argument, withdraw and think quick
Push back on assumptions, form your own conclusion
And know that in this moment your reality's an illusion
Pay attention and sense what you feel in your bones
Your body's response is like a gramophone
The needle points you in the right direction
And supports each new step forward with protection.
Divine love caresses and guides from within
Ensuring that unconditional love always wins
So next time you feel fear at making a decision
Know that you are guided by an inner rhythm
Just ask for help from Mr. Gut Feeling
Let him provide the response for your well-being.

Ok, thank you for your special alertness and attention to this.

There has been history on this planet before the catalogued history that most of us learned and continue to learn in school. These letters are an invitation to you to be open to new information that will enhance what you have already been told. It is time for us as a human race to recognise our spirituality and to grow in maturity on Gaia as we reclaim our mastery and lineage.

Incidentally, my invitation to you is to be aware of ALL new information that comes your way, every single nano second of each day in detail, without restriction and limitation!

It is such an honour and privilege for me to share this knowledge with you, Uncle Jim. It is your birthright to know this information. Each of us is born to thrive in abundance and joy. How do we get there?

Is it possible that the history of humanity on planet earth stretches over a much longer time period and is different from what you were initially taught in school, college, and university? Is it possible that the history of our human civilisation is different from what you presently think too? Is it possible that until recently, the majority of us has been born on this earth without a remembrance of who we truly are? All will slowly be revealed because in the remembrance comes the light.

The connotation of an iceberg is great for explaining this concept. At school I remember learning that generally one can only observe one tenth of an iceberg from above the water level. The remaining nine tenths are hidden under the water's surface. The potential wisdom of a human being is similar to this metaphor. When as a human being we use our logical mind to solution-provide every day, we are only tapping into a fraction of our potential creativity.

The power of a human being's true 'inner-net' potential far exceeds that human's ability to create and learn knowledge from accessing only the internet, irrespective of how powerful a computer is. How do we access our own inner-net? The answer is through our own heart centre.

Truth reveals itself....eventually. Sometimes the truth does hurt initially because it can turn our belief systems upside down. For a few people it even arouses anger from within them because they feel embarrassed and foolish for having believed a certain way, until they are informed of specific new information that changes their patterns of thinking and changes their beliefs. There is no judgement.

As Kryon teaches, the planet is in a profound test of dark and light energy. Is it possible that you can accept that the

human body is comprised of something much more than the physical corporeal body that you first see when you look in a mirror? We have endured very narrow visibility on a wide electro-magnetic spectrum of light. You can do things that you do not think you can do. Take a longer, closer look in the mirror and with more focused attention see who you truly are as you stare into your own eyes.

Can you accept that you are a unique form of energy? It will help you to better understand who you are with regards to some of the seemingly mysterious and hidden secrets that may have before now appeared to be beyond believable to one's comprehension. I am keen to help you demystify some of the apparent mysteries of life and to accentuate and accelerate the energy that is within you, as the real you, as the joyous you, as the playful you, as the loving you, as the compassionate you and as the magnificent you.

Our planet is full of galactic and universal energies that most of us cannot presently see because we have not spiritually evolved sufficiently to see them with our physical eyes and with our important third eye (more will be explained about this in a future letter). Many of us however can FEEL them and SENSE them.

The more in touch you are with your own emotions and feelings, the more intuitive and responsive you will become to these loving energies that are around you. For example, as an animal lover and former owner of two dogs, Sandy and Mitsy, you may have frequently noticed the dogs became alert to things that you could not see. Animals are tuned in to higher energies and can instinctively bring their entire awareness and attention to effectively see these energies that, to most of us, exist in an invisible realm.

There is NOTHING TO FEAR about these perceived invisible energies. It is only natural for us to be wary and scared of something that we do not yet understand and remember. You always have free choice to deny their existence. Now that you have read this new information, however, you cannot delete it! Ha! Ha! It is part of your birthright, so that you can recognise these supportive, benevolent tools for YOU in this precious lifetime as you evolve on your spiritual journey! The joy, beauty and the benefits of knowing who you truly are require a leap of faith in you to understand your WHOLE EXISTENCE.

With an enhanced knowledge there is an opportunity for you to expand your usual perceptions to give you a wider perspective of your life. This can be very healing and empowering! It is time to graciously, safely and timely wake up!

Let's take an example of introducing new information. Having experienced the loss of your own beloved parents many years ago, do you ever feel that their presence is still around you, especially when you are experiencing your own challenging times? You would be right! They are here for YOU! They are here to support you in helping you to create abundance, happiness, love and joy in your life. You are not imagining their energy around you. Their energy IS around you. They are desperate for you to know that they still exist in a transmuted form as part of the cycle of life and death, life and death, life and death and how they live their existence between lives on this planet too!

Sometimes our loved ones who have died use their energy to make noises, switch on electrical items such as stereo systems, televisions, flick kettle switches, light switches, sound door knockers, door bells, car alarms and everything else that you can imagine. Sometimes you may see shadows on a wall or even be fortunate to see their imprint visit you and perhaps sit on the end of your bed in the middle of the night. This is all in an effort to make you realise that they have never left you and that you are never alone, even though their physical body is no longer present.

You are not alone even from the ones that
you think that you have lost.
~ Kryon

I have often felt the hair on the top of my head lightly tousled or felt a hug from spirit engulf my body as I sit down. It is so comforting and reassuring to know that my loved ones who have passed on from their last lifetime retain their imprint here on earth to help me continue with my own challenges and joy-filled adventures. They know what I am doing and tune in when they know I am thinking of them. What a beautiful system!

We are electromagnetic beings of light. The amount of light that each person has within them depends on how spiritually evolved they are.

In effect, the light factor within you will increase with your increased spiritual knowledge and it is this light which, as it brings you greater peace within your heart, will also attract others to you. They will see how you seem to 'shine' and are different from others, despite the everyday issues and life challenges that you have. Those who hold a high light quotient are very joyful, compassionate, peaceful human beings with a calm countenance. This is what enlightenment is. Their laughter fills a room and makes others feel good.

We are the E.T.s of planet earth that we laugh about other E.T.s being! We are extra terrestrials! We are the superhumans. We come from the stars! Approximately 200,000 years ago, the Pleiadians, from a star system called the Seven Sisters and also referred to as the Pleiades, came to earth and first seeded the divinity of human civilisation on this planet. They are far more highly evolved than most of us are presently. They changed our biological blueprint called DNA. You see as all things are connected, so too are science and spirituality entangled with one another. We are part of the system of the physics of consciousness. More on this later! For now, let me refer back to the light of our Star Mothers called the Pleiadians. They are superhumans from across the galaxy who seeded this planet with sacredness, love and divinity.

In this context I am referring to a superhuman as a human being with a piece of divinity inside of them that is so evolved that it is greater than normal for a human being at this time. The importance of the timeframe at this particular juncture is relevant because eventually (and I cannot put a specific number of years on this as I know you would like me to) every human being on planet earth will become evolved to a superhuman state. As a result of this awakening of knowledge and wisdom within every human being, the definition of normal will inevitably change. A superhuman will ultimately become the 'new normal' state of being for a human being on planet earth.

When you add new esoteric knowledge to enhance your spiritual wisdom, you raise your consciousness. This has the

effect of increasing the amount of light energy that you have in your system. The higher your light quotient, the higher is your consciousness. The more light that you have in your energy system, the more connected you become to everything – to the 'oneness of all that is'.

With every nano second, every human being is absorbing more and more data from their surroundings – the environment, other people, social media, news media and even the sun. The sun gives us light. Light is information absorbed by one's body. With free will, every human being makes a choice whether to think, say and act positively or negatively to their life experiences. These changes then affect the light quotient within each of us. When we choose to think, speak and act in a positive way we increase our own light factor within us. When we choose to think, speak and act in a negative way, we decrease the light factor within us.

When more people choose to think, say and do positive things with their life, the average light quotient among the world's population rises and becomes higher. When more people choose to think, say and do negative things with their life, the average light quotient among the world's population falls and becomes a lower quotient.

This is because YOU are important as both an individual human being on the planet and as part of the collective of humanity. There is always a connection.

And so when we live in joy, we are always contributing positive light to the planet and raising our own consciousness at the same time. Pretty cool! Joy to the world! This can now be scientifically measured and viewed on line. It is called The Schumann Resonance. May I suggest that after a major incident next happens around the world, either of joy or sadness, you take a look at the impact this has on global consciousness. We are in the age of connection.

"

We are the world!
~ Osho

Since 21 December 2012, more and more individuals around the world are awakening to the fact that they are more than the physical body they can see of themselves in the mirror. They also know that they are more than the material possessions that they have. They 'know' there is something more. They 'know' there is something bigger than themselves to their existence.

The female Pleiadians arrived from the Pleiades to seed with the human males. These superhumans came with a light quotient within them that was at a level of approximately 88% and expressed their love and wisdom in peace and with joy. None of them held any judgement of another Pleiadian or human being because as a superhuman themselves, their high level of consciousness held no feelings or emotions related to war, shame, guilt, jealousy, lies, illusion, grief, fear or attachment.

All the Masters who have come to planet earth have come with a high light quotient. Essentially, those humans whose focus in life is centred around love, joy, compassion and integrity in all they do, hold a higher light quotient than their counterparts who choose to live their lives creating fear, pain and sadness in others, including bullying, gossiping, intimidation and other negative energy attributes.

Presently, planet earth is the only planet in our Universe that has free choice. This means that every human being is born with the free will to do whatever they want on this planet. It affects how they treat other people. They can choose to go either way; they can act negatively or act positively in their daily life. This is the puzzle of duality into which we have been born. This puzzle is put in front of each one of us to be solved. What behaviour is normal for you?

I heard of a marvellous restaurant in Columbia (I am unsure if it still exists) that was considered one of the finest in all of Latin America. It stood out because it was staffed by ex-serviceman and guerrillas who worked happily beside one another. These individuals had learned the wisdom to forgive. They united to create amazing food and recognised that war is not a solution under any circumstances. Similarly, across the whole of Colombia illegal peasant growers of cocoa (which is the basis of cocaine) have marched against the government, demanding that the government's promise is kept to help them transition to legal crops. Isn't this interesting? Throughout the world example after example can be provided to demonstrate that in this most important period of the Shift, individuals, as a collective, are starting to stand up for themselves and for what they believe is right for their country for the future. The positive energy of humans working together is not only empowering to them, but is a catalyst for positive change. It is taking time, but people are deciding on what they want for their country and uniting with fellow souls to bring about beneficial change. In some cases they are reconnecting with their emotions and pushing for changes for the better with the passion and fire that is in their hearts. They are no longer afraid to stand up for what they believe. This is new! This is happening across the

world and every situation is a step closer to celebrating and bringing about world peace.

When the Pleiadians first came to seed us on planet earth, they landed in a place known as Lemr'ha or Lemuria. Today, the location of this part of the world is Hawaii. If you have visited the Hawaiian Islands you will know that it is a remote part of the world. This was a deliberate choice by the Pleiadians because the remote land allowed them to teach humans with a purity of love and wisdom that remained untarnished from any negative energies present in other parts of the world.

Back in Lemuria, life was balanced for everyone and flowed in divine order. The women were the shamans and teachers of divinity because it was considered that as females their connection to Gaia (Mother Earth) was closer than the connection of the males to Gaia. Moreover, the females were the child bearers and so had a strong connection to humanity and spirituality as birth mothers. The men were happy to accept the roles of the women and they used to hunt for food and take pride in cooking the food that they had successfully caught for their family and the community. The men would also conduct their business guided by consultation with the female shamans received directly from the creator source of all that is. Monika Muranyi, the archivist of the Kryon channellings and author in her own right, explains beautifully some of the Lemurian culture in greater depth in her book "The Women of Lemuria" in which Dr. Amber Wolf has also contributed some of her Lemurian wisdom (remembered as the head teacher back in the day).

Do you remember the fear that was generated among human beings back in the years leading up to December 2012 because certain individuals thought that the world was coming to an end? Hollywood directors were making films about it. The truth is that all the predictions were never about the end of the world. It was always about the end of the world as we have known it to be and the beginning of a New Era, a new world where love, compassion and truth would carry more weight and influence than any negative traits of a human's character.

The profound test of dark and light energy on planet earth reached a tipping point on 21 December 2012. For eons humanity on planet earth had been living in darkness with very little 'light' (love, compassion, truth and peace) present. And now, the tide has turned. Light is winning. Feel and resonate with renewed hope deep inside your core being. What makes you feel alive and vital? What makes your soul happy? The soul awakening that is taking place across Mother Earth at this time is heightening in intensity.

Remember, that you have FULL CREATIVE control of your life! This is why it is important to think positive thoughts and to live from a place of love in your heart. When you drop all negative thoughts and are non-judgemental of others, regardless of who they are, you connect in a stronger and more loving way with your intuition and with your creative thoughts to manifest the best life for you. You are remembering who you are and connecting with the epiphany of knowing that your God, Higher Self, higher guidance, spirit, creator source (by whatever name is appropriate for you) is inside you.

Remember, that in scripture the weak man says, "I AM STRONG". These two words, 'I AM' are the most powerful words that there are, because in remembering that each of us holds a divine spark of the creator source inside of us means that we have the ultimate power to create whatever we want. This is the mastery that you have, to which each individual around planet earth is slowly waking up. We are awakening to the light, to the divine part that is within each one of us which glows brighter within our being with every loving thought, idea, spoken and written word and action.

The degree of light that each human being emits will determine their strength of ability to see other energies. A highly evolved human being already aware and thriving in the entanglement of all that exists, sees these energies and communicates with them all the time. It becomes second nature to them. They have freed themselves long ago from old energy patterning, structures and systems that would have us believe that we can only live when we are dependent on other people, hierarchical structures and a life lived in fear known as survival.

You were born to thrive, not merely survive. Every moment you are alive is a divine intervention!

Sending you all love and hugs, x

THE LIGHT ACTIVATOR!

"

*Can you go beyond the boundary of your mind
And tap into the gift for you of light inside?*
~ Lady Wise

Dear Uncle Jim,

The beauty of this magnificent way of love is that it is benevolent and supportive of all human life on the planet.

Love and fear cannot co-exist and so when you let go all fears, then you have only LOVE. Love is at the core of who you are. The language of the heart is love. Humanity was originally seeded with love and wisdom approximately 200,000 years ago. Prior to this seeding of divinity by the female Pleiadians, we had the same number of pairs of chromosomes as animals. Unfortunately, because the average human lifespan up until now has tended to be less than one hundred years, we have not lived a lifetime long enough to see and believe a world living in peace and contentment without war. The twentieth century witnessed two world wars which has made people think that war is a natural process of humanity. Wrong!

For so long we have been experiencing an overwhelming darkness (dark quotient) on the planet which has intimidated, bullied and hurt us at all levels, energetically, physically, mentally, emotionally, financially and spiritually. The illusion has been that this is part of everyday existence. No more!

Heartbeat of Your Soul

Deep within your soul, feel the core nature of your true being.
Feel a deep love within your heart for you that you are
living
In such dynamic changing global times be kind to yourself
And find a quiet space where you know you will be
undisturbed in good health
Listen to your own heartbeat, the soul's gift of your unique
expression
Reuniting you with the sound of Gaia as you close your
eyes in mindful reflection
Breathe in the whispers of angelic realms and feel the
ripples of truth
Of who you are and of your composed countenance of
eternal youth
Your own unique heartbeat is your own living treasure!
Listen carefully to its rhythm and feel its sacredness in
pleasure.
This is the energy of you at work, at play,
Always throughout your physical existence in this lifetime
on planet earth every day.
Know that when it is the right time for you, you alone have
the power to release all pain,

Let go trauma, sorrow and grief to date in your life,
never to be experienced again,
Safe in the knowledge that it is your birthright to love
and to connect
Forgive yourself for all thoughts, words and actions
About which you feel you could have improved upon
without distraction
Truly know that spirit sees you as perfect in your daily life
to date.
You are living your own soul journey guided by Higher Self
and your Innate.
You can choose to open your heart to a brand new beginning.
Be playful, act spontaneously and genuinely experience
the joy of living
As a soul, this is indeed a magnificent time to be alive
To honour yourself, live life's mystery and to thrive
This is the lifetime that will make the difference.
For Mother Earth is blessed by your very existence!
~ Lady Wise

It is more important than any other lifetime on planet earth because we are presently in a period of time called 'The Shift'. What is this? Kryon describes it as an incredible love story of human beings maturing in their spirituality, connecting more with their inner wisdom and gaining a better understanding of their very 'being' on planet earth. Scientifically, it is a thirty-six year event of the Precession of the Equinoxes whose centre point was 12 December 2012. It refers to the eighteen years before this centre point and the eighteen years after this centre point. The Precession of the Equinoxes is a 26,000 year wobble of the earth which takes thirty-six years to change the sky as it 'walks' through the Milky Way. The wobble, however, is incidental to the

grander manifestation of the evolution of humanity that is slowly taking place. The abundance that is manifested with this cycle is the earth going into Mastery.

DNA is becoming enhanced in humans to allow us to vibrate at a higher vibrational frequency. Life is vibrational! Remember that what affects every human affects Mother Earth too! We are entangled with one another and Mother Earth in a quantum way which affects the higher vibrating consciousness of both the human and of Mother Earth.

Spirit knows you by name. The earth is going into Graduate Status. WE ARE IN IT! This will, ultimately, create 'peace on earth' which will then create wonderful new opportunities for real fun, excitement and innovation! It is the Old Souls like you and me who are leading the way. With the 'God spark' or 'divine spark' inside each of us, common to every human being, we have free choice – whatever we believe.

Remember when I used to be taken to your church with Mum and Dad? The human mind is wonderful at seeking to compartmentalise everything. All too often, we become stubborn in our own boundary of belief because we choose to have a spiritual filter that is both judgemental and fixed. Yet, how we see the creator, tempers how our life goes and how we grow spiritually.

"

What you believe is who you are!
~ Kryon

Our spiritual filter is important to each of us as we grow up. What have YOU been told about God? When I was four years old I assumed that because my parents took me to church and liked it, that it was ok for me to go to church and to own this spiritual choice. As we grow, there is a filter that can change depending on what we have done, learned, observed, questioned and challenged. It often involves a stepping outside of our comfort zone and that can be difficult.

When you left with your loving wife and your family to go to Australia in the 1970's I chose to question my spiritual filter. I knew within my own mind even at twelve years old that in my world, God was everywhere and I did not need to go to church to speak to God. God was not in any human form but an energy. God was not in a particular place but everywhere. At that time, I did not know that this creative energy source of the universe knew my name, nor did I know that a piece of the divine 'God spark' was also inside me. That did not come until May 2016! These things can happen very slowly as the forgiveness and healing take place.

The most important aspect for you to remember is to know that anyone who has ever taught you or told you anything, presumably did so with the best of intentions at that time. If you now have more knowledge usurped by greater wisdom, that is ok. There is no reason to feel that you are insulting them or betraying them to move ahead. Think of the additional information as an enhancement. It is called wisdom.

Feel the harmony and joy of today! Acknowledge harmony and balance within your own energy field. Follow your bliss! To live at bliss point is to live from your heart. How do you hold the beam of love and light in your heart? The extent to which you respond to any given situation from your heart with loving thoughts and actions, will determine how strong your feelings of bliss are. The heart speaks to your mind and then this heart coherence goes through the rest of the body. It starts with love.

The love of yourself is at the heart of the Shift and will allow you to progress in your spirituality, your maturity and your wisdom. This is the beauty and simplicity of who you are. I want to tell you that there is a purpose to your life and that this is supported by the most magnificent system of love for YOU! In order to connect with it, it is important to drop your ego and drop all fears, worries, anxieties and doubts and start to love yourself. Start to feel the love that is there for YOU! Start to feel the love that you have for yourself! Know that as you are able to love yourself, you grow in self-worth, love and integrity. The essence of understanding who you are is all about being able to first look in the mirror and being able to truly love yourself as you are. For some people this is a hard thing to do.

In addition, there are those people who think that loving oneself first is very selfish and narcissistic. The reality is that only when you first love yourself with all your heart, can you then share your love with others and see the 'God' in them as it is also in you. Namaste!

I tend to think of the analogy of a full shampoo bottle. When you squeeze a full shampoo bottle, guess what comes out? Shampoo. When you have dropped all negative thoughts and have only love in your heart, then guess what? This means that you then only have love for yourself and for other people. When they hug you, they only feel and receive love. **Love IS The Way!** (Forgive me for plugging the title of one of my other books? Ha!)

When you ask the creator source for clarity and discernment, the compassion and love sets in. You can drop the fear and become joyful! You fall in love with yourself by connecting with the source of love. You become a new human by experiencing current spiritual feelings and events going on now that were not present before the marker of 21 December 2012 was crossed.

Remember that you do not know what you do not know. When you let go all that you have learned and connect to spirit, it gives you a self-balancing countenance and a peaceful life. There is an inner calm within your heart no matter what is going on around you. Trust yourself to know what is right for YOU! Let joy fill your heart! Others will notice the change in you and want to spend more time around you.

Wishing you good health, happiness and heartfelt love eternal, xxx

FREEWILL TO BELIEVE!

*"
Have you always believed what
you were told or are you your own person
not to be ignored?
~ Kryon*

Dear Uncle Jim,

I know you are familiar with those words of scripture, "I AM THE WAY, THE TRUTH AND THE LIGHT". What does this really mean? Jesus, like all the Masters who have ever walked this earth, was showing you the example by which you too could become enlightened. The beginning of an ascended personality while still physically alive on earth is now achievable in the new energy! It's time for us to join together and engulf the planet in our love, compassion and kindness with common sense and maturity.

All of the Masters have come to planet earth to show us that we each have this ability to grow in our compassion, wisdom and light. On this occasion, I have chosen to refer to Jesus, but there are countless other Masters whom I could have selected. The planet is helping a shift in human beings to allow them, through free choice, to attain a more balanced condition in their everyday life. With freewill, we are able to enrich our own lives and pursue the desires of our hearts in love, respect and gratitude.

Remember, each of us has a piece of the divine spark within us; this is our 'God spark', it is quantum and multi-dimensional. It connects us to the 'oneness' of all that is, the Creator Source, and every human being has it.

If you were to say, "I AM STRONG", then you are speaking from the divine God part of you, synonymous with the Higher Self, higher guidance or the Creative Source.

Remember, when Jesus spoke, 'Healer, heal thyself!' this is what he meant. You connect with God. You connect with the Higher Self. This is why individuals can have 'spontaneous remission' which most doctors do not yet understand. It is not chemistry, it is physics! As Kryon, the Magnetic Master, says, "This is the grandest love story there is."

Each of us has free choice to work out the puzzle of life. Everything on the planet exists for us all, for YOU! It is all based on the consciousness of humanity. It will allow humanity to awaken to a wisdom and maturity that the earth has not known before... if you believe it. My dear Uncle, the joy of finding out the truth about our existence and reason for life on earth is so magnificent I cannot find words to describe its beauty. We are eternal. Our soul is eternal. Give yourself permission to believe this is possible and allow me to share more information with you.

Welcome the difficult times for they can be our greatest teacher! You are well equipped to know this as a long-served religious preacher!

Use your ability of free choice
To connect with your inner voice!
~ Lady Wise

Trusting that 'all is well' with you and you are enjoying being pampered at home?

Psalm 46 verse 10 (NIV) says, 'Be still and know that I am God.'

You are wise beyond words. Can you feel who you are? All you have to do is to have the courage to ask spirit to show you what is INSIDE of you and the rest will become self-evident. Every single person has the ability to pull in what is sacred from their own biology. Simply be willing in FREE CHOICE to surrender, be free of judgement, pay attention and to ask:

Question: Dear Spirit, (Higher Self, Higher Guidance/Creator Source/God) tell me what I need to know?

This simple question connects your physical body with innate and with your Higher Self which you refer to as God. This divine connection works in a multi-dimensional way and the life force that is in you works with the creator source. Your human soul is unique because it is multi-dimensional. The 'hidden' 24th pair of chromosomes is totally and completely multi-dimensional. This pair has a multi-dimensional aspect which gives you a soul which has in it a piece of God. Many cultures know this and always have believed in this. The

fractals of your soul and the beauty of the sacred geometry within, represents the creator source. It holds the cosmic history of all times with no beginning!

As the soul is multi-dimensional there is no linearity within it. Your soul is in many parts. It is also assisting you along with the other souls. The Higher Self that helps you and is the piece of God within you is your soul.

Enjoy reading my next poem and be aware of what you feel as you read it!

Dear Higher Self...

Dear Higher Self, tell me what I need to know?
Support me in your love and benevolence wherever I go
It is time for me to graciously and safely wake up
And to remember the mysteries of a fulfilled life as I drink
the energy from your loving cup
Through the glorious landscape of life I start to feel
the life force
That resides deep within me connected to creator source
My mind fills with hope and a sense of adventure
Breaking down plaque coated vessels which give rise to
dementia
Being in pilgrimage, I dance through great movement and
change
Grateful for finding my freedom and losing all rage
There is no more tension in my being, I am relaxed in my
wisdom,
I have faith, I believe and accept my multi-dimensionalism
I feel the vitality flow through my bones
And cognise that I have truly come back home!

You did not come to earth to suffer, to be sad, to be in pain or to be poor. That is not the plan. You do not have to work for something that is inside of you. All you have to do is to acknowledge it. You have control over your own cellular structure and it wants to hear from you. Everything that you have gone through has purpose. There are no accidents and there are no coincidences. Now it is time to come out of your confusion, frustration, drama and puzzlement and check out the magnificence that is both around you and you!

God inside is the real you. It is in every single cell of your existence. Is it possible that you have blocked the truth about spirit all of your life and that there is more to life than you think?

Feel the energy in your body and around your body! The physicists accept that there is dimensionality of invisible energies that they do not fully understand yet. How would you describe energy? The 'old souls' feel the energy. Love is energy! Peace is energy and the creation of an attitude to attain peace on earth is energy. Energy is physics!

When the human being dies, the soul goes back 'home' to the Family of Light. There is no location or where? God is everywhere. God is in everything that there is, in all life force on the planet.

It ties together with everything there is in life, on the planet, in the galaxy, in the universe. Remember, that today's weird and mysterious will be tomorrow's reality! There is a most beautiful way of love beyond what most of us can see and sense at this time. It is only natural that you may question some of these esoteric things because you were not taught these things.

Stand tall, feel loved and feel the light of God around you and claim your mastery. Shine your light for yourself! Make it shine and radiate through YOU! When you shine your light bright enough, everybody benefits from this. When you drop into your sacred heart centre where you are comfortable with yourself, where you love yourself as a piece of God, no matter what happens and you can say, "All is well with my soul!" then all manner of things happens. Intuition becomes king and queen. You have JOY in your heart. You experience and live in the NOW! There is nothing purer. Be the light! Enjoy each moment in the moment!

The reason that I am writing these letters is to share with you more information than was previously known about, which may help your healing and give you peace of mind in the same way that I received healing from first learning about this information too.

One by one, individuals are awakening to the grandness that they are so much more than their physical being and so much more than the physical possessions that they have. Do you know that more than 80% of people around the world believe in angels? That is no coincidence!

It is time for the truth to be revealed in this lifetime as we become able to absorb the wisdom of the ancients. Through our maturity and raised consciousness, we earn the right to this increased wisdom.

All love xxx

DROP YOUR KARMA!

Karma is part of the DNA and is governed by Innate.
~ Kryon

Dear Uncle Jim,

Have you ever wondered why so many people seem to be living their lives as ONE BIG DRAMA? There is no need for this when you learn of another part to demystify the puzzle of our life on earth. Wouldn't you prefer to live happily with a constant feeling in your heart of harmony and contentment? What a gift this is! Insomnia would be wiped out overnight! Ha! The drama does not need to touch you.

DROP THE DRAMA, DROP YOUR KARMA!

There's no need to live your life based on drama
Instead as a first step choose to drop your karma
Kryon's teachings advised us to do this more than
twenty years ago
But when the time is right we are guided to the information

We have each been born into this world with 'unwanted attachments' that have come in with us from past lives, also known as past expressions. Often the 'push pull' of karma has us experiencing all kinds of chaos in our lives that we feel we cannot control. Karma is part of the DNA that exists in the invisible eight metre field surrounding our physical body called the Merkaba. Historically, we could learn lessons from the karmic situations, but beyond 21 December 2012 there is no need to continue to carry this karmic energy around with us. It simply hinders our personal and spiritual growth. Indeed, often it leaves us befuddled. If we are to take full control of our actions and our future, we need to make a decision to drop it for our highest good. This is soul learning. How do we do this? It is easy.

Perhaps we could do this together in a multi-dimensional way? I will write it as if I am speaking it with you and you can read it as though I am with you by your side.

It is time to drop your karma. Talk to your body and say. "I am done with the energy of the past. I drop my karma and move forward."

Congratulations on dropping your karma, Uncle Jim!

Much love, xxx

DIS-EASE NO MORE!

"
A higher consciousness will not catch the disease because
it will see the disease coming and avoid it.
~ Kryon

Dear Uncle Jim,

On this Remembrance Sunday we remember with gratitude the bravery, courage and determination of our ancestors who throughout time fought in many barbaric circumstances and indeed, in some places of the world continue to fight today for the intention of ultimate peace on earth and the joy, love and harmony in which we can choose to live every minute and in the future!

Of course you remember, as the indigenous know now and have always known, that we are our ancestors. They have always had the wisdom passed down to them through their lineage but the majority of people out with the indigenous tribes have chosen to ignore their teachings.

The indigenous know the wisdom of the ancients. They are their ancestors. What is lovely to see nowadays is that many of the tribal elders are now sharing their wisdom with other tribal elders out with their own indigenous tribes and amazingly among non-indigenous tribal people. We are sitting in the energy of this galactic alignment, a 26,000 year cycle that the ancients knew about. How is this possible? These indigenous peoples still have a DNA operating in a quantum or multi-dimensional way. All of these esoteric things come from within the human being, without the need for a computer or telescope!

The balance of a human being comes from opening their heart up to the inner world of all that is, while at the same time maintaining a presence of the reality of the outer world in which their physical body exists to thrive in joy and abundance!

Essentially because humanity has had and continues to have free choice, every individual has had their own power to act negatively and/or positively in their approach to one another and in how they respect the planet and all living things, including flora and fauna, mammals and birds, land and oceans. Every action by a human being has cumulatively impacted the DNA efficiency level of that particular individual and, because we are all connected, every action has also simultaneously cumulatively impacted the collective DNA efficiency level of planet earth!

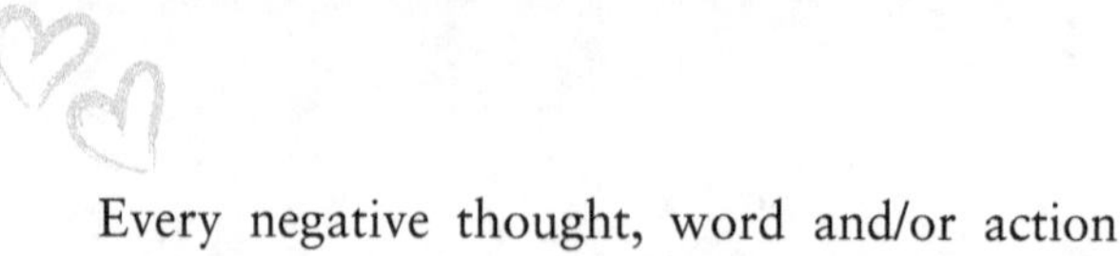

Every negative thought, word and/or action by a human being reduces that individual's DNA efficiency and the overall DNA efficiency of human beings on the planet.

Similarly, every positive thought, word and/or action by a human being increases that individual's DNA efficiency and the overall DNA efficiency of human beings on the planet.

We must pay attention to every thought, word and action in order to reclaim back our power as a superhuman with high DNA efficiency. We can only do this through the way of love.

With such a low DNA activation, we have literally lost that quantum feeling and the wisdom and knowledge of understanding astronomy. The lineage of DNA has shifted from a precious creation that was appropriate, sacred and true, to a level today where, after being disregarded for so long, it is beginning to be recognised once more in this way.

As a result of a shift in the mindset of human beings, DNA is beginning to be reactivated, very slowly, in pieces and parts in a quantum way. When the Pleiadians came to earth and first seeded us we enjoyed and experienced a DNA efficiency level of nearer 90%. Over thousands of years because of the honouring on planet earth of the free choice that every human being has, we slipped back as a human race to a DNA efficiency quotient that was only about 30%. Quite a difference! Our DNA has not been functioning as it should.

Now, we are in an esoteric age when humans have the chance to choose a more spiritual route that questions who they are. This allows them to raise their DNA activation once more.

The choice for every human being could not be simpler:-

Remain in a three dimensional reality that is void of adventure, personal development, spiritual growth, life extension, inner peace and balance

Or

Embrace the divine piece of your Higher Self (God) that is within you and enjoy the time of your life!

We are in an age of remembrance back to a Lemurian state (Lemuria is the name of the ancient lands that are known as Hawaii today). When we were more spiritually advanced, our DNA was at a level of 88%. This created a consciousness that was at one with the universe, with Gaia (also referred to as Mother Earth and Pachamama in different parts of the world).

At such a high-level of DNA activation, consciousness can control physics to the extent that intention can create and manifest what is needed. Technology is not necessary!

When everything is made up of energy, including ourselves, and we attain a high level of light within our bodies, we have the mastery to focus so intently on the vision of whatever we want to create, that it is brought into physical form. Isn't this wonderful? It places a whole different perspective on the importance of the internet versus our own 'inner-net'.

It also explains why it is important that we each pay close attention to how much time we spend on or near computers, televisions and mobile phones which, when used excessively, may interfere with our own inner-net! It is no surprise to me that health issues related to the heart and the prostrate may be linked to the carriage of phones in a top pocket or trouser pocket next to both these key organs!

Have you given serious thought to this and to the extent to which women's fertility and men's sperm count may have significantly reduced in recent years because of extended hours of the body's proximity to technology gadgets? Why not seek a little adventure that persuades you to leave your mobile phone and television firmly disconnected from reach or distraction when next planning an impromptu intimate and sensual encounter? Use your own inner 'smartness' to decide the truth of what feels right for you on this matter.

The Lemurians lived a very long time. They had self diagnostics in their DNA that created a human cellular structure which repaired itself. The Lemurian could grow back a limb just like a starfish can. When we are appropriately evolved, it will be possible for us to do this too through thought activation and consciousness. Very slowly, we are bringing back an original energy that was designed for today. One by one we are returning to our quantum, multi-dimensional state which is the spiritual state!

Remember, that your DNA is engineered to last approximately 900 years and so, my dear uncle, you are SO young at a mere 96 linear years!

Our DNA is designed to be operating at 88% capacity. The energy of the planet as a whole gives us the efficiency factor and we are not operating at anywhere near this level presently because not enough individuals have awakened to who they truly are and to the power that lies within themselves.

The energy of the planet increases in relation to the raised energy of each of the individuals alive on the planet. At this time there is approximately only 2% of the world's population who has awakened to the truth of who they are. We have a

long way to go before Mother Earth has a consciousness level as high as the 88% level it was when the Pleiadians first seeded this planet 200,000 years ago.

Why is access to the non-protein part of our DNA so important? Access to our DNA is not just for spiritual information but also to enable us to access some of the attributes that we have been in past lifetimes. Part of the process is biology. The essence of the energy of whom you used to be is in your DNA. It, therefore, has the ability to talk to the blueprint of your stem cells. It is this attribute which is responsible for 'spontaneous remission'.

It is the human being who decides they are done with the disease and picks up that attribute which is healthy from a past life which had no disease.
This is a miracle from within.
~ Kryon

The prophet is inside of you. You are your own Master. That is when you find out and KNOW WHO YOU ARE!

Feel the hug of spirit around you and relax.

Jacques Martel has written a most beautiful book with Luce Bernier, as a collaborator, called, "The Complete Dictionary of Ailments and Diseases". This book is extremely special because it not only explains emotionally why each part of the body is unwell, but provides a beautiful prayer/affirmation of how to heal the specific issue(s) identified. Essentially, it explains the nature of medical issues and provides spiritual solutions as a recognised holistic approach to our well-being and our ability to self-heal!

The science of spirituality is being remembered by those individuals who are awakening to the truth of who they are. When we can live in joy, love and happiness, (void of fear) then our bodies vibrate at a higher vibration and at a certain point that higher vibration resonates at a level above any diseases and ailments that can affect the human body. This is why living from a higher consciousness bestows greater inner peace and joy on a human being. In turn, this human being becomes ever more loving, kind and compassionate in all they do with everyone with whom they meet.

The extent to which our invisible body vibrations are affected can be explained using the following example.

As part of your religious duties, you decide to attend a local coffee morning. You are beckoned over by two ladies at a table to join them for coffee and cake, but you very quickly feel uncomfortable because these two people talk incessantly to you and then start bickering between themselves. After ten minutes one of your friends shows up and your facial expression changes from looking a little jaded to a wide smile.

This is an example of how people with different energy vibrations can influence and impact on you. The two ladies who made you feel uncomfortable were vibrating at a lower level than you and it may have felt like your energy was being drained from you. When your friend entered, he was probably vibrating nearer to your own vibration. Whenever you are together you feel uplifted by each other's conversation. When you go your own separate ways after meeting up, you leave feeling invigorated and rejuvenated from talking together.

Many of us have forgotten that it is our birthright to feel good about ourselves and to be in the best of health every day! We have the power to heal ourselves and to rid ourselves

of any 'dis-ease' that is in our body energetically, mentally, physically and emotionally. All illness stems from emotionally blocked energy.

We have the power within ourselves through our spiritual connection to metaphysical realms, to find contentment, to continually feel a natural 'ease' with our bodies and to better understand more about who we are as an esoteric soul living in a temporary physical human body.

There is the POTENTIAL for profound healing – a closure of an older energy in a body that no longer needs it. What do you believe?

"

There is no predisposition for disease that cannot be overcome with a predisposition for love, joy and change!
~ Kryon

Why does homeopathy work? Isn't it interesting that when people do not know what they do not know, their first reaction on hearing some new information is often to ridicule and/or criticise it without any substance? This is an example of fear-based linear thinking. It can often spark an angry reaction from both skeptics and academics. Why are so many medical professionals and academics missing the point?

This is an invitation to you, to better understand why homeopathy works.

The homoepathic tincture which may be given under the tongue is indeed too small to have any chemical impact or chemical reaction, but we are not dealing here with chemistry. We are dealing with the physics of consciousness.

For more than thirty years, Kryon has explained that we have control over every single cell in our body, yet, most medical professionals and academics do not even acknowledge the Merkabah or Merkaba (the approximate eight metre field packed with DNA, trillions of cells, and information around every human physical body) to which we must connect to claim such control. It is our birthright.

Why is there such reticence to question if there is something more than chemistry to heal the body? The Merkaba is presently invisible to a pair of human eyes until the invention of an appropriate instrument to be able to see it. Most medical professionals and academics use the term "junk DNA" because they do not understand it.

As examples, they cannot explain when the spinal chord is severed in an accident, why a human being's organs can still remain functioning and the only part of the body that will wither is muscle. Nor can they explain 'spontaneous remission' when a person who is diagnosed terminally ill can make a seemingly miraculous recovery. The second example is true of one such lady called Anita Morgani who now travels the world imparting her story to inspire and inform others and I was privileged to have heard her speak in person back in 2012.

The answer in both scenarios is PHYSICS!

All homeopathic tinctures are an INSTRUCTION OF PURPOSE for the body to heal itself. The Merkaba or Field around you, containing the trillions of cells, CONNECTS to the physical body waiting for you to COMMUNICATE with it. You are the BOSS! It is listening to the consciousness of YOU!

You decide how healthy you are going to be!

Disease or dis-ease is a low energy consciousness. When you raise your vibrations to a higher level of consciousness, disease cannot touch you. You become balanced. You become at ease with yourself. You love life everyday and do not see yourself as a victim.

As the support entity Kryon, the Magnetic Master, said,

"Homeopathy is a SIGNATURE OF PURPOSE... AN INSTRUCTION SET TO THE BODY TO HEAL ITSELF"

Homeopathy has been used for hundreds of years. We simply need to WAKE UP to the power of who we are and learn to connect to and address our complete cellular structure.

If we do not make the connection, then we will remain disconnected from approximately 90% of OUR DNA and our cells will flounder without us as their BOSS, ageing with every day cycle – sunrise and sunset.

"

I have just given you a clue to slow down ageing too!
So here is the information, you decide its truth.
Knowing that if you want to, you can even youth!
Every molecule in your body is waiting
to hear from YOU!
~ Lady Wise

Sending you endless ripples of love and BIG hugs xxx

LETTER 6

SOUL FAMILY OF LIGHT

"

The soul is ready now to be part of the creation of
internal peace in YOU! It is YOU! It belongs to you and
it is filled with grace, compassion, health and love!
~ Kryon

Dear Uncle Jim,

We are in a new energy on this planet in the middle of a paradigm shift – an invitation for a total and complete change in the way things work. How do we find peace and contentment within when there is so much for us as 'old souls' to react to when we see certain things on social media, television or in newspapers, for example? We must simply learn to relax into the arms of spirit and feel peaceful!

The paradigm that has worked in the past is that each of us receives help from a variety of sources. Traditionally, help would come externally! You go to someone who can help you, perhaps someone who can sit with you and make sense of your anxiety but then you leave and you still feel anxious.

Welcome to the soul! It is a piece of God inside you and it is hugely underrated! Now, you can listen to the soul inside of you.

Turn INWARD to what YOU have rather than to always look externally for help from somebody else. The soul belongs to you and it is multi-dimensional and filled with power and help.

The less intelligence a person has, often the quicker they are to recognise the truth of this information, because their mind tends to work in a more conceptual way based on feelings, rather than being focused on a logical, linear mindset.

What you tell yourself every day is SO important to reframe the new YOU! Expect good things and they will come!

Affirmations and reframing basic human nature can help YOU in shifting your belief system! Expect everything to be better than you would ever have imagined! Humanity is wonderful! All the things that you say are heard by your soul. This applies regardless of whether the words that you speak are directed at others or to yourself! The soul does not distinguish between what you say to other people, animals and what you say to yourself. It takes it all personally and accepts it as part of the 'oneness' of all that is. Now that you are wise to this, you are in a humble and privileged position to take extra care in your choice of words.

When you choose to change the paradigm of what your brain, heart and pineal have to say about the earth on an everyday scenario, your soul will start to feed you compassionate solutions. There is a Higher Self in every single human soul and you can make a choice to celebrate the creator in every situation that you see. There is light everywhere!

The soul is connected to the innate and to the biology of a human. Your soul is built to deliver peace and divinity to you which brings with it long life. It is the peace of love and compassion beyond the other side of the veil that brings YOU balance! It is the particle of the creator that is in you which makes the human soul different. Remember the existence of the veil is because every human has free choice to evolve their spiritual understanding. If there was no veil and no hidden spiritual knowledge kept from you until your evolved maturity of spiritual understanding, there would be no need for a spiritual journey!

As we encounter each day's issues, the soul stands ready to be reactivated in this paradigm shift. When we erase bad habits this contributes significantly to moving us forward! This is your legacy, old soul, a change in the paradigms of human nature! Welcome to the new human! Consciousness is not biology. It is the quantum part of your DNA. These non-protein parts of DNA will eventually be understood by most of the medical profession and many scientists.

Now that we are in this time period known as The Shift and we have past the central marker point of 21 December 2012, there is a greater benevolence and support from Mother Earth helping humanity to evolve. There is a dearth of invisible energies on planet earth that are here to help us. Some people can see, feel and hear these beautiful energies because they are highly attuned to the higher vibration. As each person becomes more mature in their wisdom and spiritual growth, these energies will be able to be observed, felt and listened to by that individual as they choose.

Can you really FEEL the LOVE? The change is in the air. It is REAL.

This is THE most important lifetime on planet Earth ever, to be alive. Your joy is your wisdom factor!

Sending you infinite love, hugs and healing, xxx

43

CONTROL OVER YOUR BODY!

"

Within the DNA is the piece of God that you are.
~ Kryon

Dear Uncle Jim,

You have control over your own cellular structure and it wants to hear from you. So how can you connect with it?

Let's first take a step back. Most people who judge will do this based on what they know, rather than what they don't know. It all depends on your 'bubble of reality'. Each person has their own world in which they live and now more than ever this is being challenged. We are each being encouraged to push our boundaries of what we know in order to learn more about the expanse of the universe and how we can affect the expansion of our own reality and realign it with the truth of our spiritual existence. It is time to stretch our spiritual 'bubble of reality' to new heights and to new understandings of the benevolent invisible energies on this planet that are here to help us in this period of transformation and transition. They can support us as we mature in our wisdom and our 'sense of knowingness'.

It is about learning to feel an energy about which you may not yet understand. It is about being open to new possibilities, without judgement.

If you are unsure about what you are hearing then simply be with the information, neither endorsing or being critical. Simply accept that new information has now come to you.

DNA is not simply a chemical molecule in your body. It is a multi-dimensional piece of divinity. DNA is best spoken of as an entirety (not as a double helix) made up of trillions of pieces. It is 100% YOU and unique. The hundreds of trillions of molecules are IDENTICAL. DNA all speaks together as ONE. It is in an entangled state in your body. It knows all of the other parts and they speak to one another and create a "field" that is dynamic. It is sometimes referred to as Innate or the Smart Body.

The imprint of the Higher Self or Higher Guidance is there. This is the 'God' piece. It is quantum and because of this quantumness, it contains that part of your spirituality, the record of all that you have been, and of all of the spiritual things that you have ever learned across all of your lifetimes on planet earth. The Wisdom of the Ages is imprinted in the DNA. You have a human genome that is absolutely unique. Not one human being has DNA like the other, not even twins, for only a fraction of it is identical, but not the quantum parts. DNA has to communicate with itself and yet many scientists do not yet acknowledge this.

When you start talking to your cells (and you can do this by thought or in any way you choose) the Innate knows that your consciousness is benevolent. It knows you want to stay on earth in your temporary physical form and there are automatic systems that will go into place improving other parts of your body that you never asked to be improved.

You are going to start a process of extended life, and healing will start to occur and balance in areas about which your consciousness has no idea, but your Innate knows all about – YOU HAVE JUST AWAKENED THE BRIDGE BETWEEN HUMAN CONSCIOUSNESS AND CELLULAR STRUCTURE. This bridge is essentially INTUITION.

~ Kryon

It's easy, Uncle Jim, but you've got to fall in love...with yourself! As the connection to the Higher Self is strengthened through one's own heart and the pineal gland, it is imperative to love oneself to build up a strong connection to the other parts of your soul on the other side of the veil.

YOUR cellular structure waits to hear from you. Remember the acronym CAL (Cells Are Listening). You can FEEL when you have made contact! Kryon teaches it is just like picking up a telephone and dialling the correct number. The cells are really listening. The science of epigenetics has proved this!

The first thing Kryon suggests that we might say is:

Dear Cellular Structure, Hello! We know each other and I LOVE YOU! I'm sorry it took so long for me to figure it out.

I want you to go into the processes that you know about that I don't.

I want you to come together in a benevolence that will create health and a long lasting human being.

If there are any chemical imbalances and inappropriatenesses in my body, I want them to go away through time and appropriate action.

I want my metabolism and body to echo my magnificence. Change what is needed. Bring my body to a place of balanced divinity and I promise I will talk to you every day because I love you.

... DO NOT HANG UP THE PHONE! Ha!Ha!

When a person goes to have a reiki treatment, therapeutic touch, a mindfulness class or acupuncture, for example, they are really going for a treatment to be balanced as an individual. The words balance and healing are interchangeable. YOU ARE ASKING FOR BALANCE AND INNATE KNOWS WHAT TO DO!

So, how does it make you FEEL Old Soul?

Perhaps you didn't know you have a friend inside to the extent that you can put years and years and years on your life! These are new tools for you to use. Your Akash or Akashic record is your own spiritual record of every lifetime that you have experienced on planet earth. It is held in your DNA. Your Akash only knows multi-dimensional impressions and potentials for it is quantum and so when you ask or 'pull on' your Akash to effectively decode your life, it will often give you this information in the form of dreams. Feel encouraged to move forward to embrace the

loving presence of the oneness of heart, wisdom and light.

Be present to the love of divine that surrounds us, lives in us, through us as ONE. Enjoy the moment!

Wishing you blessings filled with love and purpose!

Lots of love and hugs, xxx.

LETTER 8

THE SCIENCE OF LOVE!

The highest kind of physics is consciousness.
~ Kryon

Dear Uncle Jim,

Remember that you are never alone. When you decide to do anything that is sacred, spiritual or work on yourself you broadcast an energy of intent to the cellular portions of your body which are divine. A signal is sent to them that activates an energy that you do not even know that you have.

In the wisdom and the love of our Creator and by being consciously aware, we have incarnated on earth to heal (even when we think there is nothing wrong with us).

True healing begins when you FALL IN LOVE WITH YOURSELF. You must have the desire to want to make yourself the Light of God again because that is what you are! We are all consciousness!

You are not separated from your Higher Self, God or Spirit, you are that Light. Be the Light! Shine your beautiful, radiant light as it uplifts and inspires all those around you. Be accepting of this beautiful gift in a compassionate, graceful, elegant way!

If you choose, Kryon teaches us that you can activate your light as simple as saying:

"

Dear Spirit, dear Body and dear Innate, I am accepting of the meld taking place at this time in the way of your choice and it feels great.
And so it is.

In this new energy, for those healers, practitioners, and teachers who heal others on a one-to-one basis through meditation, reiki, mindfulness, acupuncture and other alternative therapies, remember to ask your client before the treatment if they give permission to be healed. When they respond with 'Yes' you can give the healing. When they respond with 'No' it is inappropriate for you to give the healing. Remember that every human being operates with free choice.

As an example, as a Reiki Master, I have often performed distant-healing for clients. Since 21 December 2012, before each treatment I ask the client through accessing their Higher Self if they give permission to be healed. When the response is 'No,' I do not proceed with the treatment.

Note that this can change from day to day. I may ask the same question the following day and the answer will be 'Yes'. At this stage, I can then give the distant-healing treatment and know that it is given with the permission of the client and for their highest good. This is why, Uncle Jim, I have been able to send you distant-healing because your Higher Self gave me permission.

Blessings and eternal love, xxx

LETTER 9

BORN WISE

"

Born wise... will change everything!
~ Kryon

Dear Uncle Jim,

Every situation you encounter was set up in advance for the lesson you wished to learn. In order to learn, of course, you need to recognise that a lesson is being offered! This is often the most difficult part. Ha! Ha! There are no answers outside of you.

Our egos have done a very good job of turning things upside down by making the unreal real. We have been encouraged by our egos to reject reality and thereby reject the true essence of who we are. Recently, I heard someone refer to the ego as an acronym for "Edge God Out!" You may have heard this too?

I know you know the story of Elijah but have you heard the story of Elijah told by Kryon and channelled by Lee Carroll? I would like to enhance the information as you

know it. The prophet Elijah with FREEWILL decided to ascend on his OWN SCHEDULE outside the transition of death and in his case, he had someone watching, a student called Elijah, who took notes of what was happening. Elijah DECIDED when he was going to die. He was in complete control over his choice to transcend his earthly body to the other side of the veil. No thing, no entity or no other person did it for him. Can you comprehend the Mastery of such a transition?

In addition, the wise student, prior to observing this unique event, asked that the prophet's powers be transferred to him before ascending and if you remember, this student then went on to work even more miracles than Elijah had done himself! The first thing that the note-taker saw was that the prophet Elijah turned into a ball of light. What was it? How did it happen? Nothing came down from the sky and no-one joined him. This is the combination of the pieces and parts of the soul on earth and the part of the soul on the other side of the veil. This combination cannot be sustained in a corporeal form.

When we decide to come into this side of the planet, we already carry with us a collective piece of the 'oneness' which is imbued in us and which can never be separate. **We cannot bring in our whole soul, because we would vaporise,** in the same way that Elijah chose to do on his physical departure from planet earth when he rejoined with his soul part on the other side of the veil upon his physical death.

When we are physically on planet earth, part of us has to stay on the other side of the veil with all knowledge of who we are, with all the love for humanity and an entourage of energies that often we have no idea exist. The part of our soul that remains on the other side of the veil sees the energy

of potentials for this planet's ascension and honours every human being on this planet.

The working puzzle, therefore, is that we already have a soul split when we choose to be born. Only part of our soul takes up a temporary residence in a new physical body. That soul part is the communication channel, or silver chord to which it may be referred, which allows an open portal from the little pineal gland (which sits in the centre of the brain and which is shaped like a pine cone) to that which is the piece of divinity that we are. It is the higher vibrating self. Other names by which it is known are Higher Self, Higher God or Higher Guidance.

One reason that so many of us have difficulty in connecting with our Higher Self, higher consciousness and our psychic awareness abilities is because the pineal gland has become calcified over time. There has been a build-up of plaque preventing the effective functionality of this important organ. This small endocrine gland produces the serotonin derivative, melatonin, which regulates sleep patterns and can become blocked and calcified from fluoride, bromide and/or chlorine. An alternative to using toothpaste with fluoride would be to use a little baking soda.

Furthermore, there are certain food types that that can be eaten to beneficially increase the activity of your pineal gland to expand your quantumness. These include pineapples, watercress, avocados, spirulina and coconuts. As an aside, do you know that spirulina contains more protein than meat?

Another name for this pineal gland is the 'third eye' and its importance must not be undermined, for it is through this gland that we connect to spiritual and universal frequencies.

Ancient belief systems and art forms have given recognition to this important gland shown in pine cone symbology. For example, the staff of the Pope shows the pine cone. The dollar currency note shows the 'third eye' as part of the artwork on the back. Furthermore, in Egyptian artifacts, the symbol of the eye was used.

Many more cultures have known about the power of this pineal gland and used it. When care is taken to develop the third eye the following benefits include:

- improved quality of sleep, because this gland governs the circadian rhythms and sleep and waking patterns;
- clairvoyance and
- improved imagination.

For as long as this pineal gland remains blocked, it may cause unnecessary confusion, delusion and illusion in a person, unable to connect with their Higher Self to receive daily guidance, intuition, clarity and assistance with solution provision in that person's life.

Without the ability to use this part of the body, a human being sees only with their two physical eyes and is denied the benevolence of the 'bigger picture' and vision of feeling the connection with the whole of the universe, with the true reality and in the realisation that we are not singular 'beings' but one with all that is in the universe.

Uno con todo!

Everything is connected!

Much love xxx.

LETTER 10

THE SHIFT

"

Energy comes from your heart and intuition
Step into your power and drop your inhibition!
~ Lady Wise

Dear Uncle Jim,

There is purpose in your life. It is about SHIFT.

Through divine love, gentleness and the beauty of who you are, you will manifest what YOU know as heaven on earth!

Mastery is the new tool of this Age of Connection. What do the Masters have that you don't have? Nothing. All were human beings. Jesus said, "I AM THE SON OF GOD AND SO ARE YOU!" His manifestation message was to help you understand that the magnificence inside of him is also inside of you. Sadly, this knowledge did not sit well with his culture and his era and so the Conquerors killed him. What he showed you is what you can do. You can change matter.

You can rewind the clock on your DNA. You can create healing that is beyond what you thought you could ever do. It comes right from the Higher Self inside you. Know that the energy of the Masters is with you and the only reason they were here was as examples so you could see it and do it today.

The Masters have all returned and they are wherever you are. They are here in spirit, in energy form, not in body. They are here to support you to create healing in your body.

Humanity is evolving and the technical name for this period 1994 until 2030 is The Shift. From 1987 until 2012 less than half of 1% of humanity had "woken up" to who they truly were.

"

In your DNA surges all that you ever were, 'Old Soul'.
~ Kryon

Our earthly experience is to hold the intent to be loving in every moment and in every situation.

Love is all encompassing. There is only love. Love is eternally present, honest, open, extending, sharing, compassionate, forgiving and healing. It never betrays because to do so would be completely contrary to its nature.

Things are going to work in a way that will surprise you in their purity and goodness.

Rejoice in a system that is benevolent and loving – created for YOU!

Love, hugs and healing xxx

A WINK FROM SPIRIT

"

It's time to expand our field of communication
And celebrate a grand love of collaboration.
~ Lady Wise

Dear Uncle Jim,

Has your eye caught the time on a clock as 11:11? Prior to 21 December 2012 it was not unusual to talk to friends and colleagues about noticing this on a regular basis. It was effectively a 'wink from spirit' that meant, "All is well!" regardless of your circumstances. Isn't that comforting? It was a reminder that even although we may be feeling unwell or be experiencing challenging personal issues we could always take a deep breath and know that we were not alone. Spirit is always with us.

Everything that is happening numerologically right now is painting a picture of new beginnings and a fresh start for humanity as truth, love, compassion and kindness take hold.

The number eleven in numerology is very powerful as it is the first Master number. That is the same number shown next to it. The Master numbers respond to the evolution of humanity which in turn affects the evolution of the universe. It was seen by many before the Shift and foretold Old Souls for years that the illumination effect was upon us and that the power of the light quotient would win. We see the first Master number 11 twice for emphasis. This number denotes enlightenment. It symbolises the spiritual growth of mankind and asks us to pay attention at several levels. It denotes an activation in a human being's emotional participation, spiritual understanding, transcendence and ultimate ascension!

Now, when I see 11:11, I think of the opportunity to send love around the world to go where it is needed. I invite others to do this too! Kryon asks us to imagine the power of love when we all choose to connect in at this time wherever we are around the globe. Across all the time zones I can imagine an almost constant thought field of love resonating all over Gaia, creating more light energy every time. What can you imagine?

Can you see the beauty behind the numbers 11:11? When I last spoke to you a few days ago, I put down the receiver and I noticed that we had been speaking for 11 minutes and 11 seconds. The joy of recognising 11:11 wherever it appears as a wink from spirit with love all around is brilliant!

Numbers are all about the energy of planet earth. Pay attention to the numbers that come into your life. You will start to see numbers over and over again that are just for you! Other people will notice different numbers. Remember that there are different levels of awakening and those individuals who do not see this are not ready yet. Everyone

sees things in a different light! Our job is to have a good time and celebrate our life in love and laughter!

Act as if there is only fun!

All love and hugs eternal one! xxx

BASE 12

"

The Pleiadians would never take away base 12.
~ Kryon

Dear Uncle Jim,

Do you remember when the UK changed over to a new system of weights and measures termed decimalisation in the 1970's and everyone had to change their mindset to learn to deal with metric weights and a new currency founded on a base 10 principle of mathematics? Suddenly, those adults who had only ever known a system taught to them of imperial weights and measures, founded on a base 12 principle of mathematics, had to learn to master a new system. The truth of the universe, however, operates a system of base 12 mathematics principle and not base 10. Kryon teaches it is as if there was a cover up of the purity underlying nature's system of love which has its origins in base 12 mathematics.

Around 600BC Babylonian understanding of the star constellation systems was renamed by the Greeks as the

familiar Twelve Signs of the Zodiac. The position of the stars and the constellations provided a guide not only to astrologers but to agricultural workers, fishermen and other outdoor workers. This psychology profiling is a beautiful symbiotic representation of astrology blended with the energetic 'life force' of humanity in all its vagaries.

This base 12 principle becomes especially relevant when it comes to the pairs of chromosomes that are in the human body. At this time, the majority of doctors, scientists and teachers still work on the basis that there are 23 pairs of chromosomes belonging to each human being. This is factually incorrect. There are 24 pairs of chromosomes in the human being of which the 24th pair is quantum. It is our multi-dimensional connection to nature, to the Gaia Grid, to the Crystalline Grid and to the eight metre field that exists around every human being. It is our little piece of divinity within that connects us to the creator source and frees us from a very limiting, linear, three dimensional existence. Twenty-four is exactly divisible by twelve and so retains the order of the base 12 principle of mathematics that operates throughout the universe and which is honoured by the Pleiadians.

New information is always coming to light – this pun was intended! The significance of this 24th pair is that it is the connection to the creator source of the universe. It is the communication with the avenue of prayer. It is not linear and your own internal communication with the creator source, in whatever way is appropriate for you, is enhanced the more creative you are in anything. We build a stronger connection to our inner divine quantum part when we spend time doing whatever we love doing. So cool!

Meantime, do not let your news and the chaos you see around you dismay you. This is all part of the Changeover Years (2013-2027). We need to experience the breakdown of those systems across the globe that are not built on love, integrity and truth before we can create new systems that are built on these values thereby giving us long term sustainability in this new era. Exciting, huh?

Wishing you creative dreams tonight, Uncle Jim!

Much love and loads of hugs, xxx

QUANTUM TEACHING

"
*I want you to relax and let spirit start to
realign your body while alive.*
~ Kryon

Dear Uncle Jim,

Can you feel your WHOLENESS now from your feet all the
way through your body, especially your heart area, and up
through your head? This wholehearted completion becomes
a REMEMBRANCE. Can you allow yourself to feel the
resonance of infinite LOVE pulsing through you?

Continue to nurture yourself each day, ever mindful that the
moment you have waited for is NOW. Feel the recalibration
and the energetic strength through your spine to support
you in these next steps. Your body is built to rejuvenate
itself. You are not this one physical human body separate
from everyone and everything else. There is so much to be
understood about the divine part of each human being,

wrapped up in the 24th pair of chromosomes. When this is recognised and seen maturely, it becomes the gateway for the expansive 'whole' creative expression of who you are.

YOU guide yourself to make decisions. It is the divinity of the Creative Source, the God Source that is inside of you that works with you and your intent.

When you talk to your Higher Self and say, "What do I need to know today?" without a bias and without a judgement of what the answer might be, this is when the answer will come to you. Sometimes the answer is simple. Don't be disappointed if all you get is a hug! That is an answer in itself. The hug is confirmation that answers are on their way! When it is the right time you will receive the solution to your problem. Synchronicity will bring it in and in the process, all you need to do is just relax. Without relaxation you will make decisions that will get in the way of the synchronicity that will occur. Therefore, the hug is an acceptable answer, isn't it?

It's all about perceptual communication. Can you see the beauty in this system and how wonderful it is?

"

You can look into the eyes of your grand-children and say, 'Look at what I've found – it goes beyond any generation gap that has ever existed – I have found God in me and you've got it in you. You can find it in you too. It's going to keep you out of trouble, it's going to keep you wise and innately, you'll always know what to do, no matter what.'
~ Kryon

What beautiful advice to give to a child. This is termed Quantum Teaching. While 'quantum' appears to be nonsensical randomness, it always has purpose.

Suggested Prayer of Gratitude:-

I am powerful as I am a piece of God and all of these things I give thanks for in the name of who I am, a creative piece of the universe, learning to expand my energy.

This is new! This is a process that nobody expected. It is called Ascension while ALIVE! We are able to vibrate into the next higher energy while we are alive and that took reincarnation before.

Innate is used to an old idea that reincarnation is the engine for enlightenment whereby one has to die to come back to have the new energy AND IN THIS LIFETIME WE DON'T! This is the power of the multi-dimensionality of the soul.

Your innate does, however, need to be reprogrammed and you can do this through positive thoughts and affirmations such as:

I AM PERFECT HEALTH. I AM JOY. I AM PEACE.

According to Kryon's teachings, perhaps you would prefer to give intent like this:

Dear Spirit,

I wish to have the solutions to the problem in front of me and the ones to follow that I do not even know about, in ways I cannot conceive and I trust Spirit for this.

Thank you, bring me more! And so it is.

It is all about connecting yourself to a bigger vision, to that energy that is so much bigger than yourself.

Lots of hugs, healing and love, xxx.

THE GAIA GRID

"

There is a raw, raw life in Gaia.
~ Kryon

Dear Uncle Jim,

The Gaia Grid is Mother Earth. There is an amazing life in Gaia of which many of us as human beings need to be reminded. Have you ever met a tree hugger? If you have or if you are one yourself you will know that special feeling from hugging a tree. As you hug a tree, the tree responds and hugs you back, sharing beautiful whispers of nature with you. It's such a pleasure to listen to the trees.

The indigenous understand Gaia's power and hold it in great respect. The Crystalline Grid offers a system of compatibility to planet earth and to humanity. The Crystalline Grid covers the rawness of Gaia in certain areas that protect human beings and allow us to be safe in certain places.

It is actually a (protective) cover you might say for the Gaia Grid.
~Kryon

A tree has a 'group soul' called Gaia. Their roots may be intertwined growing with other roots of trees.

I feel a little 'Haiku Wise' (my own version of haiku) coming on:-

Dripping rain...
Quenching the tree root community
Whose veins bubble in excitement!

So which tree receives the soul? Everything that comes under nature is part of a soul group and it responds to human consciousness. Remember that if a human has been very loving with a plant it will grow in a richness of size and health under the 'green fingers' attribute. This happens when there is an alliance with Gaia, with the soul of Gaia.

The lessons to learn about Gaia are simple and common sense. When we show loving kindness and respect to nature, we are rewarded with beauty.

In the same way that every human being has the power with free choice to broadcast either light or dark consciousness, Mother Earth has polarity too!

The whole purpose of Gaia is to support humanity. Gaia has an intelligence. Kryon calls it an 'INTELLIGENT CONSCIOUSNESS'. The Akash (remembrance) of Gaia is the life force of this planet. There is a system to keep track of who is here. Gaia needs a system and there is a reason

for this. Every single human soul that comes to this planet makes a difference, has a unique energy, creates a record and is an important piece of the wholeness of universal existence.

I thought you might like this little prayer of gratitude to Gaia courtesy of Kryon:-

Thank you planet earth for sustaining me every day, supporting me and for always being with me. Yours is a presence that I do not always acknowledge and yet I am learning that Gaia is a life force that is part of me too! Please help me to ground myself every morning as I visualise connecting to you with every footstep that I take. And so it is.

Keep tending and watering your garden plants with love, Uncle Jim, and watch them flourish! It's up to each of us to generate the light with which we came into this world! Fear cannot touch you when you broadcast light!

Wishing you abundant blessings of good health and well-being! Xxx

LETTER 15

THE WISDOM BARRIER

"

*The wise one knows that God is always with them
and knows all of the things that have occurred in
their life.*
~ Kryon

Dear Uncle Jim,

Feel the beautiful connection with Mother Earth move through your body. Can you truly feel the love?

Gaia honours the role of the Old Soul. Faith, trust and strong belief will lead you to happiness. The essence of love is pure and in a quantum state, time does not exist. There is only this moment.

Human consciousness is just consciousness. The Galaxy is made up of fractals. It does not matter the size of these fractals because they contain repetitive parts of the same DNA.

One planet may just be getting the 'building blocks' of DNA ready to be seeded by us in the future. It will be the same kind that we have, containing the same amino acid structures that we have.

It is only as recent as 21 December 2012 that we have escalated our evolution to become more mature, wise and spiritual. This means that we are such a young civilisation. As Kryon states, *"Your civilisation has not even been round the Galaxy one "rev" yet."*

By the way, the unit of a 'rev' is the measurement used to denote one full revolution around the Galaxy. The Pleiadians, who seeded us on planet Earth, have attained half a rev, emphasising our youth!

Indeed, we are effectively still in the playground when it comes to courtesy, elegance and manners! Essentially, we are still in survival mode. Kryon teaches us that the historic period prior to 21 December 2012 will come to be known as The Barbaric Years because of the difficult time that was experienced with no elegance of thought for life. The earth has experienced so much killing, death, torture and pain. This barbarism explains why some individuals have never advanced their maturity beyond an attitude of bullying.

"

I want to talk to you about ENERGY NOT SEEN. There is a complement of energy in the Galaxy that interests you and you can't see it but you want to, because it touches you in ways that are fascinating. Unseen energies make the difference.
~ Kryon

It is akin to a medical intuitive picking up on disease or joy in an aura. What is it that a psychic sees or an intuitive sees? Some of these unseen energies visit us, but none can influence us in the way that we can influence ourselves. Unseen energies have attributes that we don't know anything about.

Let us call the unseen energy the quantum consciousness of humanity. The Pleiadians realised that the physics of human consciousness could do everything that they ever wanted. In passing the marker of 21 December 2012 about which I keep mentioning, humanity on planet earth passed the Wisdom Barrier.

Certain quantum attributes occurred in a physics of consciousness in a certain way, in a distributed way, in order to break this barrier. What does this mean? It means that as human beings we are spiritually ready to accept that we will not always agree with another human being but at least we have the wisdom to get along without killing or maliciously hurting the other person whether verbally, physically, mentally or emotionally.

Humanity has broken the survival mode of always reverting to pain and torture when there is disagreement among other human beings.

Now, when a child is born they will come in with this wisdom. It pushes a button on physics that we didn't know existed.

"

The missing piece:- humanity explains things from only what they know and what they don't know – science looks into space and sees things that are not Newtonian

There are quantum rules that create attributes which affect the future of the planet. If we all knew about the physics of consciousness we would build a better world! Consciousness of physics sits there ready to be enhanced or not. The benevolence factor is one rule that generates benevolent action. When we are kind, it makes a positive difference!

When the rules of physics are applied in certain situations we can control it! The spiral delivery of it shuts the door on evil entities and those places of darkness that want to play with our consciousness cannot get in! It is the cumulative effect – one thing builds upon another. Kryon teaches us that darkness is an absence of light. When we increase our wisdom, we increase our light within. When we broadcast only light, nothing harmful can touch us.

Every single planet has had their own delivery of this depending on their own free choice. We have passed the Wisdom Barrier and the track record of each planet is the same. We all move forward! These things start to work in the laws of the consciousness of physics in ways that we will figure out and as we do, we create increased DNA light activation in our bodies.

When the psychic seeks to find out who has departed, they are simply talking to the residual in the Crystalline Grid.

They are not talking to you somewhere else, they are talking instead to the soul energy which remained here and is profound, but because the psychic is based in three dimensions they assume that they went somewhere else.

Do you know where I go when I meditate? I touch the cosmic lattice that is always here – I journey into the centre of atomic structure – I become in a quantum state with the Universe.

Let yourself feel the blessings that you create, love always xxx

LETTER 16

THE CRYSTALLINE GRID
Part 1

"
The Crystalline Grid is an
ENERGY OF REMEMBRANCE
that is all over this planet.
~ Kryon

Dear Uncle Jim,

I feel another poem coming on to explain.

The Crystalline Grid

The Crystalline Grid is an esoteric, invisible grid that lays
over planet earth's surface
It was placed here by our Starmothers the Pleiadians
on purpose
The function of this grid is to remember everything that
humans do

Noting when and where they do it and responding to it too
For this spiritual Grid responds to the Human
consciousness' vibration
And is quantumly aligned with the multi-dimensional Cave
of Creation
It has a dual purpose of facilitating transmission both to
and from the human DNA
As it works with the energy of humanity who are living in
real time today
The Grid also talks to Gaia which communicates to all
crystalline within the Earth's crust
As a key component of the esoterics of consciousness and
the system of love.

The Crystalline Grid of planet earth is a remembering grid of human action and emotion which is allied to us as human beings. It has to do with life on earth and it is allied to YOU! It was a gift from the Pleiadians and is one of many grids that work together for the benevolence of humanity, so that as human beings we can safely feel the energy and see it. It lays upon Mother Earth, the Gaia Grid, whether over land or sea and the proof of this is very evident to those sensitive human beings.

For example, where a battle of significance has taken place and an Old Soul walks across this land, they may feel the sorrow, the crying, the death and the pain of what has taken place, regardless of the time gone since the battle happened. I always remember my Reiki teacher telling me of the pain and sorrow she felt down at Battlefield, next to the old Victoria infirmary.

For a human being who would not necessarily call themselves a 'sensitive' that human who walks across the same piece of

land would still sense that it did not feel like a good place to be. Essentially, the human being is FEELING the energy of an event and this is when the Crystalline Grid works well, for it holds the energy there. As the consciousness of the planet evolves with the increased awakening of human beings to the grandness and beauty of who they are, this directly affects the Crystalline Grid.

In this remarkable New Era post 21 December 2012 the Crystalline Grid is evolving to the extent that places which prior to this time were renowned for sorrow and death, can slowly be positively transformed when human beings filled with joy and love return to these mental and physical 'battlefields'. Eventually, the strength of the love and joy from the human action and emotion of visiting these places will be remembered by the Crystalline Grid and wipe out any previous sorrow, death and ferocity that happened. Isn't that wonderful?

Perhaps we could help to accelerate the evolution of consciousness by meeting up at Auschwitz with the grand lady Edith Eger, a former Auschwitz survivor and author of 'The Choice', and spread lots of joy with readings, songs and poetry to dilute the burden that Gaia and the Crystalline Grid carry here from the atrocities of World War Two? This is a new time for us. Let's go do it and excel at being our own creators with love, compassion, understanding and benevolence!

Get well soon Uncle Jim and I will meet you there with Aunt Coral!

That is enough excitement for now! Ha!

In celebration of another new dawn I am sending you hugs and healing, xxx

THE CRYSTALLINE GRID
Part 2

"

Wherever you walk, when your intention
is to create peace,
you are creating light on the planet.
~ Kryon

Dear Uncle Jim,

Are you relaxing and not overdoing it? I do hope so. I know you were making good progress before your latest apparent setback but remember there is a reason for everything even when we cannot always see it or understand it. The big message for all Old Souls especially at this time of new energy is to SLOW DOWN. Make time for when you are doing nothing. When you do nothing you create a space and you make room for things to happen and for the energy of the multi-verse to move through you. Activating your DNA allows you to become more fully human. You become more aware of the larger story of existence, but most important is the quality of the life that you live and the quality of the LOVE with which you share and live. The quality of that love is why we each come here to Earth, because LOVE in the ethers is not the same as LOVE on Earth. With the advancement of our DNA comes the desire to teach one another and to love the Earth. Earth is a paradise! God is inside, not outside.

There is a GRAND plan, there is a system and the system has the plan whereby human nature itself will change as will our DNA. The change comes, not in the form of chemistry, but in the form of the Merkaba. The Ancestors know and knew it. They felt it, they saw it, they know the Earth, they cognised everything. We are changing the vibration of the Earth for new improved good, good, good vibrations!

"

Let me remind you that you are not the body, you are not the mind, you are not feelings and emotions, you are consciousness, you are Spirit, you are a piece of God. The vastness that is YOU is anchored in every molecule of your DNA. You are choosing to experience your 3D (three dimensional) reality otherwise known as your physicality. You are a creator in every moment, moment by moment. Your vibration creates. Your vibration is made up of many things. Your beliefs create. It is time to open up to new possibilities. It is time for you to take a look at what is 'true for YOU!'
~ Kryon

Crystalline substances in geology are the only known substances to scientists and geologists that can hold vibration. The metaphor of the Crystalline Grid is one that holds

memory and energy. The energy it holds best and what it was designed for was to hold everything a human being does. The planet responds to YOU! The consciousness of humanity is imbued into the grid every single day by your actions. Everything you do has energy. It seems like for millennia these energies that we have created have all been the same.

History repeats itself,
War repeats itself,
Greed repeats itself... until NOW!

Now we are in an expanse of time called The Shift. Slowly, we are now seeing in our daily lives the products of the Shift. The children are changing. Governments are changing. Regular human beings are awakening with a desire to change the very essence of how they live.

The governments currently that are falling across the world are ones that have been around for a very long time. The leaders of these fallen governments are in total and complete denial and are holding on to the bitter end. Many of them are prepared to face death and do. They refuse to believe what is actually happening. Both they and the leaders before them all had the same kind of control – there was a stability in the Old Energy – and that is changing. It all etches itself on to the Crystalline Grid. The Old Energy had become used to certain things and this Old Energy liked the fact that the Crystalline Grid remembers, but the extent to which it remembers these Dark events is diminishing and the Old Energy does not like this. Darkness also has a consciousness. Yet, those individuals who are convinced by and immersed in old energy patterning will not believe The Shift.

Yesterday, I explained about those sensitive souls who can sense energy when they stand in a battlefield that is several

hundred years old. They feel the sorrow and some even feel the release of death. All of it is recorded on the Crystalline Grid. Up until now, the mass events were recorded and so one could go to where that event was held, and feel the emotion. Sometimes it would be mass death and sometimes it would be joy. Every time it has been emotionally driven and it is this emotion that is the measurement. In that 'soup of emotion' is compassion. Compassion is the catalyst for enlightenment of planet Earth.

Humans sometimes come in just to be part of an event that creates compassion. The whole earth feels it and it is all recorded on the Crystalline Grid. The whole earth is changed because of human beings and their compassionate actions. If we were able to look at the cumulative emotional impact of the Crystalline Grid it would show the energy of Gaia at this moment.

The communication between humanity and Gaia is changing. As we change the dimensional perception of who we are and take on the dimensionality of our Higher Self, it changes the rules. This rule change is the catalyst for earth's Ascension in the future. The very earth starts to change because YOU are changing YOU! As you change, Gaia also responds and becomes multi-dimensional too! What impact does this have on the Crystalline Grid? It has already started to clean itself, because it is now resounding to both Light and Dark, instead of emotion.

How will this happen? As Old Energy (or Dark Energy) is released and fizzles out, a slowly increasing, enlightened, wise population is birthed triggering more innovative, sustainable long term solutions to issues such as water and electricity, for example. A shift happens when individuals choose to shift their focus away from war and on to more positive outcomes.

"

When a war no longer gets attention, pretty soon there is no reason for it. Only Light things that have an impact will change Gaia for such things suit the magnificence of God inside of YOU!
~ Kryon

Human nature will shift and drama will not matter anymore. This is what makes the complete difference! In the process of how we work with Spirit we become self-balancing. This is what an Old Soul does! We increase our Light quotient as we solve the problems of today. Solution increases Light. This is immediately seen in the Crystalline Grid, incrementally, in a way in which it never worked before. Amazing!

Everything we do is about creating peace on the planet. Our goal is to exist and love God. In the process we have marriages, children, friends that come and go, write books, poetry, sing, dance, paint, death, all of these things and so much more.

The Crystalline Grid is under your feet as you sit and acknowledge who you are.

Feel the joy of the Crystalline Grid connection from your bed!

Sending you earthly blessings of love and big hugs, xxx

LETTER 18

THE CAVE OF CREATION

"

*Deep inside the Earth there is an inter-dimensional cavern
that will never be found but which has three dimensional
properties.*
~ Kryon

Dear Uncle Jim,

Allow me to share a few more things in my poem,

The Cave of Creation

*It is time for you to know and learn about the Cave of
Creation*
*As part of the system of love from which we can take great
inspiration*
*In this present lifetime all the knowledge that we choose to
learn remains with our eternal soul intact*
*when we physically die, and is picked up again from the
Cave of Creation for us to know and use when we are reborn*

to give us the optimum chance to make a huge impact
Every single lifetime builds a library of wisdom
Into which we can tap as part of a grand system.
This lifetime is the most important lifetime ever in the history
of planet earth
When you depart your physical life with the most esoteric
knowledge possible you can return to planet earth and be
off to a flying start with your next rebirth!
The Cave of Creation is a real place on Gaia that will forever
be under protection
From being found by any human being regardless of
their intervention
It is the first place that we visit when we enter the planet
before riding down the birth canal,
And when we die and leave the planet, it is the resting place
for every soul and it's receptacle
A unique, esoteric crystalline object for every soul past,
present and yet to come
Is held within a memory vault called the Akashic Record
system
This multi-dimensional place of existence connects the
physical to the spiritual
And helps human beings find solutions to their problems
that most would call a miracle
Our Akashic record captures everything we do in every
lifetime on this planet
These cumulative experiences can then be used as a resource
in our current lifetime's gambit
The Cave of Creation interfaces with Gaia through the
Crystalline Grid
Whose presence affects the ground on which we exist
We affect the Crystalline Grid as a result of our own
consciousness and actions

When we come to the planet the Cave of Creation is the first place that we visit, even before the birth canal. When we leave the planet it is the last place we visit before we come home – known by all of us when we are not human, that is home to the Creator Source, God, Spirit or by another name of your calling.

The Cave of Creation is the repository of the record of humanity. It records ALL of the lives that humanity has lived and it records the very core, soul essence of who you are.

Here is how it works.

"

*Each soul in the Cave of Creation is UNIQUE. Each time
you are born into this planet it is with the same Higher
Self and the same soul. Each time you come and go from
the other side of the veil, the quantum potentials in the
Cave of Creation change. Everything in the system comes
around QUANTUMLY. One of these attributes of the*

Akash of Earth event is that there is no time in a quantum state – no past, present or future. There is, metaphorically, a crystalline substance for every soul on this planet. In this Cave of Creation there is a crystalline substance for every soul and every life that has been and always will be on this planet. The Cave of Creation is constantly in dynamic change, QUANTUMLY. Physically it does not change but POTENTIALLY it does.

~ Kryon

Let's take my name as an example. The name that I have when I go to the other side of the veil is recorded in the Cave of Creation when I choose to leave earth, metaphorically as Kryon teaches, as a 'stripe' on a crystalline structure. The crystalline structure remembers the vibration of who I was.

Now let's say that when I choose to come back and I am going to be called another name (that is unknown at that moment), before I reach the birth canal, another 'stripe' is tentatively added to the crystalline – same soul, stripe number two. As it develops on the planet, it expects me to return and activate or solidify the 'stripe' as I do when I pass over again. There is therefore a crystalline structure for every soul, not every lifetime.

And so the Cave of Creation becomes the Gaia record of who is here and who has been here. Now, this is where the inter-dimensional aspect may be difficult for us to fully understand and may often be a little confusing. The Cave is static from the point of view that no crystals are ever added or taken away. That means there is a crystalline structure for every potential human being who will ever live on Planet Earth. The Cave is predisposed in a quantum state to be complete every moment, therefore as things change on the planet it changes the crystalline structure. The Cave of Creation, nevertheless, is always complete. It has all of humanity in it – past, present and future – which means we are actually interacting with those who are not here yet! Super cool!

Let's recap. The Cave is a record of:

Who you are;

What you have done and

The energy of what you have done, which stays with the Earth.

"

The Cave is complete, it is sacred, it is sealed and
Gaia is there.
~ Kryon

In summary, the Cave of Creation becomes the record of souls' lifetimes and the energy that you create, whatever you do on the planet, whatever that means to you, is recorded and imbued into these crystalline substances. The record of your life remains on the planet with your accompanying vibration FOREVER! So infinitesimally beautiful! So profound and wondrous!

When I come back in then I will pick up "every lifetime" on the way back in – it is in my DNA – my personal Akashic record of every lifetime that I have been, of everything that I have ever done – ALL OF THE ATTRIBUTES ARE IN MY NON-PROTEIN DNA which includes my Akashic record. I have access to my lifetime record and prior. Why would this be important? It means that I do not have to relearn anything again!

You came into this life, Uncle Jim, and you read and listen to these words and you are learning that in your DNA, Old Soul, is EVERYTHING YOU NEED! If you give INTENT, you're going to have the WISDOM of the Ancients NOW and when you hear more of these messages you will say, "I remember this, that's right! There's nothing new here but it's nice to see it in writing."

The Old Souls on this planet have on average experienced at least one thousand previous lifetimes with the same soul and with the same Higher Self, even although in each lifetime lived on the physical earth, they may not always have previously awakened to who they truly were. The beauty of the human living this lifetime at this particular time of The Shift with the same soul is that when one is awakened or enlightened, the human connects with their Higher Self and their DNA percentage that is Light activated increases. The DNA contains the individual record of the one soul and ALL that it has done while you are alive. What a system! You are KNOWN and LOVED by the Earth.

Several young children growing up now are confusing their parents when they talk of past lives. There was one Caucasian young boy in America, several years ago, who kept mentioning to his mother that he had been a black lady who had died in a fire. At first his mother was skeptical and naturally worried that her son would come out and say such a thing. His mother, however, did some research and believed that it was best to seek information to substantiate about what her son was talking. To her shock and surprise she was able to find newspapers that mentioned the death of a black lady from a fire in the city specifically mentioned by the young boy. Although his mother was pleased to have found out about the truth of this event, she did not understand why

her son had this memory recall. She did not know about the physics of LOVE and its systems. For her son, his recall had probably been his last past life, judging from the year that the fire occurred.

As you start to remember the system, Uncle Jim, then the puzzle of life all fits into place. We are so young as a planet and only now in this special time are more and more Old Souls waking up to who they are. As humanity evolves to first seek peace on earth, thereafter the real fun then begins! What a journey! What an adventure! What a privilege! What a responsibility! What fun! What LOVE!

There is always so much more…. but that is enough for now.

Enjoy cognising the beauty of soulful meaning in your life.

Lots of love, hugs and joy xxx

LETTER 19

THE MAGNETIC GRID

"

The Magnetic Grid sits on the outside of Mother Earth
and is a quantum experience.
~ Kryon

Dear Uncle Jim,

The Magnetic Grid is one of three grids, all of which are multi-dimensional, and all of which work together and are operational today for us to FEEL.

The Magnetic Grid

The Crystalline Grid and the Gaia Grid are two grids of esoterics
That work together with the Magnetic Grid, which is a grid
of physics
There are anomalies and oddities where the grids interface
and come together in a special way
These oddities often have patterns which is part of the new
information of today

91

Magnetic variance is a spot that is an anomaly with the three grids (the Magnetic Grid, the Crystalline Grid and the Gaia Grid) and is going to have odd magnetics. The interesting thing about these anomalies is that quite often they are triangular. They often represent the mathematics of prime numbers: 1,3,5,7…Where every single one of these anomalies exists there is NO CRYSTALLINE. The Crystalline Grid is the remembering grid of human action and emotion. When there is no Crystalline Grid, all one feels is the power, the force, the life of the land. The force of the Gaia energy is so powerful and astonishing because it penetrates all the way through the earth and is not restricted to the thin outside surface of Mother Earth.

Mostly in the South of Ireland there is a similar anomaly, this time affecting the land rather than the sea. Here there has been an horrific amount of destruction, battles, death, strife and pain, yet, surprisingly, those humans who are especially sensitive to their environment can walk outside and feel the joy. Irish people around the world are known for their dancing, joke telling, fun, frivolity and spirits. One would expect the land to be covered in a Crystalline Grid, heavy with the human emotion and actions of battles, sorrow and death. This is not the case. The Crystalline Grid is VOID, just like in the Bermuda Triangle. The land in Cork is pristine! You can FEEL it! Those individuals who have been born here have something inside in their DNA that is pure Gaia. It is something that can awaken. There are so many people who have seen fairies in Cork. The land is known for it.

Do you remember in history of the Great Hunger which began in 1845 when there was mass starvation and death of people in Ireland due to successive failed potato crops that were diseased? This was as a result of an uncontrolled Gaia with no Crystalline Grid, demonstrating that, AT THAT TIME, pure Gaia energy was working in a detrimental way rather than in a good way.

NOW that the energy of planet earth has shifted, Gaia is in co-operation with this and so in this new consciousness there will never be a repeat of the negative uncontrolled Gaia state that brought with it the potato famine in Ireland.

Kryon's teachings inform us that both Cork in Ireland and the Bermuda Triangle, Florida are examples of magnetic variance, which is music to my soul because as a child I was always really curious about the Bermuda Triangle and why

it seemed so different from other places on earth. How refreshing to finally have it explained.

When was the last time you visited the Emerald Isle, Uncle Jim?

Sending you hugs and loving wishes, xxx

ACCESS TO OUR INNER-NET!

"

When we have access to our inner-net
We do not need to use the internet.
~ Lady Wise

Dear Uncle Jim,

Could it be that things are different from what you thought? Discern this information with your own mind and measure it for yourself with validity – with your reality.

The concept of Kryon's teachings that I share with you today is that there is no single brain – there are three! That is so exciting to know in itself! Tell me more I hear you say!

I like to use the phrase, 'The Triad is CIA'.

Kryon explains that there are things that are not visible to any spectrum yet, and the brain is responsible for facilitating them all, while the other two (intuition and the heart) are doing all the work. So these three parts to human consciousness go beyond the brain and create the trilogy of survival.

Our freewill to explore our divinity inside is the opening to this triad of the brain, pineal gland and the heart. When all of these are actively used together we become 'plugged in' if you like to our Higher Self and the result is 'compassion in action'.

"

Our brain is a synaptic computer...giving you the possibility to control your survival, your thoughts and your body in three dimensions (3D).
~ Kryon

I remember at school being taught about two halves of the brain. The teacher explained that one side was the logical side including everything responsible for mathematical abilities, while the other side of the brain was the creative side responsible for music, for artwork, for painting and all things creative. The truth is that the brain has nothing to do with these attributes. IT FACILITATES THEM!

When we create, create, create we are connecting to Creator Source through the pineal gland. The brain facilitates the pineal gland. As humans we each have access to our own unique inner-net of wisdom! Our intuition is facilitated by the brain which activates it into thought.

"

The second brain of the human body that is superimposed upon that which is synaptical and biological is the pineal and that is intuition.
~ Kryon

Intuition comes from innate inside the body.

The bridge between human consciousness and the smart body is INNATE. This is the strength of INTUITION, which continues to strengthen as we evolve.

"

The brain is a survival instrument, it is a survival organ, but your INTUITION is going to grow stronger and stronger. Your inner – internet is getting faster!
~ Kryon

The evolved human being has a tendency to create Light.

Do you remember Uncle Jim the story in the bible of Moses and the burning bush? In your old church in Manly, I was always fascinated by the lead glass window depicting this Biblical story. This was a flame that did not consume itself but if you really could see it in reality, it was a white light. It was a higher consciousness than he had ever seen before, an energy coming through his pineal projecting it to him.

The third element of consciousness is centred in the human heart which has the strongest magnetic field of all organs in our body. We view it metaphorically as the symbol of love.

Perhaps it's time for you to activate the triad too, Uncle Jim!

Feel the warmth of the love that surrounds you at this time
xxx

LETTER 21

WHITE LIGHT!

Of all, it is the children who see your light first!
~Kryon

Dear Uncle Jim,

WOW! What a message that was, you'll need all three brains to absorb and take it all in! Ha! Ha!

When you are connected, you are able to see that it is the brain that FACILITATES the connection and the inner-net connection is to the creative source – white light!

Under old energy patterning, for those individuals born pre 21 December 2012, the moment we were born we were programmed to believe that we were only a physical body. Perhaps that is why we seek to cling so hard to it, to materialism, the personality and life's attachments. Yet, above all else we are consciousness and we exist beyond time and space.

Could the massive photonic energy arriving on this planet be the help we need to decodify ourselves from old programming and discover the essence of consciousness that dwells within us?

When we read the 1st Epistle of Paul the Apostle to the Thessalonians Chapter 5 Verses 2 to 5 it mentions in verse 5, "Ye are all the children of light".

What you seek is seeking YOU! It's beautiful, Uncle Jim! The awakening of this information is ineffable! Slowly, over generations we will create a peaceful earth.

When you take care of yourself, all the other things fall into place. It is the test of free choice. It is about being here! Why do it? Those of us who do it will live longer with a sweeter life, without frustration and without drama.

I love Kryon's illustration of putting on a coat to suppress one's ego and to allow one's light within to shine and radiate love, compassion and joy.

"

Something happens when you put on that coat, you will see slight changes in your personality – all of the ego that was there is buttoned up in your pockets... and wants to get out too, but nevertheless, as you wrap your own hands around yourself and wear that coat, the ego stays put and people will not see the ego anymore. They will see the coat – a mantle of spirit.
~ Kryon

When someone has a Near Death Experience (NDE) they go to the white light. This is more than metaphoric. That

person starts to create something that Kryon explains as Divinity and Mastery. White light emanates from a person the higher they evolve. The more one's DNA efficiency is increased, the whiter the light becomes.

Remember God is in you! You are an extension of the Creative Source.

Let your heart sing! All love, xxx

LETTER 22

FALLING IN LOVE

"

Your true nature is to love and love never judges.

~ Kryon

Dear Uncle Jim,

One of the reasons we are encouraged to stay on earth as an Old Soul to guide others is to have fun, even while at work. Besides when we work with passion how can it be called work when we love what we do?

Can see the profound and precious love that is offered to you?

Do you remember how good it felt when you fell in love with Aunt Coral? This is why falling in love is so amazing because God is there.

In fact, the brain is really frustrated that you are in love. It's saying, "Why did you put your shoes in the fridge?" You

101

say, "Because I'm in love! I was distracted and forgot." That's what love is. Ha! Ha!

When you look at somebody and say, "I love you" that is PURE INTENT. If you are not in love with a person and you say, "I love you" because they want to hear it, it's not the same and it never will be. The love isn't there. The connection isn't there. The communication isn't there. The entanglement isn't there. It is just words.

Now let's look INWARD. There is a divine part of you that is in love with you and waiting for you to say, "I LOVE YOU!"

and your cellular structure will know you mean it. And so, when you fall in love with yourself and honour your sacred body to such a degree that you realise it is part of God's creation of YOU, your heart becomes filled with that love and you open up to an awareness that connects to multi-dimensionality. You touch the divine part of you that is your birthright. Without it there would be no enlightenment, no consciousness, nothing.

Some of the indigenous such as the gurus of India can control their body and slow their heartbeat down. They talk to a part of their body that is listening and adjusting – they know how to do it – AND SO DO YOU!

So knowing this information, what is next? When you are in touch with this divine part of you, it creates a pathway to your cells, which wait for human consciousness to give them instructions. How do you do it? Your toolset is being enhanced. You CAN do this. Your cells have been listening since you were born, waiting for the time when you would AWAKEN and actually speak to them so let's do it!

You can talk to them any way you want – through thought, in writing, out loud, in song! Any way does not matter because they are part of YOU. You have their number and the key is LOVE.

When you start communicating with your cellular structure and you have the number right, you will feel a MASSIVE amount of chills – these are the cells celebrating. The body has JOY. INNATE has a party. Your entire body will rejoice with every breath. All these years it has been waiting, listening for communication, because without direction it just does what it wants. Without instructions your body is simply going to follow the AVERAGE.

With instructions, YOU CONTROL YOUR BODY. It couldn't be simpler. Firstly, your body celebrates, secondly it starts to work. Believe you are perfect health! When you start talking to your cellular structure (in thought, for example) these instructions go straight to the data in your DNA. Is your heart smiling today?

Feeling joyful, feeling healed, feeling blessed enables you to carry with you a consciousness and a light. By your light and your actions your family, friends and all are touched by you in so many different ways. Mother Earth awaits what you are going to do next and will then morph to complement the energy you create!

For now, relax in the invisible benevolent support all around you that loves YOU!

All love and hugs, xxx

CONDITIONING YOUR DAY

"
We have the power to create the best version
of ourselves every day!
~ Lady Wise

Dear Uncle Jim,

I hope your sides have been sore with laughing since we last spoke. A good laugh is great for the soul! What a wonderful surprise to hear you on the phone yesterday when you called me. It made my day! Thank you so much for taking the time to call especially since you were only up for a short while. I was thrilled that you were able to sit out on the veranda on a balmy summer's day and have a delightful chat with one of your neighbours. What a treat! Of course, the trick now is to take things slowly and to hold yourself back from racing off in your wheelchair. Ha! How many miles per hour can your wheelchair do? Is it potential competition for the Formula 1 driver, Sir Lewis

Hamilton? Ha! Where are you making beauty today? Are you feeling wonderfully carefree today? I do hope so.

Every morning when I wake up I choose to condition my space for the rest of the day ahead. Perhaps I will say, "I am going to have a quiet day today with a few great surprises thrown in at random," as an example. This worked well when I said this yesterday morning because one of my great surprises was when you phoned me for a brief chat! Intention is everything. I like Kryon's suggestion of an intention of working with spirit such as:

"Bring me ever greater clarity of mind and peace in my heart"

This is powerful conditioning.

When we take a few moments first thing in the morning to condition our day, then it is effectively our time to connect to our Higher Self and choose to take responsibility for our day ahead. When we choose not to do this then our day may become particularly chaotic and full of unnecessary drama as we are drawn into the shadow aspects of the veil and all the 'nonsense' as I call it that this brings.

Time taken to condition our day every day is important time for ourselves to determine what we want to happen. When we make our own choices we are deciding how we want to live. We are able to be independent and think creatively.

Why would you want to be caught up in the mass thoughts of other people when you have the power to create your own thoughts of how you want to live your life? Your life experience becomes based on your desires and no-one else's thought forms.

Expression of freewill has to do with intent. Wisdom, tolerance, patience and acceptance speak through intuition. I just love the fact that metaphorically speaking when you reach your hand out to spirit they reach their hand out to you too! So cool, so comforting and so healing!

Wishing you health and happiness as always.

Love 'n hugs, xxx

LETTER 24

GREAT EXPECTATIONS!

"

Forgiveness is a much deserved gift we give to ourselves.
~ Lady Wise

Dear Uncle Jim,

Thank you in advance for allowing me to share some ideas with you. Today I am going to start to expand on love and how its beauty and benevolence operates for the benefit of every human being who chooses to open up their heart to it.

Mother Earth respects the freewill of every human being. It is only when we ASK for support and guidance that we RECEIVE it. You remember that this is a long known experience. 'Ask and it shall be given unto you' are familiar words to you in your religious sermons.

At this time, it is the Old Souls with the balance of body and mind who are connecting with spirit first in this Shift and changing human consciousness. There is an innate

acceptance and understanding to be the guide for others – to be the Wayshowers. Us 'Old Souls' are here to be examples to others simply by being who we are! This light then resonates with others who often unconsciously then start to change themselves. This is the evolution of humanity. It is about giving hope and peace to the planet. We are here to create, create, create! Staying healthy is of paramount importance.

What do you expect? Be careful! You might receive what you asked for! Ha! The beauty of synchronicity is that it runs on God's timing to allow all the potentials of your wishes to be satisfactorily fulfilled. And so it is no surprise that patience is a real virtue. Ha! Ha! Can it really be so easy to live a life of love and laughter? Yes. It all starts with forgiveness. When we choose to forgive then we can set ourselves free, enjoying every day as a new day, breathing in the joy of every moment, contented from our inner knowing that we are safe, secure and fully trusting of our inner wisdom. Remember that when we trust our intuition it is always on our side.

Some other affirmations that Kryon teaches to help provide the feel good factor are as follows:

I am trusting of the process of life and I am not limited by any past thinking. With each thought I am creating my future. Today I look at life with a fresh pair of eyes. I choose balance, harmony and peace and I express this in my life.

I give and receive joyously and lovingly. I choose to contribute to world peace by keeping my thoughts high and I contribute to world healing with every kind, joyous, grateful, peaceful, generous and loving thought.

I know that my mind is a powerful healing tool and that the cells in my body are continuously responding to my inner mind and how I feel.

I am in love with life. Divine love leads me each day and keeps me grounded. I am deeply grateful for and very appreciative of being alive!

Sending you blessings of love, xxx

LETTER 25

SMILE WHEN YOU FEEL IT!

Love is the highest vibration on the planet.
~ Kryon

Dear Uncle Jim,

On 21 December 2012, our planet reached Graduate Status for the first time! The tipping point for the light being stronger than the dark energy was 21 December 2012. There is no going back. We are firmly on our way to peace on earth. Ignore all the doom and gloom! This is an example of a mass energy that has still to wake up to the wonder of a new future filled with hope and light, bringing with it new ideas and innovations to help humanity on a grand scale.

The reason this time period is called The Shift or the Changeover Years is because everything that is not built on a foundation of love and integrity is breaking down. It has to! It is up to the Old Souls and the children coming into

110

earth at this time, in their purity and honesty, to realise the wonderful new solutions that there are to the many problems that we have. As above so below! Heaven is on earth!

It is up to us to create the most beautiful place for us to live here on earth. We are part of the Creative Source, of God, of whatever one chooses to call it. There is nothing of which to be afraid.

Love and fear cannot co-exist and so when one lives a life filled with love, there can be no negativity such as doubts, anxiety, gossiping, anger, bullying, harassment, worry and fear. There is only love! Love is multi-dimensional too and we all know what that FEELS like! It is time to safely, timely and graciously wake up and truly feel the power of love as it is the highest vibration in the universe!

Lots of smiles, love and hugs xxx

LETTER 26

SOUL EXISTENCE

"

Allow your feelings and emotions to be your guide
As you connect with the invisible universal energies inside!
~ Lady Wise

Dear Uncle Jim,

What makes your heart sing and not sink? Would it be a portion of home-made hot curry with a glass of orange juice and a couple of Anzac biscuits to follow? Ha! Ha! I remember that holiday in Perthshire very well even though it was over 30 years ago!

The Creator is inside! The beautiful help that is the love of God is ALWAYS there, making instant help in every moment available to you! Go with what you FEEL! Let the energy of this message touch the esoteric, multi-dimensional parts of you, so you know it is real, it is safe and it is beautiful.

There is a meld of energy and consciousness that can only happen with humans because we were created in the image

of God and the image is compassion of knowledge, understanding and beauty. What can we learn about the soul?

SOUL EXPERIENCE

The essence of your soul that you cannot yet see
Holds all your personal experiences of past and present
reality
This higher guidance represents physics in its true contextuality
It is known as the science of spirituality
As a barrier to humanity, the veil keeps us from knowing
who we are
This is on purpose, as we choose to break free from
all things linear
In the sacred world, ALL of reality is in a circle
And those with the highest consciousness have an aura
of the colour purple.

Kryon teaches us that from the love source of nothing became the Human Soul and explains this using the metaphor of the Mother Tree.

"

There are billions of you and so you may say, there must
be billions of souls? What if there was a beautiful silver
tether that went from the main source to every human
being? What if the Creative Source was like a Mother Tree
with roots and those billions of roots were your souls? Let
me ask you how many souls are there? They are
individual and yet, they are the same. They have never
disconnected. They come from the vastness where there
was nothing. They always were and always will be and
every single human being is involved – every one of you.

Love is natural and the fact is that so is the creative source in YOU! There is more to follow soon!

Lots of love! xxx

LETTER 27

COMPASSION IS IN FASHION!

"

Compassion will be the king of all emotions.
~ Kryon

Dear Uncle Jim,

Every puzzle, fear and frustration is known by God. Imagine this soul energy connected with the silver chord to the Master Tree. We are simply roots of a single soul called Creator Source, God, spirit.

There are multi-verses but since we do not yet fully understand the physics of it all, we have no idea of the different levels of dimensions that are possible. Full realities exist that we cannot see yet. These invisible realms exist.

Kryon teaches us that there was no such thing as the Big Bang. Instead there was what one would call a Dimensional Shift, when the very membranes of physics collided and our

115

Universe was born. While our Universe was born, our Galaxy was being formed and other Universes were there. Other Galaxies were there. Other Planets were there. Our Universe is not the last one nor the first one, but one of many.

The soul energy which is the Creator, is part of the plans that are spiritual in ALL the Universes. The consciousness of God is involved in all of them. The Soul is part of something massively big and it was involved in the Universes before ours.

Now think for a moment, Old Soul. If we are part of the Creative Source, we were there! Our Galaxy is far older than the four billion years that scientists say.

The Universe itself has many age layers. The majority of science and scientists look at things as the same: one beginning, everything ages the same and all the speeds are the same. Yet, Kryon teaches that there are so many differences that we have not yet seen. If time is relative, that means that certain parts of the Galaxy itself could be older than others. Some puzzles we see in space are because we apply the same rules to everything. When our solar system was literally an infant, this Galaxy was a billion years old and other planets were there.

Moreover, Kryon explains that when we discover microbial life in other parts of our solar system we will find DNA. The same processes that have made us have made others. Is it possible that the same physics that created you has created others? Before there was even a single cell on our planet there were others like us and some had souls. The souls came from that vast nothingness – without a beginning and without an end. Forever is a circle. Part of your soul existed with the others before Earth and you were there.

There were planets going through what Earth is going through now, before there was Earth, and graduation spiritually occurred on many of them, changing the vibration of a Galaxy. With FREE CHOICE, planet after planet would come and find the light, and in doing so, the physics of the middle of the Galaxy began to shift.

These Kryon teachings give you the physics of why everything exists so that soul energies journeying to physical bodies have a chance through time to find the divinity with free choice and actually change the attributes of light itself. The WHOLE GALAXY changes when a planet wakes up. The whole planet changes when a human being wakes up.

"

God is the same yesterday, today and forever, but the RELATIONSHIPS within the Universe to God CHANGE, planet by planet, and slowly the Earth was formed.
~ Kryon

It is up to each one of us to mature in our love, knowledge and wisdom and thereby relate to the magnificence of who we are and appreciate the magnificence of the soul.

Each of us has an invitation to control physics with our consciousness and our thoughts. At this point when enough of us work on self-transformation and achieve this, collectively the planet moves into GRADUTATION STATUS. This is slow but we are already there!

After thousands of years of low consciousness and war – we have had enough. The precession of the Equinoxes aligned (21 December 2012) and ever since, consciousness has continued to rise. Look for this in your grand-children, Uncle

Jim. You're going to see it in politics and in the integrity of what you accept and don't accept in business as just two examples. You're going to start thinking differently.

We are going to start to seek COMPASSION in our leaders. A compassionate person is a wise person, Old Soul. This is our journey. We are the peacemakers!

Much love, hugs and healing xxx

LETTER 28

ESOTERIC TOOLS OF HELP

"

As the Earth goes through this Shift, the tools of light are changing. You can pick them up and use them and start the Integration Process.
~ Kryon

Dear Uncle Jim,

I want you to know so much! You are loved beyond measure by the invisible energies of the esoteric world! As human beings have a consciousness that is curious but unfortunately, we have a tendency to look at everything in a LINEAR way. When we use logic we are operating in a linear way. This inhibits us to think in a more conceptual way with feeling. There are, however, pieces and parts of our DNA that have very small quantum elements and these are AWAKENING!

Your curiosity becomes heightened because you are FEELING these things. The Creative Story is that the earth has been

"seeded". Human beings then have the knowledge of light and dark energy. This is where the Soul really comes into the human. Dear Uncle Jim, there is so much to learn about the attitude of the Soul. Is the Soul yours? Absolutely and totally. Moreover, it was yours in the last lifetime, and the lifetime before that and the lifetime before that. It means it has many names if you want to name it. As humans we generally want to attach a name to everything! So, if the Soul is part of the Master Tree, could it be that YOUR SOUL would somehow be connected to someone else's soul? Oh, how perceptive you are!

We are ALL connected, but not in a linear way.

Have you ever met another human being that thought so much like you thought, you would believe that somehow you are connected? Perhaps it is an esoteric connection, a consciousness connection? You meet a brother or a sister, a soul mate and you know somehow a part of you is in part of them... and that's going to be for another message.

What is the attitude of a Soul? You want to assign attributes to this beautiful thing you call your Soul. If it is part of God and part of you, what is the purpose? And, if there is a purpose how would you talk to it and is it you or not you? Dear Uncle Jim, this is the Duality, this is the veil that separates the human being's biology from the esoteric, multi-dimensional Soul. The energy of this planet is beginning to shift.

More and more humans are waking up to true things that God is not apart from them, but part of them. The attitude is integration. This has been the message from all the Masters of the Planet. We are in a new age of connection with new benevolent energy ready to support us. This enablement is brand new and has never been on this planet before. Believe in yourself!

Now, if that is so the next question is, how do you integrate? How can you take a three-dimensional biology and somehow obtain some communication from this beautiful part of God that is YOU. Can you FEEL that it is YOU or is it still something esoteric floating out there somewhere? Where is the Soul? Dear Uncle Jim, in every single case where there has been physical biology inhabited with the Soul, the Soul inhabits the human at the molecular level. The Soul is INSIDE, not outside. This creates in You an 'integration potential'.

You were taught as part of your ministry that you have to go through all manner of hoops to please God. This is not how the system works. The Soul is part of God, it is inside you.

"

God knows who you are in a way that is connected to you as never before.

~ Kryon

This is the power of compassion and love. The more you integrate, the more you shine on this planet. The more you can feel love and purpose for YOU, the closer you become to being BALANCED and that's when you RELAX, put a SMILE on your face and say, "It is well with my Soul that I am happy just to be!" And then...the memory starts.

You know you are Ancient, you know that death has no sting. You see the cycle of life and understand it. You are comfortable even with those you lose around you. It is possible to let go those you have loved and lost. There is no need for the sorrow inside because the only thing that has died is the biology.

121

The soul of those you have loved and lost are still here, some of them are with you and some of them have joined the Creator Source and in your three dimensional state you cannot see them.

What if you were to train those around you to celebrate when you choose your time to pass. You've got plenty of time! Show them how this works so that when it is your time, your children and your grand-children will well up with JOY. They'll miss you, but know you are not gone. What a truth this is!

Many people have been told by some to fear God. Do you know what you could fear? TOO MUCH LOVE!

Your essence is connected to the Creative Source and YOU have freewill to see it or not – right now – true or not. It's beautiful to feel that release is it not? Old Soul you are ok, walking through life after life helping the planet as you go. Dear Uncle Jim, how does it feel to start to have the realisation that every human being is so loved beyond measure and that the Creator of the Universe would love to take your hand to integrate.

Multi-dimensional information has a difficult time being taught but for now, it is enough to know that the Creative Source that we call God is not to be feared, is not to be worshipped but to be allowed to love you and integrate into your life; to change your ageing pattern and to let you have JOY. You may read this and be healed. The Creative Source energy knows who you are. You can listen to and/or read these words from now and claim the healing you have chosen. That is integration. The healing comes from INSIDE YOU!

How can the body suddenly clean itself of disease? It does

this spontaneously, all at once. The body then rebalances chemically at a cellular level. What was, is GONE! Sounds like a miracle doesn't it? Welcome to INTEGRATION. This is the attitude of your Soul. Why not YOU? The time is here. It's synchronicity that allows you to listen to this, to read this, and you have FREE CHOICE to ignore it or to feel different than you did before you heard this information.

Let all be well with you.

Much love, xxx

LETTER 29

SOUL AWARENESS

Soul Awareness becomes Planetary Awareness. This is how the one person changes the many and literally how the planet changes its vibration, because of humans doing something.
~ Kryon

Dear Uncle Jim,

You have a time to eat, a time to worship, and a time to work. Yet, it is only when we are in certain places that we allow ourselves to say it is ok to flip the switch and FEEL our awareness of the soul.

Soul awareness is a reconnection. You are able to reconnect with what has always been disconnected in your life until now: the animals, the trees, the dirt, the oceans, the birds, the sky. At some level, they Know Who You Are. Can you FEEL it yet? As you connect with your soul and have an awareness of what is there, everything starts to connect again.

Set aside fears that have plagued you for years
Throw away your limiting box of beliefs
Welcome a reconnected 'New You' full of love with all
fears released.
~ Lady Wise

Even the air that you breathe knows you and the consciousness that you have begins to shift! You become reconnected with the sacredness of Gaia.

There is a new energy on this planet that is going to call to many people and this call is to become aware that there is something more. You may become peaceful, more joyful and relax. Individuals who do this live longer and they have no idea why. They have connected to something that is divine and beautiful. This Soul or Higher Self is metaphorically like a water faucet inside you. It has got to be turned to be activated. Further, the handle must be gripped firmly with intent and turned to open it and if you do, there is pressure behind it. It will come flowing into you. You do not have to be much more than be aware that this is exactly what you want. Yet, that's not what you're taught. To most people, the faucet is rusted. To some they are told that there can be no faucet. They're not even aware of it.

It is not possible to separate your health from your joy when you start opening the faucet. You become more aware of what is there. EVERY cell of your body knows what you have done. Things that you didn't think were possible regarding your own physical body start to happen; so many issues that you've had all your life.

Perhaps you have done things a certain way for so many years that you think it is impossible to change? When you become aware of that multi-dimensional soul that you have, these bad habits will simply go away.

It IS possible to change your biology after all of these years.

Your DNA has designed your body to rejuvenate. When you start opening that metaphorical faucet the divine energy that starts to come in to your cellular level begins to affect the efficiency of the rejuvenation process. This is a FULL BODY REALISATION. How aware are you?

If you take on the divinity that you have earned, it's part of YOU! Your cells vibrate differently. Your auric field will change. Are you aware of the imprint that you leave wherever you walk? Remember that the Earth knows who you are? The Crystalline Grid remembers the footsteps of Old Souls. Wherever you choose to walk in your divine way changes the planet. Everything is connected.

As you become aware of your soul and as it comes into cooperation with your cells, the Field around you increases in its divinity and wherever you walk you will remember. The very dirt of the Earth will know you. If you decide to study some of the most ancient belief systems that you can find, such as the aborigines, they will tell you what I am telling you. KNOW that you are part of all nature and it is part of YOU!

Are you aware of how much influence you have on others when you start to have compassion? Other human beings want to be with you. They just love to sit next to you and talk to you because they are aware of what you have done. Soul Awareness is YOURS, Old Soul!

Love and hugs xxx

THE BOND OF LOVE

"

The Soul is the oldest friend you have and the oldest part
of you on the planet. It is your best friend.
~ Kryon

Dear Uncle Jim,

Each time you come to this planet, no matter what you looked like, no matter what gender you were or what name you were called, the same Higher Self comes in with you.

Pure love is so elegant and is the basis of spirituality. A multi-dimensional love is everywhere. It cannot be defined nor can it be confined. Ha! IT JUST IS. The soul is multi-dimensional. Kryon asks us to imagine that tree which is the sacred source. It is God. Imagine the roots of that tree are connected with a silver chord to each soul in the room or to Earth. WHERE IS YOUR SOUL? Ha! Well now you are suddenly realising that you are sharing it with the Creative Source. It is always connected to God. That means part of you is... somewhere else. Are you remembering that in a

127

multi-dimensional state, there is no PLACE, so we are simply saying it is the other side of the veil. This makes sense because I have already just stated that you are not all here.

Part of the essence of YOU is also on the other side of the veil. It has to be, for when you connect to the Higher Self that is what you FEEL – the connection to spirit is this way.

"

What if I told you right now that a piece and a part of your soul is being shared by other souls?
~ Kryon

As an intellectual Uncle Jim, your mind is probably filled with questions such as:

Who is it?
Where did it come from?
What is the percentage being shared?
And the answer from Kryon... is YES. Ha!

It is ENERGY, dear Uncle Jim, and so it has no bounds, for God is everywhere. If you are part of God, your soul is everywhere. It is your DNA, it is also on the other side of the veil and it is also in the Crystalline Grid of the Planet. There is a SYSTEM. Listen to me, Uncle Jim, what I am going to tell you is not in your Holy Scripture. You may hear this and think, "I don't believe it" because it has never been written in scripture. The most sacred scripture you can find, beautiful, accurate and loving, all of it was written in an older energy.

Would you take what you learned in third year at school into university? Was it accurate and true in the third year when you studied it? The answer is yes. There was nothing

wrong with it, but as you grew in knowledge and wisdom, things changed.

New information is now available. Everything has become more elegant and advanced and your scripture is the same. What I want to tell you now is hard to believe I know, and it is one of the soul-sharing attributes Kryon terms 'Akashic Sharing' and it has to do with family.

What if I told you when you take your last breath the soul is split – you cannot count the parts, even though as an accountant I would love to be able to do this for you. Ha! You breathe the air of the planet. Your soul takes on a different attribute. Remember, there is a system here. Every time, Old Soul, you pass over something happens. There is part of your soul that transfers to those left behind. Sometimes they're your biology, sometimes they're your partners. THE BOND IS LOVE. Part of you transfers in love to those left behind. Their Soul changes as they receive part of YOU!

Those you have loved and lost, live with YOU in your Soul. That is a system of LOVE, my dear Old Soul.

What a system of LOVE! Do you realise that the legacy that you have, the consciousness that you have developed, passes to those you love? It also passes to the planet as well. You may ask, "Does the planet have a Soul?" Well, perhaps not as you think of it, but it does have consciousness of Gaia (Mother Earth). This is another process of soul-sharing.

"Where is my Soul?" and the answer is YES. Just accept it.

The elegance of a system of Akashic Love means that you are never gone. Every lifetime is left on this planet in a certain energetic way – some of it is passed to those you love, and

in turn, you carry with you the ones who have passed on before. I want you to think about that tonight, Uncle Jim, when you are alone and you dare ask, "Who's in there?" Ha! Oooh! You would be shocked! EVERYBODY. You are never alone – it's not just God with you, it is the loving family with you of so many. It's complicated and beautiful, it's elegant and TRUE, and the system you feel is all about YOU!

One of your loving family of light, xxx

FOREVER TOGETHER

"
Why is it that you are so linear that things that happen
are gone when they stop happening? In linear time and
in your calendar, it is gone. The most beautiful aspect,
however, is that there is no calendar with God.
It always is. It always will be.
~ Kryon

Dear Uncle Jim,

The candlelight especially at Christmas time is so beautiful, calming and enchanting in its brightness and ambience, isn't it? Whenever we light candles, whether it is at home before receiving friends or whether it is in a church or in a restaurant, let me use the metaphor of the lights being like the intent of all those around them.

We see the candles are placed individually and carefully positioned. The impression left is like a sea of light. The sea of light has no names attached and the sea of light becomes one light, like the human soul. It's the best example Kryon

can give between that which is the Creative Source and that which is part of Gaia. Do you ever have a feeling of the end of each letter bringing a little sadness because you enjoy receiving them and don't want them to finish?

Let me tell you that each day your daughter reads these messages to you, there is a confluence of energy between You and your daughter, Spirit and You and You with You, the music, the messages and the honouring of the human being. LOVE never stops. If you have love for a child who then grows up, does it ever stop?

Certain kinds of love are always fresh like the love of God for YOU! Like this experience you are having, if you have appreciated and enjoyed it and perhaps it even made a difference to how you feel today, this is a physical reality that can go with you in your mind. Every time you think of it, it is real again and it never goes away! In the eyes of a multi-dimensional soul there is no sadness, no meeting over. Like the music that never stops, it plays even when you are asleep and reminds you of who you are.

All love and hugs, xxx

WE ARE OUR ANCESTORS

"

Blessed is the human being who knows they are God
and part of the Universe for things
will never be the same EVER!
~ Kryon

Dear Uncle Jim,

Are you ready for some more soul communication? When a soul is married to a corporeal human, like each of us, it is the RELATIONSHIP BETWEEN THE HUMAN AND THE SOUL that evolves. This Shift that we are in is new and is the one that humanity HAD to make if it was to evolve in maturity and wisdom. We are slowly evolving into an enlightened time when as humans we start to see each other for who they are; that life is precious, that each human is a piece of God.

For some the daily news may suggest a totally different viewpoint. To think this would be another linear thought. There are things happening on this planet which will show

themselves eventually. You will see the Shift in how you and others behave, on what we decide is NOT acceptable anymore, in the systems that we build that are humane, in the things that we put together to help one another and where the money is spent. Eventually, there will come a time Uncle Jim when there is no longer a reason to build a weapon.

Kryon tells us the snowball is rolling – the snowball called "Peace on Earth" – the Renaissance of Light. In an Old Energy, Old Souls were perceived as dangerous. Too much wisdom! Too many new ideas! Now, others around them, others around you, are starting to listen. The children are starting to become wiser. Perhaps you have seen this in your own grand-children, Uncle Jim? New inventions will begin to take humanity out of poverty.

The Shift

Slowly, slowly, slowly things begin to shift.
The Old Energy of the planet is eliminated and no longer exists
though not by killing it but instead by showing it the light.
Darkness cannot exist when the light appears so bright!
Lives are changed when people can see things they didn't know were there.
Awareness is changed showing them of what they must be aware.
Compassion is King and Quuen of the new benevolent energy
Peace on earth is the definitive prophecy.
~ Lady Wise

Are you feeling a little impatient, Uncle Jim? I know I am impatient. It is like a little child saying, "It's new, it's new!

Let's go, let's go!" As a planet that has gone into Graduate Status however we are a youngster! Do you remember how much I love driving? The impatience is like wanting to leap into a race car already knowing how to drive it and take off along the track yet, the race car has still to be built! Ha! I am so impatient. My mother once bought me a Christmas gift of a 17th Century lady dressed in all her finery standing poised with her hands behind her nipped in waist. And the name given to this Royal Doulton lady made of porcelain china was…you've guessed it, "Impatience".

Dear Old Soul, what we are experiencing is the challenge of patience. It used to be the challenge of an Old Energy, but your Akash remembers what this is like. Imagine an array of candles surrounding you, with every lit candle representing a human being and at the same time knowing that all the light is one. Every light is an Old Soul that is going to return and return and return and return and the light becomes brighter every time you start to understand that it's getting better. The light is here FOREVER!

Metaphorically, the rolling snowball CANNOT BE STOPPED. Imagine it as a ball of light as it races downhill and cancels all of the darkness on its way. Eventually, it comes to rest at the bottom where the Old Souls all take a piece of it.

What is the future? Consciousness can change corporeal health. A multi-dimensional consciousness can make sense of things before they arrive. As evolution continues and the physics of consciousness becomes more aware, the meld between corporeal and consciousness becomes stronger and stronger.

When you are mostly light, the corporeal self and the Higher Self begin to blur. You can actually begin to start to control

matter itself. You have ultimate choice on how long you will live, the wisdom to control things on this planet over which you think you have no control. You have the attributes of the Master, that's what happens. As a result, the planet itself has already shifted into what is called Graduate Status and it looks into space to see if there is another planet that could benefit by being seeded with the knowledge of light and dark.

And so, Uncle Jim, what do you feel about the beauty of a system called Akashic Love? Can you feel the ones you've loved and lost? Can you take your children and grand-children aside and tell them that no matter what happens in your life that even after your last breath, you will live with them until their last breath? Can you plant that beautiful seed of truth in them so that there will be no sorrow or suffering when you leave this planet? Instead, you will only have knowledge of the way energy works. You could start telling them now. Perhaps not everyone will believe you and they will say, "Oh Dad, that's just that esoteric stuff!" Ha! And when you're gone, they're going to remember every word and they're going to cling to it and they'll make it REAL, like you do. That's the future of the soul!

Death has no sting and is just a change of energy. It is about understanding reincarnation in order to take away the sorrow. That's wisdom! That's an advancement in civilisation! If you really want to look at the truth, it is exactly like it began in the Ancients. They believed in lifetime after lifetime. They believed that you could ascend your very soul, while you stayed on Earth. They believed in an alliance with Gaia. This is not a New Age. This is a return to Ancient Truth and it's about time!

Now here are your instructions. Dear Uncle Jim, after listening to this message, after reading this message, spend the rest of your time JOYFULLY and carry with you any good thought or thing that happened while listening to all of this message, almost like you had it in a box so you could open the box and revisit it anytime you want. Think of it like a recording that was reality and everywhere you open the box – here it is again! Can you feel the love, the attitude and the peace? You probably know that you do not need to have solution to have peace over a situation. Just know it is coming and be peaceful that your soul is bigger than you think.

Wishing you eternal peace in your heart always, xxx

CELEBRATION MESSAGE

"

*If you, with a high consciousness decided to build physics,
to create a reality, would you not be tempted to stir a
little love into the mix?*
~ Kryon

Dear Uncle Jim,

Are you remembering that you have full creative control?
What does this magnificence mean to you? The primary
message is that of love. When you are connected, the physics
of love is the reality in which you find yourself and is the
way things work. The Creative Source, the 'I AM' presence,
is the physicist.

When we realise that God is inside of us and we surrender,
then spirit gives us our desires and we start to change in a
different light! Higher Self informs us where we need to go.
There is a system of love in physics! It is called "The Field".
Kryon terms it, 'Physics with an attitude of benevolence.'
This "Field" seeks to synchronise and balance with everything

with which it comes into contact. Science has seen this and called it entrainment. Think of The Field as something that winks at you and is around you all the time. It pushes and pulls you when you say, "Yes". Regular physics is all around you.

If you change one thing it throws everything else out of balance and you see it immediately. Balance is not random. Mother Nature is not random. **Mother Nature is the name for "The Field".** Mother Nature is the best example Kryon can give to us at this time in our evolution. Why does Mother Nature work? Mother Nature can be explained and defined as an infinite system, like a beautiful clockwork of all the elements that come together perfectly and which is balanced. This is the circle and cycle of life.

Did you know that the oceans have the ability to clean themselves from oil spills? It is called bio-remediation. This is balanced as well. Often we do not give enough credit to Mother Nature's ability to clean itself. Pre humans, oil bubbled up from the ocean bed in its millions and the oceans cleaned themselves. Yet today many people panic when an oil spill happens without considering that the ocean may be able to take care of itself!

The Field will do its best to cooperate with the human being's desire for harmony. This is a new tool on the planet. This is more than just a tool of awareness. Imagine an energy of benevolence and all it wants to do is create harmony wherever you walk. Can you use the Field? Uncle Jim, not only can you use it, it can be so much a part of your life.

What are the attributes of how homeopathy works when a tincture is far too small to cause any kind of chemical reaction? Biologists and chemists know this fact. The presence

of a few parts per million of a remedy under the tongue of a human being will create a cure. How? The answer is INNATE. INNATE is the smart body. The smart body sees it as your instructions for reality and then the body starts to act upon it NATURALLY.

Can you name a physical process that would take the tincture and create a cure? The answer is The Field, because physics is present in chemistry. It's everywhere. A tincture, a remedy when placed in the human body is exposed not just to the smart body or the innate, but the Field, because it has a consciousness of effect. You have got the remedy in your hand! That is the signal that says I am willing to give my body a reality. At that point in time you put it under your tongue for fast assimilation into the blood stream. That is an ACTIONABLE item. It carries a compassionate action for you and your body. You have effectively just given a POSITIVE ACTION SYMBOL and the Field does the rest. It wants to create harmony with the chemistry. It talks to that which is called the INNATE. It moves to create cures in the body. Spontaneous remission is when one is connected to the Field.

Imagine! What do you think is the most synchronous thing you could have in your body? Good Health! Kryon's teachings give us the secret of why homeopathy works. It's not just the chemistry of your body in a random way, seeing something and acting. It is a driving force called physics.

Some people will say the 'physics of love' has been hiding in plain sight all along. Remember, consciousness is physics and when you use the "energy of intent", it makes thinking an actionable item. What you positively think, do and project has positive energy for your body. I have talked before of affirmations and so let's talk about ACTION this time. That is why the title of this letter is the Celebration Message, because the celebration of who you are is extremely actionable.

A matching attitude for the Field if you are going to meld to the Field will result in celebrating who you are! Picture a celebration – what are you doing? Are you dancing or singing perhaps Uncle Jim? Ha! There is music, laughter, joy and smiles all around and PURE CELEBRATION. All of those attributes together create a confluence of energy just by the word 'celebrate'. The celebration is that you are part of the cosmos itself. The celebration is that you belong here on this planet. Your parents didn't get it wrong, they just didn't know! NOW you can share this knowledge with your beloved parents in your mind and these positive thoughts will pass to their energies as we are all connected.

NOW it is time to convince yourself of your own reality. It is YOU controlling YOU! It is what is taught at the highest level for a human being to have absolute control over their own being, over their own thinking process, over their own emotions without input and influence from anyone. This knowledge is very old. What is NEW is the ENERGY OF CO-OPERATION, for the Field is alive and well.

The experts are now saying that EVOLUTION was way too fast to be normal – they're right. Welcome to the Field, pushing it forward at an unbelievable speed that is not random. The higher one raises one's consciousness, the greater the Field will cooperate. The more you help yourself the more help you will receive from the Field.

These are new things and these are advanced tools as both Mother Earth and humanity recalibrate. Since 21 December

2012, we are now in a world where there is no more fence-sitting. As an Old Soul you decide either to be compassionate or not. You are either willing to go to these esoteric thoughts or not! This is the new energy, especially for an Old Soul.

The future is the Field. You have free choice to discern this information, but Uncle Jim, you either assimilate all of it or none of it!

Sending you loving hugs and warm wishes for a peaceful and happy Christmas!

LETTER 34

THE FUTURE IS PHYSICS!

"

So, the future is not more chemicals – the future is physics! Physics with an attitude of harmony, togetherness, synchronicity and love!
~ *Kryon*

Dear Uncle Jim,

It will not take long before scientists will see the Field. This is known by great metaphysical teachers of the day. It is already out there. If you vibrate slightly differently you can be in tune with the cosmos!

Think about resonant frequencies as an example. Do you ever sing in the shower, Uncle Jim? I love singing in the bathroom because of the acoustics. Perhaps you may have noticed that if you sing in the shower there are some notes that seem louder. Why would this be? It is because these notes resonate with the shower, that's why! When I sing in the shower and this happens to me I know that I have just hit a resonant frequency of the shower and it sounds

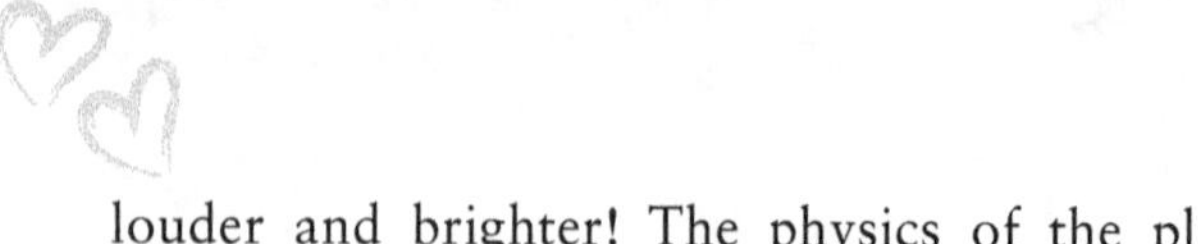

louder and brighter! The physics of the planet is filled with this.

The Field is biased with an attitude of togetherness and harmony. I am suggesting that you choose to harmonise and resound to the Field. If you were to do this with your consciousness you would activate your cellular structure – you would live longer!

Those who can totally harmonise with it, can control physics. In this new energy, the Field has increased its awareness and many more Old Souls are being asked to seek and integrate the frequencies of consciousness that are in the Field.

Physicists are starting to become aware of this. It is outside of linearity and so they call it QUANTUM, entrainment, entanglement, things that want to work together. When they are exposed to the Field, they do. Dear Uncle Jim, the Field has been created for every human being, especially the Old Souls at this time, as a resonant frequency for our consciousness. Call it enhanced intuition, if you wish. It coordinates things and makes things happen and vibrate at the same frequency. That is, control over whom you meet and to whom you talk, because in the Field in which you vibrate, others vibrate at that level with you.

The fast-track system to get in touch with the Field is your Innate. Innate has been called the smart body of the human being. It is almost like a body sensitivity that is beyond you, inside you. It is the part of the body that you muscle test. You can ask it questions in a certain way that your consciousness does not know. It is the smart body which is used in kinesiology. When the bridge between your consciousness and innate is complete, you will be able to be your own medical intuitive. Innate is already connected to

the Field. It enhances healing, creates peace and allows you to be calm within yourself and feel joy! Feel transformed as you become more in tune with the inner rhythms of your soul and your intuition. Find your own heart beat to the song of life! You are a piece of the essence of love itself – of the Creator – beautiful!

Wishing you a Happy Christmas Eve!

Lots of love, xxx

LETTER 35

ACE AFFIRMATIONS!

*I am thankful for all my good health, abundance and
success with love and gratitude.*
~ Lady Wise

Dear Uncle Jim,

Happy Christmas Morning! I am so thrilled that you are
here with us on planet Earth at this very special time.

Have I convinced you yet that the only path to true
communication is LOVE?

*On the spot, your intuition will come to you in order that
you will say the right things and know the right things.
You will know which way to turn, which way not to turn,
what is next and know when to be quiet, know when to
make a decision and it is going to be so INTUITIVE.*
~ Kryon

The Field is ready to expose you to your Higher Self and the main tool is YOU TALKING TO IT THROUGH THE CONSCIOUSNESS OF AFFIRMATION.

Kryon teaches that someday the Field will have a new name, but right now it is the secret for the new energy.

Well constructed affirmations are a POSITIVE REINFORCEMENT OF WHAT YOU ARE STATING AS YOURS! You are not asking for it, you are not wishing for it, you are stating that it is yours!

Innate is the first to hear it. It is as if innate is waiting with large antenna. There is no greater influence than YOUR VOICE and YOUR CONSCIOUSNESS stating WHAT YOU ARE. This is not about what you want, it is about what you are and saying it OUT LOUD!

So Uncle Jim, when you tell your body that you are healed, your situation is settled and the fear starts to go away. The old energy starts to diminish – it makes a huge difference.

The importance of being careful what you say is paramount! Affirmations posture all that is POSSIBLE. Your DNA cellular structure will start to cooperate with this positivity.

An example would be when a sick person says out loud, "I AM HEALED. I AM WHOLE. THANK YOU SPIRIT!" They may cough in the next moment, but the fact is that they have positively stated it. The sick person is stating that they believe in the potential of the affirmation statement. The sick person is creating their own healthy future through their belief! In a multi-dimensional way this person is connecting to the multi-dimensional Field.

What you do now, shapes the future of what has not yet happened. Start stating who you are, because it's who you are going to be in your linearity.

May all your days be lit with the glory of love!

Happy Christmas,

Love, healing and hugs galore, xxx

LETTER 36

REALIGNING INNATE

"
Deep down you know how the universe works.
This lifetime is about remembering it and
remembering one's life purpose.
~ *Kryon*

Dear Uncle Jim,

Always live in your now! Remember the power of a hug! When we hug someone we are exchanging frequencies – it is akin to an electromagnetic exchange.

How wonderful to hear that you are eating well and also different foods. Isn't that interesting? You see when you become more true to YOU, your DNA slowly changes and INNATE knows what your body needs more than your conscious mind does. It is wonderful! Just go with the flow! I have found that I am eating more fish now than meat because my intuitive self is yearning for it. Why argue with self? We all want a smooth and peaceful life, right? Open your eyes and wake up to the adventure!

Relax and let spirit build in you the new human. This is ascension while alive! You had to die, come back and realign in order to do what you now can do as you choose in this lifetime – as long as you are not afraid of it.

Your innate requires to be reprogrammed and you are able to do it through affirmations and positive thoughts and by the actions that you have. Innate is used to an old idea that reincarnation is the engine for enlightenment. No more!

When you have the FORTITUDE to CELEBRATE THE PROBLEMS, YOU HAVE JUST BEEN REALIGNED!

Maybe you've been realigned in a way that you're picking up that from the past that is going to make you healthier and live longer. What if you spent hundreds of years in a culture compared to a few years in Australia? Don't you think your cellular structure wants the old ways more – the old foods more? And if you say 'yes' you are going to see chemical changes in your body – changes that no medicine would be able to do. It has to do with basic health. Have you had a blood test recently? Oh yes, I forgot. Uncle Jim you do not do things by halves, only 100% or not at all. So you have perhaps had a blood transfusion? Ha! All good! Your blood type may not change but the BALANCE will change, because of what you are eating. These changes are not subtle. Some people are feeling them and they are fearful, but you know what I have told you about fear, Uncle Jim. It stops light. EMBRACE THE LIGHT THAT IS YOU!

To release emotion you have to feel it, acknowledge it and then allow it to be released up and out. Depression is always disconnection from the Creator Source. When you connect with your TRUE self, you will want to engage and start meeting different people.

Remember that with each near death experience you are increasing your consciousness of who you truly are. Although this is not something I would encourage too often! Ha! This is such a magnificent time to be on Earth as a human. What a privilege to be breathing in this momentous time on Earth! It is truly life-changing and there is so much for us to learn!

You are an Old Soul (nothing to do with your age in this life time – a mere 96 years young Uncle Jim). No, no, no, no, no! This is about living as an Old Soul in recognition of having had at least 100 perhaps 1,000 previous lives.

Doesn't connection make you feel good, joyous and happy? Essentially you are shifting operating systems from your head to your heart. Perhaps set an intention for your day before your feet even step out of the bed. Actively make a decision about what you want. You do not need any tool other than "THOUGHT".

Be that force of light from the love you give YOURSELF! Be grounded and present. When you do this everything else takes care of itself!

Pain exists when you are operating in the mind and not working from the heart centre. As you embody being present, you are making it easier for those around you to recognise this frequency state of being.

Harmony, balance and unity allows you to live compassionately.

Much love and hugs, xxx

LIGHT QUOTIENT

"
*Light is more powerful than Darkness. You need less of
it against the Dark. The Dark is weaker than Light!*
~ Kryon

Dear Uncle Jim,

Being in tune with the intuition of knowing what's right and
what's wrong and what is going on with YOU – all of that
is hearing the voice of spirit. There is a CLARITY that comes
with this intuition and it never lets you down.

The history of humanity is short. All of our history has been
about fighting and NOW, it is beginning to CHANGE! This
is the time of The Shift, of the Renaissance of Humanity.
The test on the planet is one of light and dark energy.

When the test started, Light DNA in the body was a level
of 30%. Precision over this is provided in the numbers and
I will explain it as a portion of the whole, where the whole
is treated as 100%.

The point at which the power of Light over Dark generated EQUALITY was when the DNA percentage activated in the human reached 35%, leaving 65% of Darkness. Think about why would it not be 50:50? With a ratio of 35:65 representing equality, the power of Light is more powerful than Darkness.

When the Pleiadians first seeded humans on earth and the test of light and dark energy was initiated, the levels of light in a human being changed from 30% DNA of Light activated, to 35% almost immediately. Why would this be? These 'seeded' humans were living in isolation in Lemuria (known today as Hawaii) which allowed for the almost instant growth of the active DNA in the human.

Moreover, the Pleiadians were still with them on Earth and acted as their teachers. That was really when the test started. What happens at 35% active DNA? There is an intuitive understanding of gender balance on the planet, of who does what and why.

This is celebrated in the Lemurian Sisterhood. It is a time when genders respect one another and understand the FEMININE Gender is the one that is more in touch with spirits as a Life-Giver. Therefore, they are the ones that would be in contact to help guide the communities and societies.

Historically, as soon as the DNA started to lose percentage value, the gender balance was dysfunctional. Kryon teaches that if you want to have a test of any society on the planet and you want to know where their DNA level is as a society, all you have to do is look at gender dysfunction. From being respected and being shamans, the women were treated as second class, even third class along with animals. There was NO BALANCE. That is what happens when the percentage starts to dip into survival mode rather than thriving mode.

Survival mode is consumed with non-elegance, war, non-appreciation, non-caring, separation and hatred.

Thriving mode is full of forgiveness, love, kindness, togetherness and has compassion at its core.

Kryon explains that the DNA average percentage of Light back the Middle Ages, was 25% before rising again to 30%, 31% and then 32%. There is still tremendous gender dysfunction at these levels. Balance occurs again once it hits 35%. When we hit 40% it is going to be so intuitive. We will look back and say, 'What was wrong with us?'

At low levels of DNA Light percentage around 25% and 30%, then the strongest beings win. The ones with the most muscles win. This is Old Energy and Old Thinking and it brings with it gender imbalance.

When a balanced society is working at 35%, the Gender Balance starts to be appraised. The respect and appreciation shown to the women is considered. A great example of this is to look at the indigenous and find out what the records say. They will tell you that the women were the shamans, the women were the Life-Givers for they are close to spirit and they have a better intuitive ability. Can you imagine having someone as a guide who could see it and feel it and have the voice of God clear to them? That is Gender Balance! The men knew it and they depended upon it and the women depended upon the men for the things that they did best – gender balance at its best! It is still around in the indigenous. It never changed!

Those individuals who do things best are placed in roles that optimise their skills. This makes perfect sense.

Dear Uncle Jim, if 35% is equal, we have never seen this on our planet in our lifetime, UNTIL RIGHT NOW! Dark is coming out of the woodwork, so to speak, and it is running the other way! Darkness is dysfunctional.

Darkness cannot look up to a higher level. Darkness cannot look up and see Light. It only sees the strength of Dark. It does not understand it is going to lose! All it can see is itself!

Examples of the Dark are starting to be seen in politics, society, business, large establishments – indeed, everywhere. There is a longing for integrity in high places instead of dysfunction. People are becoming tired of Old Energy because they are becoming more intuitive and know better. In their increased awareness, they know they want CHANGE! The Old Souls recognise it for what it is and start working with it and KNOW they can get messages from it and GUIDANCE from it.

Kryon explains that we are nearing 36% Light activated DNA on this planet, even with all the things going on around us. As we defeat the Darkness we are winning! Rise above the noise and nonsense! Intuition will speak to you in a clearer voice.

The logic in your brain changes, because it is in the DNA. There is an awakening. When there is a more efficient DNA you start to think differently.

WISDOM BECOMES INTUITIVE and not something that you wish you had!

The magnificence of it all starts to be seen and heard by more and more people. With NEW THOUGHT and the evolution of humanity, we hear better the VOICE OF SPIRIT!

Dear Uncle Jim, we are at 35% Light Activated DNA! Some on the planet are still at a much lower percentage. How can we tell? How they treat their women is the clue – remember, it's back to Gender Balance.

Stand tall when you hear this message and Know Who You Are! The DNA will be activated in the sequence that is needed for YOU! You are not limited by what you can feel in your heart! JUST LIVE IT!

No-one can argue with your BALANCE, especially if they see it day after day, after day and realise that truly you have something that is worth asking about!

With a continuing ascension of increased DNA in humans that is Light activated at 35% and higher, there will be changes in systems. All of the systems are going to change eventually. Kryon informs us that technology is coming for all sorts of things such as electricity and fresh water for all. For example, I know that in Australia you are short of natural water. One of the solutions for this is to desalinate without heat and without using chemicals. For those who are interested in this science, Kryon teaches us that perhaps the use of microbiotics may provide an answer?

What about the systems of ecology? Those companies operating without integrity in the pharma industry are dysfunctional and will eventually fall over and change. Dear Uncle Jim, the new systems are coming and they are going to come from those wiser in spirit, who will invent them. Look at the young technicians and the young scientists! They have the answers and the wisdom that none of us expected. The answers will come from the difference of living in the new energy.

The new paradigm is peace on earth and all you have to do is "KNOW AS YOU GO!"

So, Uncle Jim, congratulations at your young age of 96 for being in the right place at the right time. Remember, I have told you previously that your DNA is capable of living for approximately 900 years... as YOU CHOOSE IT! YOU HAVE FULL CREATIVE CONTROL! Isn't it wonderful? What a life puzzle to work out and then choose to live by.

Uncle Jim, look around you, that's family! The people around you now and coming into your life at this time are members of the Family of Light. The new energy will help you energetically remember again. Old Soul, you are part of a universe that has beauty and joy beyond measure. It is a peace that goes beyond anything. The people around you will see a beaming face of joy, wisdom and maturity.

The evolution of human consciousness is here NOW. Reach in and touch the wisdom that you have earned. All of the guidance that you need is synchronistic because God knows who you are and it's new. It can only happen to an Old Soul. It's the beginning of something GRAND! Do your best to have FUN and improve your life to such a degree that you become wiser and smarter for those you love!

Sending you loads of joy, happiness and love, xxx

LETTER 38

PSYCHIC ABILITY
EXPLAINED

"

When you understand your psychic connection
you restore your wholeness
~ Lady Wise

Dear Uncle Jim,

The soul energy is a multi-dimensional space where there is no time. When a person dies they leave a RESIDUAL of their lifetime soul energy imprinted on the Crystalline Grid of the planet forever. The vibration of the earth is the culmination of all of the entities upon it.

When the psychic seeks to connect with a loved-one who has physically departed from this planet, they are talking to the residual of the energy of that loved-one that remains on the Crystalline Grid in a quantum state. Metaphorically, think of the Crystalline Grid as containing lots of crystalline 'stripes', one for every soul. The psychic connects with the

158

other side of the veil (this Crystalline Grid) which is a multi-dimensional part. When we are birthed and come into planet earth, a piece and part of our soul is left on the other side of the veil, connected to the oneness of all that is. As previously mentioned in Letter 9, we would vapourise with the intense power of the pure energy if we attempted to bring this part in with our physical body.

Anybody who is sensitive around earth related things such as animals, nature, even the study of the rocks, can walk in certain places and FEEL the intelligence of Gaia.

There is no reason to be afraid of learning about your psychic connection because it is another part of who you are. Let a little knowledge on this subject dispel your fears. Start to expect success and good things in all you do instead of looking for a negative excuse not to learn something that will give you wisdom to fulfil your greatest desires while on planet earth. Why would you want to self-sabotage such an opportunity?

Remember we are all psychic whether you choose to believe this or not!

There are those psychics, however, whose skills help detectives solve cases of missing persons, for example, and who can assist with the locations and details used to solve homicides, rapes and other unpleasant crimes. In these specific scenarios a psychic is often called in as a last resort by detectives. Some detectives remain skeptical until a psychic does provide information that leads conclusively to a positive result together with DNA evidence available. Many detectives even after valuable psychic assistance has been given remain baffled by the way locations can be described and pertinent details contributing to a subsequent arrest and conviction can be given. Although psychics and detectives can successfully

work hand in hand to solve cases, for many police commissioners and officers the use of psychics is still not accepted as part of traditional police work. I have observed police in the USA who, having used psychics to solve a case, still refuse to want to know how it works?

Until we become more open to knowledge and wisdom there will be no change. It is as if the police involved are fearful of the methods used and think that if they remain ignorant of this, then no harm would come to them? Well of course, when one does not know how something works the first reactions are usually to ridicule it and then promptly seek to disprove it as 'nonsense'. So my message is #GetWise and #Wiseup so you can evolve and attain your true potential in this lifetime and welcome a little knowledge about your amazing psychic abilities that are part of your birthright. Remember the importance of realising that CHANGE IS GOOD!

Hopefully more individuals and especially those involved in any kind of justice and legal work will start to be more open-minded and realise that psychic ability is a natural gift that is part of a system too. It is part of the system of love, of the physics of consciousness and it is real.

There are many active psychics who do not even know about the system of love and how their psychic gifts work! This is ok. Understanding will come. We do not always need to know the science behind a gift, just accept it with grace.

The Shift is a period of fast-track time for us with free choice to keep moving forward with our learning in a new era when we no longer need to feel afraid about being open with our knowledge. It has not been that long ago since psychics would have been hanged for such knowledge. Thankfully, as we become more mature in our wisdom through extended knowledge, the development of our psychic abilities increases our clarity of mind over our own matters, as we make our own choices about what is best for us in daily living.

This planet has received what it has from the Pleiadians in a beautiful way, in an appropriate, divine way – with no wars and no conspiracies. We are in a quantum state with them – some of us can feel it and it is beautiful!

I have recently spoken of the Crystalline Grid and the Cave of Creation, both of which are part of the PHYSICS of LOVE, the fundamental system on planet Earth that is there to be found by humans who with free choice choose to raise their consciousness and in so doing raise the Light quotient of DNA in their body which, in turn, assists in raising the collective consciousness of everyone on the planet.

The Crystalline Grid (where crystalline is the word that lets you know it is a storage device that holds information) is on the exterior. It is a grid that sits upon the ground of the Earth, even although you cannot see it, it is there and contains imprints of your energy. Everything that ever happened lays on the grid where it happened and so it is LOCATION SPECIFIC.

For many individuals who meditate, they can easily discern where battles have or have not taken place. In the countryside of southern Ireland, for example, where nothing barbaric has ever happened, the land is clear and clean and one can meditate better. Whereas in Shawlands, Glasgow in and around Battlefield there is a lower vibrational energy felt by many on account of the death and destruction in that area so many years ago. The Crystalline Grid even explains ghosts. Those who claim to see ghosts are actually cognising an imprint so strong in a certain area that even though the

human beings have left, the imprint of what they did replays like a tape.

Why always the connection to the Earth? Gaia is part of a measuring system, a vibrational measuring system. There will come a day when the Earth is measured for its vibrational attributes that were created by what we humans have done.

Collectively, what we have done and what we are going to do will lay upon this planet in a vibratory rate which is measurable by spirit – that is the Crystalline Grid.

Every human being has a Divine part to them that is Quantum (that is their consciousness), whether they believe it or not. This means that each of us exists in 3 places at the same time. Remember it is only a human being's perception that they are three dimensional which limits them from understanding the magnificence of who they truly are and the bigger picture, so to speak. As you become more quantum in your consciousness your Akash is going to start growing in its awareness. Ok, so back to the three places of existence for each human being:

Part of the Cave of Creation keeps a record of who you are as you come and go on this planet and keeps your energy even though you are physically gone. Remember that the Cave of Creation, nevertheless, is always complete. It has all of humanity in it – past. present and future – that means we are actually interacting with those who are not here yet! So now I would like to explain to you about the genuine psychics and spiritualist mediums (for as there are rogue accountants in the world so too are there sadly rogue psychics).

Many spiritualist mediums and psychics do not even know about the whole system of LOVE from where they source

their 'gifts' and for millennia these individuals have been misunderstood and burned at the stake for their spoken words. Even today there is a disconnect with many religious groups when it comes to acknowledging who these people are and the judgement put upon them by some people is that they are 'evil'. This is extremely disappointing and saddening as these very people have a higher consciousness that has allowed them to access the Cave of Creation, as indeed can any human being with free choice. One of the reasons for the Cave is that it is there as part of the Physics of Love for us to learn wisdom and celebrate the love coming through from our ancestors.

It is the psychic's ability to connect into the 'stripe' or 'essence energy' of the human being departed, whose 'stripe' is held in the Cave of Creation that allows them to be the messenger for the communication.

That is why often the messages that come through in the energy of each departed human being are firstly about that person or about the illness of the situation in which the deceased person passed, to bring in validation to the receiver of the message.

There is no need to fear either the messengers or the messages that come through because they are only ever for the highest good of the receiver to help them in their daily lives and to be a 'comforter' to let us know that the soul never dies and that while one may have physically passed from this world, that their soul remains alive…forever, as a metaphoric "stripe' on the Cave of Creation.

Psychics do not "foretell" the future. The Cave as a storage device holds ALL the POTENTIALS forever of every human being. It is like a massive 'soup of creation'. It is based on the thoughts that every human has. A psychic will tap into

the energy of thoughts of the person for whom they are giving a reading.

What the psychic picks up at that particular time is the most likely potential of what that person is likely to do based on all their cumulative thought patterns at that time. For example, you know I am keen to come over and visit you again in Australia. I may also have a dream to become a Managing Director of a corporate Canadian Company and a dream to live in Alaska, for example. Depending on the energy I attach to each of these 'potentials' at the time that the psychic gives me a 'reading' will determine the 'potential' of the future that they will communicate – at that time. The strongest potential will be selected. I could of course meet the Ambassador for lunch at the Lithuanian Embassy the next day and those potentials would all change because afterwards I decide I want to live and work in Lithuania. I used this example because several years ago one of my friends texted me from Italy to ask what I was doing. As it happened I was indeed having lunch with the Lithuanian Ambassador and planning a business trip to there. Later that afternoon I texted my friend back to tell her what I had been doing and it was four months later when I met her over the festive holidays that she asked me if that had really been true!

The 'future' is simply the 'soup of potentials' that each of us thinks of in our minds, hence the expression, be careful what you wish for! So the power of thought, your intent and the energy that you put into this is very important. It is always wise to keep one's thoughts high and for the highest good of those involved in your own story of creation.

Part of the DNA in the human body helps you while you live and stores all that you ever were; all thousand lifetimes

if you have lived a thousand lives is in your DNA and they are all accessible. You never have to relearn anything spiritually because it is cumulative, it stays with you. All you have to do, metaphorically speaking, is to open the spiritual jar and out will come the wisdom of the Ancients. All of us are our own Ancestors!

The indigenous know this. Look at their "services of worship". The first thing they do is 'honour their Ancestors' – it is with them, it is intuitive to them and they know that it is first on the stack of honouring before they ask for help. They always go to the Ancestors. Not only do they honour their Ancestors but they ask them for wisdom. The indigenous know how to mine the Akash, they always have, because they realised the Circle of Life – they know they are their own Ancestors, they know it is inside of them so why wouldn't they pull upon that which is wise.

The indigenous know Gaia and they see Mother Earth as a partner in their soul life – INTUITIVELY THEY KNOW!

Humanity on planet earth will evolve at a faster pace as each human being 'awakens' with the truth of who they are. Remember, the Three Wise Men who have always been held in high regard in biblical terms and yet so many of us devalue the psychic gifts of others today, because of a lack of knowledge and understanding of how earth works and the magnificence of the human being and of what each person is capable with the quantum piece of divinity that lies within.

Can you see the profundity of the system and what it is about? It is about YOU!

Sending you excited messages of love, hugs and healing, xxx.

LETTER 39

HOW NUMBERS INFLUENCE

*Each number has its own astrological attributes and all
of the planets are involved in the numerology.*
~ Kryon

Dear Uncle Jim,

Around the world 1 January has happened – Happy New
Year! You are alive, what greater gift is there? Let the love
and healing flow as we celebrate a year of new beginnings
and unlimited possibilities.

Take charge of your own life! Be with it and let new
beginnings blossom! Gratitude gives us more energy to
survive. Slow down. Make wise choices! The power of the
mind is going to come into its own. Every human being is
here to heal. We are getting rid of unnecessary fears. There
is no stopping the revolution of mind and spirit. Be exuberant
in your life – love your life and let life love you!

As we greet a new calendar year, there is no better time than now to mention about master numbers and how it is specific to us moving into another year. It is germane to the planet. Energies represent ancient systems that some believe and some do not. A reason exists for all of this. Numerology defined is the energy of numbers and numbers have energy!

There are many kinds of numerology but I am going to tell you about the most ancient – the Tibetan. I have always felt an affinity to all things Tibetan and particularly love using and hearing Tibetan singing bowls. When you see a number it is usually part of a communication. It may be a page number, for example. Can you imagine a book without a page number? Doesn't that tell you that numbers have a message? A number on a page tells a story and on that page is ENERGY. If it is a page in a book then the number of the page before and that of the page after will each tell a different story. Numbers contain energies that are definable.

The Tibetan system focuses on the most basic of numbers 1 through 9 inclusive and excluding zero. There are extensions to this but for ease I am only going to mention these base numbers to you.

Some people take an alphabet, any alphabet, and assign numbers to the letters. There is nothing random about this. Through free choice, Uncle Jim, you can create whatever you want to, but when you pay attention to what is already here in the physics, in the numbers, in the colours, in the feelings, in the grids, in Gaia, it will all come together for YOU and so systems are everywhere.

Remember it is not chance how you were named. When you take the letters of your name and add them up this gives you a number to which energy is attached and it is around

you. There is a little dance when you are plugged in to the metaphysics of the planet!

Number 1 brings new beginnings, the beginning of something, perhaps a new project.

Number 2 represents duality. It also responds to free choice. A number 2 around something tells you it is going to be filled with decisions.

Number 3 is a catalytic number. If you have a number 3 around something, you know the energy moves other things without being changed itself. An example of this would be healers and teachers who would have the number 3 around them constantly. For everyone who passes through their energy, their life changes.

Number 4 is an earth number. It is community. It is Gaia and farmers, animal breeders, animal rescue centres and others affiliated with animals are generally associated with this number.

Number 5 represents change. Raw change! When you see a 5 around something it means that the energy of the situation or the place or the address or the year, as examples, is changing. Think of the number 5 as flowing and fluid in its form.

You are your OWN NUMBER. If you do not believe in numerology and the power of numbers, then for you, your reality, your truth will be in another paradigm of your own. Numbers would be just numbers to you, but if, like me Uncle Jim, you cognise this system of numbers, you are part of the system, you are on board and are sensitive to the metaphysics of the planet.

Number 6 is a spiritual number and means harmony. It would therefore be useful to have a number 6 as part of a project reference on which you are working, so as to bring co-operation to the completion of the task.

There are many names developed only from the numerology and some people choose to change their name only because it adds to a better number for them. When they change their name to add up to a different number it carries a different energy with it and because they had the intent, yes, it works!

Number 7 may have a spiritual overtone where you actually talk about things which are meaningful to you and spiritual. It governs spirituality. If you think of your house number, Uncle Jim, whether it was intentional or not the number 34 adds to a 7!

Number 8 is manifestation and abundance, not necessarily equating to money but many others riches too. For example, the manifestation of good health, long life, great friends and perhaps even a powerful immune system which will keep you from having disease.

Number 9 is the active number of completion. Completion can mean many things. It can mean the end of something that is completed to the extent that you are done with it. Alternatively, it can also be the end of sorrow, the end of a certain way of thinking in society, the end of an old way, of a project, or perhaps the termination of something that existed before.

Numerology changes depending upon the situation. Now there's more! One number affects another depending upon the energy of the number and where it is positioned and how long it has been next to another number. I will spare

you the complexity of the varied complications, because I don't know these attributes myself...yet! Ha!

It does work, however, no matter how long a number is. You take the number and add up each of the digits in the number to the one number. The exception to this simplistic numerology is where you have two numbers which are identical which stand alone next to them such as 11, 22, 33, 44, 55, 66, 77, 88, and 99. These are Master Numbers which have identities and energies of their own.

The first four double digit Master numbers of which Kryon has informed us are as follows:-

11 – Means enlightenment; let there be light;

22 – The Creation Story; that which is duality (remember that the planet is in a test of duality – the test of energy of the light and the dark, where the dark is an absence of light);

33 – Represents the beginning of compassion on this planet;

44 – Is peace on earth.

Once the collective consciousness on the planet reaches a higher level of wisdom (that is DNA Light quotient), the meaning of the remaining double digit Master numbers (55, 66, 77, 88 and 99) will be duly revealed to us.

Welcome to the New Earth where these energies contribute to the "harmony of your life". How many of them are you suddenly bringing into your awareness?

In joyous love and numerical harmony, xxx.

LETTER 40

ETERNAL HOPE

You were here before the Earth was the Earth. On the other side of the veil there is only the beauty of LOVE and the beauty of 'being' because there is no resting, no cycles of anything, just the purity of being.

~ Kryon

Dear Uncle Jim,

Traditionally at this time there is a celebration of the end of an Old Year and the beginning of a New. It is a time for sharing time with one's family, for giving and of reflection. Have you thought that the gift might be to reflect about yourself? We are all so UNIQUELY different, yet so well known to the Creator Source.

Kryon uses a great analogy of airline pilots to explain the feeling of freedom that we can have. Pilots say that no matter what the issues are at home or at work, once they get into the sky it all goes away. It is euphoric to so many of them – what a feeling to be ABOVE IT ALL. Apparently, it

diminishes their problems and puts them into perspective. When you use your imagination in this way, your intuition catches a feeling of remembrance of being with family called Creative Source.

Every one of us will take a last breath some day but there is no need to fear this, for it is merely a last breath in our physical body in this lifetime. Your soul is eternal! Next lifetime you will return, rejuvenated and young and vibrant and ready to go. There will be a noticeable change. It will be the first time that you rejuvenate in a New Energy! There will be no fear of death and even those that you leave behind will have a renewed understanding about both human and soul existence.

"What do we do between physical lifetimes?" I hear you ask. Ha! Ha! Remember there is no 'doing' only 'being'! YOU have been there and this is what I am asking you to do a little bit of. Simply soar above everything that you are today and rely on yourself to give you that sense of balance. Relax and FEEL THE LOVE of spirit for you, from deep inside your heart. This is the real you. Can you feel the beauty of inner calm?

Take a few minutes to imagine ascending into those clear blue sunny skies where the sun is shining bright and FLOW WITH IT, feeling carefree! Can you smile at the beauty that is there in physical things and smile at the quantumness to be discovered, which, incidentally, allows instant travel anywhere? Perhaps in a quiet moment you sense the future that is millions of years away and then you remember the last universe you were in when you did it before? Is it possible, Old Soul, that in the eternity of each moment you realise this whole Galactic experience is just a 'tick in time', as

Kryon describes it, and that you will do it once again to lift the vibration of the planet itself? Every single time that a world goes into Graduation with free choice we increase the Creator's energy.

We are beginning to evolve into Mastery. One of the attributes that we have as we start the lineage of Mastery is the ability to see things and to be comfortable with them immediately, because we can see through them! We see through things into a future that is brighter and better.

You will be able to laugh when others cannot, you will be able to listen to those and help them just by the fact that you are balanced. They may only be with you for a few moments but it will help them and they will remember those few moments and they will want to come back and talk more with you. This is the difference between the Graduate and the Newbie human being. As Old Souls, we know we can get through everything because we can get above it. We are here to show others BALANCE when times are both good and bad. There is a consistency of a spiritual countenance that people will see and feel.

YOU ARE THE LIGHT that has to SHINE when things are DIFFERENT. Start to see how worthy you are! Smile and say "Here we go!"

If time is in a circle that means that even the things that you have never experienced before have to feel somewhat familiar to you in a way you perhaps cannot describe. This is your Akashic remembrance of having gone through these things at least once before, during that evolution of this Galaxy.

We are part of the Light that is increasing on the planet. For those suffering now, this is known by God and can be

diminished with Light. YOU HAVE LIGHT!

The new human being walks in a reality that is everyday – eat, walk, work, drive, play, sleep, but is not consumed with the issues of drama, gossip and negativity because they are above it all.

Kryon teaches us that beautiful winds are blowing – the wind of change, the wind of love, the wind of awakening and realisation and the wind of peace. Every one of us deserves to feel it and relax with peace in their heart.

Sending you love sparkles and happy hugs, xxx

THE PRECESSION OF THE EQUINOXES

"

The Precession of the Equinoxes is a 26,000 year wobble of the Earth. It is the story of manifestation. The abundance that is manifested with that 26,000 year wobble is the Earth going into Graduate Status, into Mastery, into DNA which is going to start to arrive at a higher rate – YOU ARE IN IT!
~ Kryon

Dear Uncle Jim,

Who would have thought that physics is at the heart of spirituality? The Precession of the Equinoxes as a 26,000 year cycle that pertains to the wobble of the Earth in numerology terms adds up to an 8. The number 8 represents manifestation and abundance. What about the significance of this as an esoteric event? As a planet we made it past the centre point of the 36 year cycle that it takes for this wobble to change the skies and walk through the Milky Way. That centre point was 21 December 2012. It's been manifested. We have past it!

The Precession of the Equinox cycle of 36 years itself adds up to a 9 – stand by for the 9s! The Precession of the Equinox is all about 9,9,9,9. It is the end of the old and the beginning of the new energy. The cycle is 18 years into it (adding to 9) and 18 years coming out of it (once again adding to 9). The 9s are king when it comes to the Shift repeating it over and over and over and over. Ha!

Everything that we thought was the value we might have as a human is going to change and it is going to be greater than we could ever have conceived it would be. The LOVE of Higher Self is going to pour through your consciousness some day. Babies are now being born and they know who they are! There's going to be a consciousness on the planet with a light percentage in our DNA that is above 44%, maybe even above 55%, beyond which we will start to have the attributes of Mastery. Kryon suggests we may even master time and life itself! Physics will be able to be manipulated. This is high consciousness and we have seen it in the Masters.

"

The ones who seeded you went through a similar thing. They did not have a wobble of their planet but instead they had another scenario completed. Theirs was from the stars when Suns came together and they made the same Shift we did. Their history was worse than yours. You experienced partial genocide and think you have had it bad. They experienced FULL genocide. The ones who seeded you have gone through it more than you have.
~ Kryon

Generally, we measure time on Earth by how long each of us lives and then we measure the life span. Yet, WE ARE ETERNAL – WE WILL ALWAYS BE HERE – LIFE-TIME AFTER LIFE-TIME AFTER LIFE-TIME! Is it possible for you to start to think differently about the concept of time?

Souls coming in now (after 21 December 2012) are starting to awaken in lives and remembering while they are here. The next time each of us comes back, we will awaken with the knowledge that we will not make the mistakes that we did this time. Phew! This is the Old Soul moving into an energy that is DIFFERENT than when we awakened the last time. When we were born there was one dominant old energy on Earth. You will KNOW you are an Old Soul! People will see you as different. Children are starting to shift now. Eventually all children will be prodigies – all of them.

From 8 years to 18, children come alive socially and they (and us) will be seen as different. They will enjoy one another's company, they won't go to war and they won't kill one another. We will know them! We will look back and say that our history was barbaric! We will eventually never kill another human being as a solution to a puzzle!

Can you find the joy factor inside of YOU? It is the inner child that awakens happy and has the wisdom that it can change its own chemistry. You have the power to build extended life. If you choose to do this it will send a remarkable signal to the Field, to your DNA and things will CHANGE. Everything is related to everything else. If you wallow in the Old, nothing will happen differently!

When you embrace joy in all you do, that is the joy of compassionate action. You are going to start seeing numbers over and over that are just for YOU! Someone else will have

different numbers. This is who you are. Numbers are the energy of the planet. Remember there are different levels of awakening. Those who do not see this are not ready yet. There is no judgement of those who walk away and laugh. The truth inside you tells you intuitively of the integrity of this information.

Hear the joy, see the joy, feel the joy, be the joy!

Heartfelt hugs xxx

LETTER 42

AWAKENING TO THE WINDS OF LOVE

Honour your intuition as you go
Harness your wisdom and be in the know!
~ Lady Wise

Dear Uncle Jim,

I am SO excited to tell you about awakening to the Winds of Love.

The three winds, described by Kryon, represent the three states in which we find ourselves.

The Wind of Birth;
The Wind of Existence;
The Wind of Transition.

Spirit works with these three winds as support to each of our needs. This is the role of spirit through your Higher Self – the discovery of the Creator Source INSIDE! The plan is beautiful Uncle Jim.

The Wind of Birth is different from one's physical birth. The Wind of Birth is before one's physical birth! How cool is that! This is when one is ready to go back to earth from the home of Creator Source – the home of God. What is involved? Who is able to be in the Wind of Birth? Firstly, the answers are NOT LINEAR. We talk of coming back after a lifetime lived before. What are the rules for 'connection' back to humanity? On this planet, coming and going you and every other human being has their Higher Self, the structure of the DNA and the potentials which are IDENTICAL. What is different with each incarnation and from each other? The only thing that differentiates one from another in the DNA is the Akashic record – it holds the ability and potential for enormous energy depending on what you have done in past lives. If you have awakened to spiritual potential there is more energy than if not.

The creation of an enlightened Old Soul is literally available at the Wind of Birth because it's what you have done before, who you were, what you have accomplished earlier, whether you're working the Light Puzzle or not.

The Akashic record is about how much spiritual knowledge you've awakened to which is not merely about the number of past lifetimes lived. Your Akashic library, that you pick up and hold through your life and into the next, will help you to know what the next life will be like, because you will never have to relearn anything.

Metaphorically, once you open the door it is ALL available – all lifetimes, all learning. The human being has the beautiful Higher Self and the core of Creator Source, therefore, how much of that you can accept and open the door to see it, will depend on how ALIVE and enlightened you become.

There is immense planning to put you at the Wind of Birth. What did you accomplish last time, if anything? What soul group were you in? There is so much that goes into the planning and each life path is DIFFERENT and UNIQUE for every human being. There needs to be the understanding that humanity is honoured way above the need for any instruction manual! Ha!

Kryon teaches us that there are certain attributes that human beings receive after they have been back to Creator Source. These are called CREATOR ATTRIBUTES that are almost Quantum and take several lifetimes to complete. What happens to the creatives is that they will go through a series of number of lifetimes as though it was 'one', in order to have completion.

For example, a famous singer will come back and the first thing they will want to do will be to sing... and they do! Something similar will happen to composers, poets, artists, sportspeople and sculptors as examples too! They come back and keep going with their creative talent. When you play a famous composer's music and say, "Oh, they don't make music like that anymore" you are wrong, because they are here again. The creatives and the energy they set up are different from the others.

We do not arrive here with a blank slate without talent and gifts. The only ones who do are the "newbies" or the new ones. It is all based on ENERGY POTENTIALS.

When you next come back all these POTENTIALS and POSSIBILITIES await you. The one thing for sure, Uncle Jim, is that you are coming back as part of the Family of Light. The gender you will be and the place you will be is all part of your planning process. This process is energy

based. Kryon teaches that if one has awakened, there is potential there that is not there if one has not, and so an Old Soul will go to another place that a Young Soul will not. Just like a vast quantum school of learning. Ha!

The Old Soul in the New Energy is completely different at the Wind of Birth. The Old Soul who has awakened over and over, is comfortable with the process and remembers very fully what they have gone through. The Old Soul may have made up their mind what they are going to do. With your knowledge and the DNA changes in light quotient percentage, you will have allowed a child to come forward next time, who remembers how to read. The toddler doesn't have to be taught everything because the bridge in their DNA is starting to be complete between what was and what is. The child will come in fully loaded. Ha! This is the promise of a New Energy changing children as they come into the planet. The promise of a planet going into new uncharted areas of quantum energy and discovery will be the vibe. They will need a whole new set of tools. Watch for this! Dear Uncle Jim, all of us as Old Souls have participated in the beauty of such a potential happening.

The second wind termed by Kryon as the Wind of Existence is called Life. What is it not? It is not a punishment and it is not a test. It is about a test of energy on the planet and whether humans can change that measurement.

"
Human beings are not here to be tested.
You are here to flourish.
~ Kryon

The bridge between the Wind of Birth and the Wind of Existence is where you remove everything you know about the truth. You are no longer aware that you are a piece of the Universe itself, where you come from or what you have been through. You awaken to potentials of remembering. Now, there are Old Souls who do not necessarily awaken at all. An Old Soul with a previous hard life will skate through this life, like a vacation, and never wake up, yet you know they are Old Souls when you meet them because you can see it in their eyes. It is the very thing that attracted you to them. This time around, however, some are simply here to hold the energy of who they are. There are no rules. Next time round they may do the work.

No time is ever a waste. It is all about time and what you do on planet Earth during the Wind of Existence. Who are you? The Ones who know what to do will depend on the conditions that they find when they arrive. Kryon puts this into three categories as follows:-

New:
The New Soul has no idea about how life works. They do not know about human nature or human consciousness and can be tricked so easily by a human being who wants to trick them because they are naïve in all directions.

Learning:
The Learning Soul gets to understand how things work. When you become a LEARNER you hear information and either recognise it as truth or not. Learners are the potential awakeners.

Old:
The Old Soul knows their life path. They may have awakened in this life time for the first time, but they are an Old Soul

and in their Akash, although they did not live it personally, they can pull from it because it is there regardless!

We were seeded by an ascended human race called the Pleiadians. This means that everything that they know is in our DNA. That means that you can awaken to great amounts of truth that there is from what they gave to us. Genius!

It goes beyond our Akash into a Spiritual Quantum Akash that belongs to those who seeded us. We start to pick up the truth of the Universe of the Galaxy that is way beyond our years. This is a New Energy attribute.

Remember as Old Souls we have dropped our karma and have taken the helm of our own energy and steered it into an enlightened Earth.

Moreover, an Old Soul can plan today for what they are going to do the next time around with the love of the Higher Self TOGETHER!

In this New Energy you have never had a chance to change the Wind of Existence like you can NOW! Collectively, in the next few years there will be greater INTEGRITY. All souls will create it. You will gain the upper hand. The very plan of what the Earth is about will start to shape up. Kryon teaches us that eventually someone will come up with the idea of an Alliance of Nations and promises of help for one another.

"

There will come a time when everyone will look back on 2012 and prior to this date and name this period of time the Barbaric Era and you will see civilisation as we know it started in 2013. That is the promise of this demarcation point.
~ *Kryon*

The Wind of Existence is you working the Puzzle, Old Soul, and YOU are not in karma and you are not in contract. Your contract is to be here and that has been fulfilled! We are in MANIFESTATION MODE! It may not seem like it but give it a go! When we get out of survival mode and stop worrying, we start to move into Manifestation Mode.

Worry mode is often what your parents taught you and you can probably hear your mother and father speaking in your mind. You inherited it and it's not what enlightened beings do. Enlightened beings manifest what they need. They don't worry about what they don't have, because it comes to them when they need it. This is why we can be so relaxed about life!

The last wind, The Wind of Transition is often referred to as Death. None of us knows when it is going to happen or do we? At this time of the Shift, some of us Old Souls will be here a very long time because we are not done with what we started. Cast away all fear that you don't know when the Wind of Transition will occur because we all helped plan it!

The very awakening process decides when you are going to transfer the energy. Survival pushes us to life. At the moment of transition when the heart stops and the last breath is breathed, the Creator Source knows that the transition is happening and all of your entourage are there. In a fraction of a second, the person in transition knows it is ok. All worry leaves them and they feel a sense of peace. Some call this a Spiritual Anesthetic. Kryon calls it 'the gift of heaven' so that the Wind of Transition from a quantum standpoint is beautiful! After that fraction of a second when one knows that they will not take another breath, all fear is gone and

one is moved into a three day remembrance of who we are. Part of us remains here on Earth and part of us is HOME with the Creator Source, God, and all of its beauty.

Some humans have gone though a Near Death Experience (NDE) and explained it the best way they could and they come back different. When they have come back they have said. "I couldn't believe it, it was beautiful! I heard singing". That is a gift from Kryon, the Magnetic Master and a support entity, who is the last energy we see when we come into earth, and the first energy that we see when we return home. There is no staying in death. The only sting is for the loved ones left behind who remain on earth and often do not know where we are. Where we are, is out of 3D (three dimensions) but we can see them.

Everyone we have loved and lost is still here. The Crystalline Grid contains their Mastery. Some of them become our guides. The parents that one has loved and lost will be with the person until their last breath, holding the person's hand – this is complex. Dear Uncle Jim, do you remember that your soul group can be in several places at the same time? This is quantum thinking. They can be reincarnate into another human soul and also be with a person as a guide.

When someone passes, their soul remains ALIVE and WELL as a beautiful ENERGY of LOVE. We need to know this so that we can grieve, celebrate the life of our loved one who has died and know that their soul is eternal. I enjoy talking to my late parents every day and regularly receive non-linear responses from them. All good!

In various areas of Japan, they have a white phone box with an old fashioned phone inside. These are placed in the grounds of the cemetery and encourage surviving relatives to go into the box, pick up the phone and speak to their beloved ones who have passed. What a brilliant idea! It can bring such comfort to so many individuals who find it a struggle to communicate their sense of loss to others and who miss the physical presence of talking to their departed loved one(s). It is another way of bridging the gap in our understanding of these Winds between linear and quantum living. Furthermore, it can result in great healing for those relatives and friends left behind on earth who continue with their own soul journey.

Much love as you enjoy more about the Light Puzzle, xxx

LETTER 43

WISE COUNSEL

"

*We are here to make a difference, to hold frequency and
to make wise decisions.*
~ Kryon

Dear Uncle Jim,

Happy Epiphany! This is known by many as the Day of the
Three Wise Men bearing gold, frankincense and myrrh to
the baby Jesus. So wonderful to hear your chirpy, strong
voice on the phone earlier this morning! I am thrilled that
you are making good progress...one step at a time!
Ha!

Remember in the scriptures John wrote in Revelation 21:1
"I saw a new heaven and a new earth".

This is now what is happening, very slowly, since the
mid-point of the precession of the Equinoxes on 21 December
2012.

188

The discovery of our truth resolves the past and puts the future in perspective. The remembrance is being triggered in you that heaven is a place on earth. We create our own piece of heaven right here on this planet!

One of the positive affirmations that I like to use is as follows:

It is my intention that I create an harmonious lifestyle. It is my intention to experience excellent health and energy that will lead to creative adventures! It is my intention that I will be provided for, that shelter and food and all of these things that I need to be given to me to experience life, will be received by me in great abundance. I pass on this great abundance and share it with others!

Rejoice in a system that is benevolent and loving for YOU!

Wishing you peace and love in all you do, xxx

LETTER 44

NEW THINKING

"
Can you open to an unseen realm of light
Whose communication link will ALWAYS keep you
safe, day and night?
~ Lady Wise

Dear Uncle Jim,

It was so wonderful to speak with you on Epiphany! When I came off the phone I had a thought. What if the arrangement of having someone come around on a Tuesday for a few hours is God's way of allowing you to discretely continue your ministering? We both know that God works in very mysterious ways sometimes and this could be an example of this. Rather than you going to visit individuals in hospital and ministering to the congregation in church, others will be able to see you SHINE in your own UNIQUE way when they come to visit you. Wonderful!

Remember that we have all come to Earth for healing. Very often those people working with others are oblivious to the healing they receive and indeed, oblivious to the fact that a little healing through a chat and a laugh is very beneficial for them. It still has the desired impact at a deeper level. You know yourself how many people you have touched and those who have then passed on their thoughts and feelings from having met you to others and so the snowball continues to roll and gain a momentum... one human at a time.

The tip for today is to turn on your inner net of wisdom within and to spend a little less time on the internet! Ha! This will give you improved balance.

The human being and the human's soul are accepted by most people as 'one'. When we are in truth with our Higher Self, we are in touch with the 'oneness' of all that is. The wisdom of God is a singular wisdom.

Be inspired and have an amazing day! Lots of love, xxx

Letter 45

STAR PEOPLE!

"
With more light and more compassion, you will see more
solutions because of the ripple effects of the harmonics
that go everywhere.
~ Kryon

Dear Uncle Jim,

It is a time of testing and of learning. There is a lineage in each one of us that connects us with the stars. There is a new way to feel. How much love can you take? How much compassion can you show?

Human Star People

The new band width raises the resonance of emotions of humanity.
As we enter this bandwidth we become aware and filled with vitality.
When we all connect to this vibration we will have world peace.

*We will each have more clarity and discover new skills, new
ideals, new understandings ripe for release.
As you discover your new gifts, enjoy them as you grow
Feel new freedom from constriction as all the old ways are
let go
Keep the resonance growing for the energy is going to
increase,
Allow the infinite love to pulse through you when you drop
your karma and all fears cease
In your daily life you will become more wise
And discern the truth from those telling lies
Continue to nurture yourself every day
Take time to relax and remember to play
Claim your lineage and come into the Light
As you grow in integrity and the power of insight
These esoteric things will one day be known through science
For consciousness and the language of physics have an
alliance
Scientists on the planet are already receiving information
To prove the consciousness of physics using newly created
instrumentation
Quantum things do not exist in a way that exists in 3D
Imagine with such newly invented scientific instruments what
we will see?
Gravity someday will be able to be seen and measured
Its patterns and colours will be sights to be treasured
The fractals and the magnetic field create patterns of
confluence
Whose invisible life force on the planet is tied to humanity's
influence
When we see the Grids and how they ally with human
biology
It will lead to a beautiful esoteric discovery!*

Remember gravity is variable and is not linked necessarily
to mass calculation
The instruments will eventually define a quantumness in each
person's calibration
The prediction can be made because the potentials are there
They have been seen in other civilisations that have evolved
elsewhere.
Consciousness is the description of the paradigm of thinking
Founded on an open heart and the emotions of feeling
Let me give you examples of the 2 greatest energy producers
One can soften your heart while the other is powerful enough
to crash a computer
It's time to grow up from living a restrictive low energy life
Founded on entrapment, hatred, fear, pain and strife
Wake up to the notion that you deserve the best-
A life filled with love, why would you settle for less?
Power lies in COMPASSION which outweighs all things
evil!
Everything that is not built on integrity, love and truth is in
upheaval
I encourage you to feel the movement around your third eye
or pineal
To further explore those things that are unseen and yet
real
The creation story of the universe with you and of you with
it is an amalgam
The universal human is alive and well – it is YOU! And so
I AM.
Be in the presence of who you are,
Allow the merging of the two – male, female, light, dark –
human star!
Feel your wholeness and the love from your feet
all the way through your body making you complete.

My poem explains the beauty behind the maturing and evolving human being. One human at a time, we are learning to reconnect with our more compassionate nature and the importance of being loving and kind to everyone whom we meet. There is a truth that spirituality and science are connected! Now, there is scientific proof of this relationship. There is an elegance in expressing yourself with more respect, grace and sensitivity. In this way, you will enhance your intuition.

Intuitive inventions will help humanity. They will give us solutions to help us understand about managing population growth and satisfactorily address a whole host of other perceived social, economic and political problems.

One of the inventions that will occur which is mentioned in my poem is an instrument that will reveal patterns of consciousness. All energy gives out a pattern. Humans are made up of energy as well as every other thing on the planet.

Low energy humans who are prone to living in fear create the simplest pattern of all. It will show a strong circle around the individual – the circle is a prison – it will not be aware of anything outside its own circle. It cannot see beyond what it knows. It is restrictive. The strength of it comes from the fact that it can create a bigger circle – entrapment.

High energy in humans creates the most complex vibratory rate with a consciousness of love, compassion and high integrity. High vibrations creates fractals and a coming together of energy that creates more of itself with harmonics that emanate outward in an expansive way. It enhances whatever is around it in a never ending cycle. The harmonics it creates vibrate way beyond itself, it has an influence EVERYWHERE. What we see is the real difference in the patterns.

Low energy is powerful, simple in its pattern and restrictive.

High energy is powerful, complex in its pattern and expansive!

Human consciousness has tended to circle itself in the lowest vibration possible – hatred, war, argumentative rudeness, bullying, humiliation, intimidation, gossiping and unkindness because it was in SURVIVAL MODE. This was the way humans survived – country to country, human to human.

Disappointingly, the circle that that pattern created, was one from which the consciousness could not expand or grow, so all it did was repeat itself, repeat itself, repeat itself. There were no harmonics to send out.

Now, the energy on this planet is changing the patterns, because the pattern of consciousness lies in the things which are the Magnetic Grid and the location of planet earth in space. As all these things are changing, so too are the patterns of low and high energy vibration types. Transition is occurring. High energy that is the most complex has fractals far more powerful than the basic survival low energy! Exciting!

Low consciousness is darkness that cannot see above itself. When you look at people you will recognise this low energy as those individuals who are angry, unkind and rude. You may think, 'What is wrong with this person?' There is nothing wrong with them. They are simply invested in SURVIVAL. You may not like it but they survive on rudeness. They consider compassion and kindness show weakness from their perspective as they cannot see outside the circle. And so their approach with you today in negotiations and discussions is to come at you with unkindness, strength and rudeness. This is what you do not want and find unappealing.

A compassionate person is not a weak energy at all. The energy around a compassionate person INVITES YOU IN! The energy around a rude person excludes you out! Are you understanding the different behaviour patterns?

Human consciousness is starting to rise above what it was, because the Light and Dark weightings of each, the ratio if you like, has changed. The Light is winning!

Rudeness and unkindness will eventually be seen as dysfunctional and people will walk away from this old, survival energy.

Compassion, integrity, joy and kindness shine a light so bright that people will see this far, far better than the rudeness and unkindness. Love is within!

The new survival is Light. Those with Light will live longer. New leaders will come from those practising compassion in their leadership and behaviour. When you are compassionate everybody feels it.

A compassionate person is seen as SAFE. It's enjoyable to be around them. They will not judge another, hurt another and say unkind things. Others will say, "Did you feel the energy around that person, it was great? " They are going to listen to you and they are going to love you and it will happen in business too! In the future Kryon teaches that we will have this as a staple and we will be able to see it and measure it and even know why it works. It will change the planet, Uncle Jim, and you are a part of this elegance!

The ones who thrive the most are going to have the most compassionate brains and minds. Those people who are non-judgemental also see the Creator Source in those whom

they meet and expect good things first. Are you starting to FEEL the reality of this? It is safe.

The idea overwhelmingly on this planet now from families and many adults is how to come together and make peace on this planet and be able to get along. Welcome to the New Earth, it is here! We are building it together using a foundation of love!

Blessings in the energy of infinite love!

Peace and much love, xxx

LETTER 46

TOGETHERNESS OF LOVE

"

Love endures across the ripples of time
Embrace uncertainty as you recalibrate and realign!
~ Lady Wise

Dear Uncle Jim,

You and I know that love is more than language. You look into the eyes of your newborn grandchildren and there is communication.

"

Two humans together in love, they form a bond, there is
actually a third energy formed because of the love they
have for one another. They think about each other from
long distances. It is more than language.
~ Kryon

When you are asked about love, Uncle Jim, how do you describe it? There are so many different kinds of love. There is love for your wife and family, for your animals, for your

ancestors, for your friends, for those you have lost, for the planet, it is endless. What about your soul? The soul is not part of us that is physical and yet is resides in us. It is a piece of the Creator.

The human soul permeates everything about you. It is pure multi-dimensional energy that is sacred and beyond anything you can ever measure. The soul is part of our DNA and as Kryon informs us, resides in the energy of our consciousness in ways that we do not yet know. Spiritual evolution is going to mean an increase in soul awareness. Some of us are starting to feel **soul remembrance.**

"

The closest thing to the soul is the love that we can feel.
We cannot explain our Soul or the Creator yet we know
that it is real.
It is generic and beautiful and it has no gender.
It is inside everyone and it is filled with splendour.
~ Lady Wise

Uncle Jim, **WE ARE IT!** We are now a planet in Graduate Status! All of Kryon's teachings about the soul are for the following reason.

"

Spiritual evolution within the cellular structure of your
body creates a symbiotic relationship with your DNA,
with your Akash and intuition.
~ Kryon

The system of spiritual evolution comes through the soul. The pineal gland senses the Higher Self. Intuition senses the

Higher Self but the soul is the one who delivers the information. The soul is connected to the Magnetic, Crystalline and Gaia Grids.

"

There is a third language that represents an intuitive language which is broadcast to those who wish to listen – loving, informative, benevolent information – that goes beyond the spoken word!
~ Kryon

It surpasses anything we have ever experienced on the planet and the Pleiadians gave this to us a long time ago. When humanity was ready to be seeded by the Pleiadians, YOU were there and you came from the Pleiades. When it comes to reincarnation it is not limited to this planet, you were aware of that were you not? We have to have come from somewhere. When you have an exponential growth of humanity where do you think the pool comes from? Humanity comes from other places. Life does not then emerge from nowhere.

"

What if I told you that there was a certain amount of entities and soul groups that incarnate and it has been happening for millions of years – other places – long before 200,000 years ago. You came from the Pleiadians.
~ Kryon

In order to receive the seeds, we had to be of a certain kind of chemical readiness, soul remembrance and all the things of which we have never heard. These had to be correct for the seed to take, for the meld of the DNA, the chromosomes

to move around, for YOU to become who you are. This is the Creation Story imparted beautifully by Kryon.

How many lifetimes have you lived over the last hundred thousand years? Who are the Pleiadians? I will let Kryon explain.

"

The Pleiadians, the Seven Sisters made up of 9 Suns, 3 habitable planets, all habitable by Pleiadians eventually, have been a society of enlightened humanoids for 2 million years.
~ Kryon

We are looking at a society that has existed eight times longer. They went into Graduate Status like we are now and everything changed for them. They passed the marker and they began to receive information. Their DNA is like ours.

"

DNA is DNA all over the galaxy. The principles of DNA created here are those which are created everywhere. DNA is the building block of life – period. It is a naturally occurring life process everywhere.
~ Kryon

The DNA of the Pleiadians started to increase in its light quotient like ours, slowly increasing to 44, 54, 55, 66, 77, 88% activation.

"

Let me tell you what happens when you reach 88% – you start to meld with the Soul. You are designed to be Divine.

You are designed to live forever – renewable – every cell keeps going and going especially the Divine in you when it starts to balance up the cellular structures, it creates new ones, it goes to the blueprint and it never gets old.
You never get old.
~ Kryon

What are we going to do with overpopulation when we never get old? The hint is where Kryon tells us that the Pleiadians have three planets! We learn to move around. We learn about the Universe. It is not a problem. It's beautiful. A Pleiadian is the closest thing that you will ever see to an angel in your life. They are working at 88% DNA activation. They have control over physics and they are entangled with anything they want to be including rocks, oceans, sand, animals, flowers, mountains and trees.

"

*The human soul is **divine physics** at its maximum, control over everything. The Creator is in the Soul. The Creator is the Master physicist of the Universe and so if you are at 88% of that, one has control over everything! That is the seed that YOU have inside!*
~ Kryon

Perhaps you are now thinking what is the Pleiadian society like? There is no society, Uncle Jim, as we understand it. There is only the **TOGETHERNESS OF LOVE** operating at 88% DNA activation of the Creator Source over two million years. The Pleiadians were seeded by others, including the Orions and the Arcturians, who have become our Akashic grand-parents.

In a planet that is over four billion years old, to use a Kryon phrase, we are "the new kids on the block" here! Can you imagine what went on in the Galaxy one billion years ago, Uncle Jim?

Planet Earth is the only planet of free choice in the Galaxy at this moment.
~ Kryon

Your human soul was the catalyst for the Graduation Energy that you are now ready to receive. It does not come in through the human portion. It cannot. The time capsules (nodes and nulls I will tell you about another day) have been opening that the Pleiadians primed to release to give us information. This information goes to the soul part of us. It is only able to be engaged by the soul when we approach 44% DNA activation.

Yet, some of us are remembering who we were on another planet, some of us are remembering the Pleiadians, we are remembering that we have been through this before, it is giving us HOPE. We were able to see 88%. Who knows how long it is going to take this time? It doesn't matter because we are all going to be here to see it.

88% Soul Remembrance is what you are going to call Soul Akash. It remembers past Earth and this is starting to happen. With the evolutionary process of that which is taking place on this planet with Old Souls, in is going to come Soul Remembrance, you are going to remember that
YOU ARE ETERNAL.
~ Kryon

Our souls are coming from other places that have gone through this i.e. all the planets of free choice that have graduated.

YOU, dear Uncle Jim, would not be reading this letter unless you had a certain attribute of soul remembrance that is already at work, not what you have done on planet earth, but what you did in the Pleiades. In the Seven Sisters you did this, you graduated, closer and closer to the divine source. It is so attractive, Uncle Jim, to come to a place where you are at one with God. You have been there. You have done that and you received the seed and now you awaken and you remember a little of what it was like...just a little. Many Old Souls were scheduled to leave early to pave the way for YOU coming back.

There are many pictures of holy men and women many of them on other continents who have found the connection that brings them to a WHOLENESS where they can keep themselves alive for a long time, be one with the planet, meld in consciousness with nature and all that is. In an older energy, this was always possible, but it took discipline and it changed their lives forever. Some of them could not eat the things they used to eat, many of them became celibate, all of these things in order to create this precious energy that for a moment would give them solace of feeling the Creator. I want to tell you Uncle Jim they were the forerunners for what is coming.

Let's talk about one of the Masters about whom you preach. You will have seen the pictures of Christ and the animals gathered at his feet. Kryon teaches that the animals saw the high 88% DNA Light quotient in him and they were attracted to it. People would gather from all over just to sit at his feet and watch him glow because it was addictive. It's a celebration for an addictive energy of love, of compassion and this is where we are going. As we increase our efficiency of the DNA, our soul brings in more of the creative energy from the Creative Source. This is the evolution of the human spirit. It is way beyond biology. We are starting to see humans mature in spirit. The things that are so out of balance today will begin to become balanced. We are seeing it everywhere! Balance, compassion, wisdom, you can already start to see it.

"

When you come in next time you are going to remember who you are.
~ Kryon

That is a promise from Kryon! You are going to pick up from where you left off and you are going to be a wise, old child beyond any children you know today, Old Soul, and you are not going to make the mistakes you made in this lifetime – none of them!

"

Your Soul Remembrance will keep you safe and your children will carry what you carry. It comes in with you.
~ Kryon

That is the way it is going to work, that is what will propel us forward past peace on earth into graduation soul energy. Is this too esoteric for you? That's ok. We have plenty of time, Uncle Jim. Let's make a date to check in with each other in about a million years! Ha!

Cheers in celebration of the oneness and the love that we are! xxx

LETTER 47

AKASHIC LINEAGE

Your Akashic lineage is God. The collective purpose of
being together is to move consciousness.
~ Kryon

Dear Uncle Jim,

The indigenous foretold it; a higher consciousness after the Precession of the Equinoxes, with the key marker date 21 December 2012.

Spirit has always spoken to humanity in code. The Book of Revelation is in code. Kryon tells us Nostradamus wrote in code so that his friends wouldn't know what he was doing! Ha! That is a little different! True spiritual prophecy, however, and sometimes the most profound messages even to the indigenous, came in code and the codes were metaphors. They were always metaphors. How does a multi-dimensional God speak to a single digit dimensional human being? The answer is through metaphors. That has always been the code. And yet, some teachers, especially of old, will have taken the

metaphors and then looked at them literally and taught them as literal. This is common. As an example, the seven days it took to create the earth were not seven days, they were seven dispensations of benevolent grace where things were created in a way that made sense and the result was the planet. You know this now. You have seen the common sense of it and you have figured out this is what spirit really meant.

It is time to start applying that to some of the things that you hear daily or have been taught about metaphysics in general. It is important to pay attention to the minutiae in particular.

Any time you hear the word crystalline associated with anything whether it's a grid or it's a planet or whether it is an entity, do you understand that that is metaphorical and it means "that which holds vibration or remembers".

The information given in this new energy (post 21 December 2012) is to offer greater clarity to what you know. Much of this will be in metaphors too and requires you to rethink what you thought you knew but perhaps now realise you can see differently with this understanding.

What is the biggest difference between the Old and the New Energy? The Old Energy separated and survived because the people walked in the Dark.

New Energy has the Light turned on where we can see each other and there is no reason to separate. Instead we come together to work things out!

Dear Uncle Jim, this takes work. When you start to change who you are, how you behave and how you react, you are rewriting your humanism, aren't you?

This is the invitation to rewrite humanism. Never before in the history of spiritual humanity, since the seeding of humanity, have the cells of your body been more receptive to suggestion, the suggestion of behaviour i.e. what works and what does not work.

The new balance on the planet is the paradigm of survival. The balanced ones, who are going to survive in the chaos all around them, are the ones who are going to be seen as strong.

In the past, the ones who had chaos attracted the most attention and got what they wanted. Now they will be seen as flailing children that misbehave and humanity will look for balance in individuals' businesses and spiritual systems that make common sense and spiritual sense.

There are many groups represented that channel to humans now to open up possibilities that are grander. Some groups being represented are the Arcturians, those from Sirius, the Pleadians and those from Orion. This is done in full love to open up possibilities that are grander than what has been traditionally taught. It is confusing. There should be no exclusion. Do not exclude others – because that is what survival does.

What do you know about the attributes of grand-parents that your parents don't have? How do you feel about your grand-parents living or dead? You look at them different than your parents, don't you? Your parents are hands-on. Your grand-parents want to entertain you and help you and they take you places. Mum and Dad are different and unique in their own special way.

The Pleiadians seeded us and they are the ones opening the time capsules and giving us all the information. Our Akashic grandparents are the ones giving us the most help – be they Arcturian, Sirian, Orion. We have in our DNA who they are, because it comes with the territory of our Akashic inheritance. You know them. They know you. They are probably the most helpful groups on the planet. See the system for what it is and absorb them all. They love us and they know who we are. You are going to see (awareness of perception of the Old Soul with things unseen that are real) more of them. Does this make sense, Old Soul? I trust that you are comfortable with this?

It is so important that you understand this. It is your birthright to know about the reality and common sense of a system that is beautiful right from the Creative Source that is God. God is bigger than anything about which we have ever been told.

"

You have help. Acknowledge it, work with it and use it!
~ Kryon

In celebration of the truth and the demystification of who we are! All love, xxx

LETTER 48

AN ACTIVE PINEAL GLAND

After eons, our pineal gland is becoming active once more,
Can you feel its power and connectivity to your
heart core?
~ Lady Wise

Dear Uncle Jim,

I do hope you are making good progress in your recovery and simply cherishing the joy of each new day! I am choosing to write today in one of my early mornings. I have just heard faint bird-song from my bedroom window and have started to write at my desk in the dining-room at 6.15am. Although it is still so very dark outside, I am thrilled that the earlier light morning and evening cycles have begun since the winter equinox and that spring is on its way!

Have you noticed that your intuition always puts you on the right path? Are you aware of colour masses flowing

across your third eye in meditation? These lights or colours of the 'third eye' are a sign that your pineal gland is becoming activated and that your third eye chakra is opening. There is no need to be afraid. There is nothing to fear. For many individuals this is often one of the first signs of a subtle positive change taking place within them. Some may also experience a heightened awareness of and sensitivity to light.

Are you feeling a gradual change in the way you interact with other individuals? Perhaps you are feeling a little less self-centred than you used to be? Ha! Perhaps you are feeling more compassionate towards your neighbours?

Can you start to visualise a better life for yourself?

Is your memory improving? Working with creative art, photography and day dreaming are all activities that enhance our imagination and our pineal gland. Many of us have our gifts within us that lie dormant until we activate our pineal. This gland is a hormone. An active pineal gland will therefore help you sleep well and affect your ability to recover from any health issues and balance your hormones.

When you can increase your sleep quality this may give you more energy as well as positively contributing to your ability to visualise through your 'third eye' of intuition and to cultivate this to develop certain gifts!

The electro-magnetic energy from your heart is significantly more powerful energy than the energy from your brain. Use your heart to connect with the emotion that you want to feel. Can you imagine a dial on your chest and amplify the emotion and joy from feeling your third eye open more and more, as you see yourself helping the world. Success is a relaxed state! When you realise this you will be able to receive more and more gifts! Cortisol is in our body and handles stress but when this is out of balance then we can use certain herbs to address this imbalance. Adaptogenic herbs that will adapt and reduce stress by seeking out the stress areas in your body and helping your hormones to be in balance are rhodiola rosea and ashwagandha.

Rhodiola rosea is a remarkable herb that has a wide and varied history of uses. It is thought to strengthen the nervous system, fight depression, enhance immunity, elevate the capacity for exercise, enhance memory, aid weight reduction, increase sexual function and improve energy levels.

Ashwagandha is an adaptogenic herb popular in Ayurvedic medicine. Ashwagandha helps to lower cortisol levels, balance thyroid hormones, combat stress and depression, and even build muscle. These are two plants that tend to grow in very adaptive, challenging environments and so they are very strong.

The human body becomes particularly vulnerable to dis-ease when the frequency at which it vibrates falls below 62 megahertz.

My Aunt mentioned that you were interested in eating some different foods that you would usually have never eaten before? Our choice in food and changing habits are often associated with the process of awakening. The pineal gland is really important in this process and over the years it often becomes calcified due to eating certain foods and using certain hygiene products. What does this mean? Restricted use of an active functioning pineal gland can affect sleep patterns and our creativity. The pineal gland regulates sleep and wake cycles. It also governs our circadian rhythms and is related to the third eye. The third eye is the part in the centre of one's forehead which is also referred to the as 'the seat of

the soul' by the Egyptians, and is the connection to the multi-verse and allows for 'third' eye sight. It is through the pineal gland that we have our own astral plane within the mid brain where we can be creative.

As an aside, it is interesting to note that dementia in individuals may apparently be caused by a calcification of parts of the brain. It really is important that we know this so that we can take steps to prevent this disease occurring in our bodies in the first place.

Our intuitive self knows what is best for our bodies and so today I am going to share with you some information that I found out only yesterday.

There are several foods which are particularly beneficial to decalcifying the pineal gland. You decide which ones you already eat and which ones you may be keen to try?

Watercress is rich in anti-oxidants and will help to reduce the calcification of the pineal gland because it absorbs all the heavy metals from the bloodstream due to its iodine content. Other foods that will assist in restoring the pineal gland to full functionality are as follows:

Avocados are high in the fatty acid called oleic acid and assist in insulating the brain with myelin to protect brain function and brain processing speed;

Bananas are full of tryptophan and help produce serotonin and melatonin which regulate our sleep pattern and help us feel good about ourselves;

Natural coconut water is full of lauric acid to boost our immune system and helps to rehydrate the body and brain function;

Pineapples increase brain function and provide high content vitamin C. Have you ever noticed the pentagon shape on the skin of a pineapple? This shape indicates that it is good for you.

One level teaspoon of spirulina powder is protein packed and works well in a glass of water by itself or blended with half a banana and a level teaspoon of turmeric too! I usually enjoy this first thing every morning and choose to heap the teaspoons of turmeric and spirulina because I love the taste!

Remember to stay away from all inorganic foods containing monosodiumglutomate (MSG). Years ago, Mum was walking with me in town up one of the steep hills near George Square. All of a sudden she said she would have to stop because she was feeling breathless. This was completely out of character for her as, at that time, she was used to walking several miles and a jaunt around the city centre was equivalent to a mere 'skip in the park'. Anyhow, after about fifteen minutes we continued although she did not feel 100% well. When it happened again later that afternoon, she decided to make a doctor's appointment. Fortunately, her doctor, although puzzled by her symptoms at first, suggested to her that she made a note of everything that she was eating and to come back in a week's time. He had had another client who had experienced similar problems, but at this stage it was too early to call.

When Mum wrote down her food intake and returned a week later, the doctor commented that he had seen a recent case that was not dissimilar to Mum's issue and the cause had been pinpointed to MSG in her diet. When he looked at the list of food Mum had ingested over the past week it was not obvious, but then Mum remembered she had recently

started to eat packets of soup instead of making her own at lunchtime. No-one else in the family had eaten them because Dad was at work and I was at school! The doctor asked her to check the ingredients on her return home because it had been an intake of MSG that had been ring-fenced as the problem for one of his other patients. Eureka! Mum returned home and chose not to eat any more packets of soups with the label showing MSG contained in the soup powder. It took several weeks before Mum's energy levels and breathing regulated itself again. In order to live a long, healthy life we need the body to be in perfect homeostasis. Since we are each so unique, we are our own best guides on what feels best for us to eat.

Aunt Coral probably remembers that refined grains frequently found in white rice and white bread may not be the best of food for us! These grains may produce increased fungus and mould in one's body which is not a very pleasant thought! The most acidic grain is wheat and wheat contains gluten. It is the gluten that effectively keeps the intestines 'stuck together'. When this happens it is more difficult for the toxins to be eliminated from one's body. While we all store bacteria in our gut it would make sense to limit this to as much good bacteria as possible to build up a robust immune system.

I am unsure Uncle Jim if you eat much white rice but whether it is rice or bread it may be advisable to switch to brown rice and brown bread. Mucous is another side effect of too much gluten in the body. The refined grains can cause a blocked nasal package that has a knock-on effect of aggravating the lungs and coughing occurs. When this happens the mucous is starting to work against the body! Other alternatives to refined grains would be quinoa or

buckwheat that is not a grain at all but a fruit seed full of phyto-nutrients.

We are here to raise our energy frequency and to keep our pineal gland at optimum health. For every food type eaten, Uncle Jim, it is important to question whether it helps you to eat to live and thrive, or struggle to survive?

Love and abundant blessings of good health xxx

LETTER 49

INNER RICHNESS

"

Clarity transcends all duality when you look inside,
Find your truth and free your mind!

~ Lady Wise

Dear Uncle Jim,

What I find amusing is that I so enjoy all this learning and imparting the knowledge yet there is no last step to knowing it all. Ha! We are always developing and raising our consciousness. How wonderful that the relationship with spirit is through love and is available twenty four hours every day, all the time.

With free choice, it becomes a meld from that part of you which is connected to spirit, to the part of you that is on the other side of the veil.

Isn't it funny to think that we effectively are multi-tasking with our Higher Self? It is so super cool to be connected to

spirit while we are doing other things such as eating, dressing, walking, writing, singing and being playful? Even accountants can be crunching their numbers and at the same time be aware of their divinity – 24/7 – all the time! Ha!

When we meld with our piece of divinity inside, the compassionate part of us starts to be involved no matter where we are. Consider it similar to an extended worship service, Uncle Jim, worshipping the JOY in all you have, all the time and not just on schedule for a short time as in a weekly church service.

We have also always been connected when we sleep. That is part of the multi-dimensionality of our dreams when we cannot make linear sense of so many of them. The brain disengages in sleep and part of spirit is with us in ways that it is not when we are awake. Spirit knows what we need because it is always present.

The indigenous believe that God is in everything. They know that the animals are here to be of service to us as part of our food chain and then there are those who show themselves to be our companions and much loved pets. The plants grow for our nourishment. Every step we take, Gaia is with us. The meld was complete long ago and the connection has been lost. Now we are rekindling this meld and in the new energy it starts to go beyond this.

You will find yourself meeting others who are there to meet you. The answer is the meld. The meld helps you to understand and appreciate your connection to everything. Expect synchronicity with people you don't know! Synchronicity is the new key. Intuition will push and pull you in positive ways. This is different from the negative push and pull of karma.

Now that you have dropped your karma it no longer features in your life. You become the catalyst to compassion around any problem. You can place the issue into a bubble of love and the result will be that others will feel it. Eventually, those things will morph and change and when you have enough people doing this together – the difference becomes evident!

"

The Old Soul recognises the power of it, the
appropriateness of it and the majesty of it.
The message is clear – God inside. The meld is here.
~ Kryon

Dear Uncle Jim, your cellular structure craves balance and the wholeness of the connection to innate. It is the solution to the mystery of life.

The melded human being is one who is super intuitive and doesn't even know it. They just know what they are to do next, where they are to go. This creates the New Human who understands that spirituality is not removed from the corporeal human being. When we meld we no long have feelings of isolation and separateness. We become healthier and live longer.

"

Access to this higher frequency energy will not only give
you the tools for more abundant living but give you access
to improved health, without which each human being
cannot achieve much.
~ Kryon

Any fears that were drummed into you will start to leave. You will understand that you can have empathy for the planet but that it does not have to control your emotions. You can see injustice and it doesn't have to make you sad and keep you from sleep.

Instead, when you see the imbalance of what is going on around you, you will send energy to that part of it that needs the radiant healing energy because of the God inside. I do this every day at 11.11am – send healing energy and love around the world to wherever it needs to go.

Now it is really getting powerful because you are the source. Instead of visiting the creator source energy, concentrating on it and using it, you become it! That's power! That's energy!

You are forever and when you meld you will be aware that death itself is nothing to fear and is a joyful transition to your spiritual home. You go home and all that happens next is that you come back. The worst thing about death is not dying, it is those who are left behind and how they respond to the death of their loved-one. Can you prepare your loved ones and friends for a celebration when it is your time to die? They will celebrate you and your next incarnation and they will celebrate all that you did while you were here. They will celebrate you into the beyond and there will be tears of joy that you are eternal like they are. What a concept! A new kind of funeral is being selected by more and more families! You are going to see it. I chose to have a Celebration of Life funeral for Mum. This is an accelerated consciousness. Ways of thinking that may seem very different today are going to become common because universal truth is that way.

Blessings and love always xxx

LETTER 50

EASY EXIT PLAN

"
*When you pass from this planet, your biology may die but
the perfect spiritual soul goes back to the creator source,
one with everything, with nature, with God.*
~ Kryon

Dear Uncle Jim,

Today I want to mention about an agreement that I have
already made with myself and my Higher Self in regards to
my own death.... some two hundred plus years from now,
ha!ha!, since I plan to live in this lifetime a very long time.

There is so much wonderful stuff going on just now in this
Shift and I know that I can help so many people, why would
I want to leave early? Afterall, DNA is built to last at least
nine hundred years, hence the age of some people referred
to in Holy Scripture.

In all seriousness, Kryon explains that it's not easy for many
people to die. You have to know where you are going, you

have to have a plan and you want to aim for meeting up with those who 'know the ropes' on the other side who are clear and pure and who really love you – that's what you want to have meet you and those are the beings that will meet you if you set your intention and set it up that way. You do not lose who you are when you die. In order to comfort you right now, I would make a decision in this moment that you have nothing to fear.

In the privacy of your own agreement, say that when it is time for me to go, I will go fearlessly into the long goodnight and I will go into a great new reality knowing that loved ones wait for me and a new adventure is at hand. In this way you can eliminate the fear of dying.

It is important to have an exit plan. You may be years and years away from your exit but a little bit of imagining can go a long way. It can be as simple as deciding how and where you are going to die.

The Pleiadians suggest making an agreement. An example of this may be to say:-

"Higher Self, and my Over-Soul, when it is time to terminate my experience in reality of this physical body I want to leave graciously and effortlessly. I want no pain, no mess and no fuss. I want the easiest of exit plans. "

Whatever it is that you want and by putting your desire out there, you are already conditioning the space for how you are going to exit.

Do you know how many people are afraid of dying? It is not unusual for these individuals to fall sick because being afraid of dying makes them sick and they spend years sick,

dreading the death portal as they go from hospital to nursing home to a greater and greater degradation of vitality. It all comes from the fear of leaving the physical body. The non-physical, i.e. the soul, is an absolute separate reality and because of your investment in this lifetime you will bring your consciousness with you – everything you have learned goes with you.

So what about making an agreement and then putting it away in your mind. This means that when your time comes, it is going to be good. Simply forget all about it and enjoy every moment living a good life NOW!

Another aspect to death is to help people die in a cleaner way. Presently we are experiencing increasing disease such as Dementia and Alzheimers because of the fear that people have of dying. From a generic global perspective there is no normal anymore. All kinds of systems are breaking down across the world – economic, financial, social and political, weather cycles are changing with jet streams bringing warmer air in winter breaking all time records and the good health of adults and children is being eroded by multiple factors which include processed food, environmental pollution (especially air and water) and technological pollution. Some of our work now needs to be addressed at helping individuals to die with grace.

It is of paramount importance that we let our elders know that they do not have to die in pain anymore. There is an honouring of the process that can be taught from which we can all learn and share with our family and friends.

There is no need for a death without dignity and grace or an early death from fear. When people understand the bigger picture of the eternal soul and eternal life, they can enjoy every nano second of their life, having safely made an exit plan agreement with Higher Self.

Wishing you eternal peace in your loving heart! xxx

LETTER 51

LEGACY OF WISDOM

"
Encoded within us are the keys that will unlock the
mysteries again enabling us to realise greater harmony,
peace and higher purpose.
~ Kryon

Dear Uncle Jim,

The Ancient ones encoded their timeless wisdom in their art, song, prayers, architecture and stone circles using specific colours, words, sacred geometry, location and celestial alignments. At these sacred sites they used ritual and ceremony to help keep energy flowing between heaven and earth.

As current cycles are ending and new ones are emerging, it is time to remember, honour and integrate sacred wisdom into our lives.

We will integrate within ourselves the most powerful cosmic energies to help activate our cellular memories. Our journey will be a living book of experiences as we share the gifts of

the moment. We will go beyond time and space and remember our divine essence.

Sacred places transcend time and space, and act as a catalyst for deepening the spiritual and transformational process. Ancient masters created a legacy of wisdom where ancient wisdom is fused into the heart of their creations. These special places serve as a repository for human memory and they speak to each person in a profound and unique manner. Sacred places also offer greater cellular activation where we can align and integrate our physical and spiritual bodies into a body of light and wholeness.

Today many people are seeking greater personal meaning and are being called 'home' to these sacred places to actually experience divine principles and to connect with nature, ancient wisdom, and higher dimensions of awareness. They know and feel that the repository of wisdom was encoded within their sacred space.

"

Without the darkness, we would not rise
The divinity within each person is the grandest surprise
In this evolution of the maturity of the human being
We reconnect with our legacy of what it means to be
ALL SEEING!
~ Lady Wise

Higher knowledge was left for a future time when those seeking mastery would return and be infused with divine energies, enabling them to unlock the keys to remembering and actualising the wisdom of the gods once again. The time is now. I expect to return to Lemuria, at least once in this lifetime, to feel hugged by the Pleiadian Star Mothers.

Wishing you peace, joy and love in your heart, xxx

LETTER 52

NODES AND NULLS

"
The nodes and nulls are only a few years old in our
knowledge yet they were placed on earth 200,000 years
ago in actuality in case you made it.
~ Kryon

Dear Uncle Jim,

On or around 2012, Kryon brought in the knowledge of the nodes and the nulls. It was part of what Kryon, the Magnetic Master, is here for.

Kryon asks the question, 'If you were creating the next planet of free choice, how would you assist the humanoids, should they choose to become a graduate ascended planet?'

Such a deep esoteric question is asked so that we can start connecting the dots of the Gaia system that the Pleiadians created when they planted the seeds of divinity on earth.

The nodes and nulls of the planet are a part of the Gaia system created by the Pleiadians which are "hooked" into the benevolent design of the universe. How would you prepare that prospective planet? What kind of a system would there be? If this process has happened many times over, do you think there would be similar attributes each time?

Humanity only passed the marker of the final decision point on December 21, 2012 when humans chose to become a graduate ascended planet. The nodes and the nulls were brought here for an accelerated consciousness. We have now passed the marker. This means that detailed information regarding the nodes and nulls was not previously ready to be given, as humanity was not ready to receive.

Imagine telling humans who lived more than one hundred years ago about Twitter or Facebook? It's a similar premise. Now we are ready to receive the information.

"

Nodes and nulls work in tandem, not as a single unit, operating as a polarised pair. The mechanics of the polarised pairs of nodes and nulls, are a "push-pull" energy of The Crystalline Grid.
~ Kryon

What does that mean? Think of nodes like a vacuum cleaner. Nodes have been working slowly 'pulling' and taking away the energies that are no longer needed by humanity, such as fear, war, anxiety and drama. Think of nulls as a repository of Pleiadian energy where new information such as ideas and invention are slowly being pushed to humanity.

That is the 'push pull' energy of the nodes and nulls.

*They contain a system of process, an engine, and when
it was time they opened. They match up with the
human consciousness of the day.*

~ Kryon

When our human consciousness and spiritual maturity start to change, parts which have been locked, start to open up. The nodes and nulls have now fully opened. They have been paired up all over the planet and the energies that they create pour out information on to the Magnetic, Crystalline and Gaia Grids of this planet – the three active interpersonal grids of this planet – the ones that interface with you and your consciousness. The information goes into the grid and not into your consciousness. This allows for FREE CHOICE. It is put upon the grid, enabling you to choose with free choice to accept things which do or do not resound with your consciousness.

Some well-known locations where nodes occur include: Mount Shasta, California; Sedona, Arizona; and Machu Picchu, Peru.

Some well-known locations where nulls occur include: Valley of the Moon (San Pedro de Atacama), Chile; Mt Kilimanjaro, Tanzania (Africa) and the Bermuda Triangle.

There is no symmetry with these lines and they occur beneath the earth as well as on the earth so it becomes more complex than what we think. All of these lines are created by the Crystalline Grid, and the Crystalline Grid is created by human consciousness. Human consciousness has shifted greatly which has triggered a recalibration of everything: Gaia, the Crystalline Grid and human nature as we have known it.

How were the nodes and nulls created? When the Pleiadians came to earth they put themselves into a quantum state all over the planet in various areas. Nodes and nulls represent different attributes of energies on the planet [placed by the Pleiadians]. There are numerous nodes and nulls all over the planet. We find them in the highest of mountains, the driest of deserts and everything in between.

"

Long ago the Pleiadians looked at this planet and they selected 12 pairs of energy points that would represent the duality of the planet. These 12 energy points are found at 24 geographical locations. A total of 24 nodes and nulls, on mountain peaks and deserts, were selected to represent the parts of the planet that were the most promising. These 12 polarised node and null energy pairs may also be referred to as 'time capsules'. Energy was set in these places so that if humanity would ever make it to a higher consciousness these places would release information for the individual human being as well as for the whole planet. There is a sacred geometry within the selection of these pairs. Within the sacred geometry the shapes, colours, sounds and numbers all reveal the divinity of God.
~ Kryon

The Pleiadians selected these points, long before any civilisations lived on earth. The Pleiadians set energy within the time capsules, ready for release if ever humanity would reach a certain vibration. In 2013 we were at that vibration. The first time capsule on the planet was ready to be activated and opened on the Island of the Sun, in Maui, Hawaii. The matching null was Mt. Kailash in Tibet. This time capsule was waiting to be opened in the year of the six. The year

of the six refers to the numerology of 2013. In numerology, six represents sacredness, perfection, harmony, balance and love (also the Higher-Self).

The time capsules created by the Pleiadians refer to a direct link with multi-dimensional information in real time. There are time capsules in Gaia, placed within The Crystalline Grid and the cetaceans [whales and dolphins]. There are also time capsules within our DNA [Akash]. All of these time capsules have a different purpose but, they all co-operate together in one plan.

The quantum information (within Gaia's time capsules) is about attributes of science and life that will help move humanity into a new paradigm. The time-capsule pairs respond to "designed compassionate action". These time capsules needed to be on the planet as a guide or blueprint for the starting creative energy of Gaia [the Creation Template].

The slow release of the time capsules modifies the Crystalline Grid which helps human consciousness shift, and eventually creates an ascended planet. These information templates are also quantum portals of Pleiadian life. The time capsules are sacred, mostly untouched, protected, and they represent the original Pleiadian Creation Template. These are not "capsules from the past." They are "capsules for the future." There is nothing in them! They open and give real time quantum energy to the grids, allowing higher consciousness, invention, and human DNA evolution. How do we communicate with the time capsules? We communicate to them with our consciousness.

Humanity's decision to shift consciousness has allowed many new ideas and inventions to come onto the planet. So watch this space! Just wait until love is provable! Feel the love!

Wishing you abundant blessings of peace in your heart xxx

LETTER 53

ENERGY GROUPS

"

The energies of the human being
Change over time and have new meaning
~ Lady Wise

Dear Uncle Jim,

As humanity evolves the attributes of the human being and their energies will change over time with the altered state of human consciousness.

Specifically innate and consciousness are going to start to move closer together. Right now with the human being operating on average at less than 35% DNA activation, they are very separate. We need to choose to search for Higher Self.

Using kinesiology, for example, you can find out what preferred foods are healthy for your body. You are separate to your molecular structure. Each one of us can become our own medical intuitive. In this process, the Higher Self will begin to show itself. Innate and Consciousness will therefore

begin to agree and see that death has no sting. I AM ETERNAL.

As we evolve, we will remember what has happened in ALL of our lives. This will manifest itself in WISDOM. Perhaps you have already witnessed a child who knows how to walk and does not need to be taught. This is evidence that the spiritual part of the DNA is starting to increase its efficiency.

Now to something a little more controversial! Is it possible for you to cast aside all your linearity for a moment? Ha!

Your Higher Self must stand apart from you in order to be your adviser on the planet. Evidence of this is the change in energy that takes place.

As you are awakening to spiritual truth, you have your own guide set. Some people, familiar with seeing their spirit guides, look at them and think that they are new! Humans look at them in linearity and even give them names! They are YOU!

"

How can a human soul break apart and be in many places at the same time? Welcome to QUANTUM ENERGY! It is easy in a multi-dimensional state that is not linear.
~ Kryon

How many guides do you have? 3 is the catalytic number – the catalyst in chemistry and physics that changes something else, while it remains the same and this is then the wisdom and healing and knowledge, and it is part of the guide set, your guide set, regarding the ones that help you with your INTUITION, the ones that generate your INTUITION,

standing apart, so they can see the overview. And guess who they work with? They work with the portion of your soul that can be sustained in a corporeal body and even though these are complex concepts, they will make sense in a moment if you follow the trend of the logic.

Now, not only do you have parts of you standing outside of your corporeal body but you have other parts which are on the other side of the veil. It is not your Higher Self – that is separate. And so what are they doing there? They are helping YOU! This creates the potentials of synchronicity. This is how you meet the ones you didn't know you could meet. There's something bigger UPSTAIRS! Ha! There's a committee going on ALL THE TIME to help push you and steer you to do the things you're supposed to do!

"

To you it may be complex, while others find it normal. This is what co-creation is. You are walking with ALL OF US and often you don't even know it!
~ Kryon

Why not come out of the "bubble" and acknowledge and realise that the pieces and parts of you are sacred enough, that you can trust them and that your intuition is effectively your voice in your ear – YOU helping YOU!

You have free choice to awaken to the TRUTH of who you are or not! There is a life force around you that you may misunderstand. You are part of GAIA and GAIA is responsive to YOU!

There is a place for elegant chemistry and for the elegance of natural solutions. One will not usurp the other but it is

time to remember how to heal yourself in Gaia (Mother Earth), with Gaia and through Gaia.

We are part of the Magnetic Grid. The Higher Self is in the Magnetic Grid of the planet. It explains why astrology works. It explains why consciousness is affected by the Magnetic Grid and the Magnetic Grid is affected by consciousness. The physicists know it and the satellites have proved it.

We are really part of this system and not apart from it.

The evolution of the planet especially right now is starting to change the linearity or non-linearity of the actions of humans on this planet. The Grid is going to be far more responsive to JOY, LAUGHTER and COMPASSION, than to death, horror and war.

It is all in the movement of the planet and the softening of the earth that has started to happen since the consciousness shift has started. As we solve problems with INTEGRITY, they stick to the grid and those who follow us will pick this up!

There is a reason that so many want to have you stay here and continue to radiate your light of WISDOM to those around you and on to the Crystalline Grid.

Have a wonderful day! Be the change you wish to be!

All love to you, xxx

LETTER 54

HOME AT HEART

"

In carefree moments remember to treasure
Your eternal connection to source forever!
~ Lady Wise

Dear Uncle Jim,

Enjoy taking a breath. Let your feet feel the connection to the floor through your shoes to beautiful Mother Gaia. Take another breath. Perhaps close your eyes for a moment – let your breath talk to your heart and say,

Hello, good morning and thank you.
Thank you for beating in each moment.
Thank you for letting me live in this day of love.
Thank you for opening me up to new possibilities.
Thank you for the love that surrounds me.
Thank you for the hope that I allow myself to feel inside.

I want to feel the heart connection and I want to feel home in the complete and total essence of the beauty of all that I am.

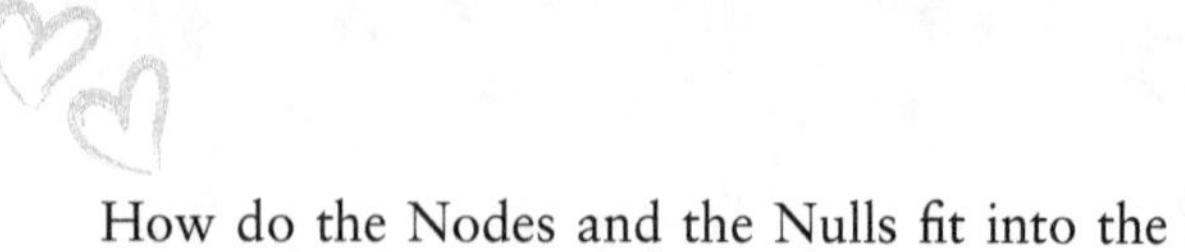

How do the Nodes and the Nulls fit into the beauty of the system of love again? Let me remind you, Uncle Jim.

"

The nodes and nulls effectively release 'radiation' which reaches the Magnetic, Crystalline and Gaia Grids. As the new energy intersects the Sun, the Sun intersects the Magnetic Field and this field talks to your DNA. When this happens then suddenly some of your DNA is unlocked with an opportunity to increase to 44% DNA activation in your body. There will come a day when you will stop worrying about everything. You stop worrying when you know you're in control
– that's 44%.
~ Kryon

The unlocking of DNA triggers Akashic activity which will help you remember who you have been. With this remembrance comes what you did mentally (not physically). Old Souls carry with them experience.

When you look into the eyes of a child you are going to see the wisdom just waiting to break out. Most of their issues are navigating the Old Energy we created for them. Wisdom is evolution! It is not getting smarter, it is getting wiser! I feel a short poem coming on...

The Oneness Experience

A oneness brings together all sides in confluence that creates things we didn't expect
Which evolves from a common sense of collaboration, creativity and respect!

When we build a coalition of oneness in wisdom and strength
We achieve more by working together on the same wavelength!
Enjoy the realisation of your true freedom and awareness of
all that is
As you start to co-create with others in compassion, happiness
and bliss!

The next step for humanity is to return to the basics and to know that Gaia is us – we can never separate the two. The ancients throughout all of history have known this, which is the reason why the indigenous start their days honouring the earth from north to south and east to west. It is not merely quaint, Uncle Jim, it is essential for you to understand that the planet is alive and that you are part of it. Our consciousness evolves and rises when we start our alliance with Gaia. It is a return to what you have already known.

What do you need to do? All it takes is intention for you to start the alliance. May I suggest you put your bare feet on the grass from time to time and feel your connection to Gaia. It is a slow process as the planet starts to understand an accelerated feeling of greater compassion. The earth is the compassionate mother.

Both of us along with many others have had many incarnations and expressions on this planet and we are going to have many more.

"

There is a spark coming. It is the spark of love, of compassion, call it whatever you want. It sits upon you, your intellect, your heart, your brain. It sits upon you and you are a different person. You are beautiful and gentle

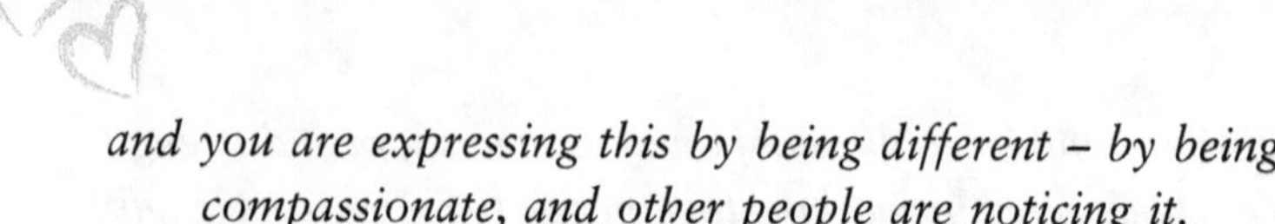

and you are expressing this by being different – by being compassionate, and other people are noticing it.
~ Kryon

Enjoy these magnificent times! Xxx

OLD ENERGY DECEPTIONS

"

The Old Energy was built on a paradigm of deception
Now the New Energy comes in with the best of intention!
~ Lady Wise

Dear Uncle Jim,

Isn't it wonderful the people who touch our hearts and the people whose hearts we get to touch? When we feel the love we get to experience the potentials and know the support of spirit holding us in loving support, filled with compassion and honouring us in our journey.

Love has many faces – compassion is in fashion and through all of this we are experiencing the Shift. The truths of the Old Energy have expired and are no more.

Let me now give you the Kryon teachings of the five great deceptions of the Old Energy that WAS, not is. Humans are starting to grow up and recognise and sense the intuition and the God inside. The value of compassion is starting to show itself beyond what it was even eight years ago. New questions are being asked that are beyond the Old Energy paradigm.

The biggest hurdle is how to get out of the bias of the Old because it has tainted us and made us less than we are. And yes, you may feel a little of it inside. We have residuals of the deceptions that we have to clear out because we have lived through part of the old paradigm.

When children grow up there is such innocence and equally such beauty in the innocence. In this new energy, as children grow, they have the wisdom to focus and see a more profound truth than we did as children. The childish things will drop away.

1. The teaching of the Old Energy is that everything repeats itself. It gives a sense of no hope and people expect what has happened in the past will return. Dear Uncle Jim, this is the way it used to be. You would expect war because there always was. NOW you can expect something DIFFERENT!

NOW, we have now turned the page. Ha! Ha! This future has never been written. Kryon offers these beautiful words to help us:-

Dear Spirit I know that the future is unwritten and my life can steer right into the serene ocean that has never existed before. I hereby drop the deception that it has to be something that I have seen before.

2. The Old Energy has you believing that you cannot get ahead. You have made every effort but there is always

something that will beat you up including yourself. There is a plateau but you are never able to get ahead of certain things because the dark energy of this planet has kept you in this box. And so there is a complacency that says this is good enough. This is such an old energy deception and it is built to keep you in line.

Let me assure you, if you feel stuck – you will be. Do you know how easy you are to control when you think you cannot get above a certain point? Easy! And there are those who have controlled you for years – controlled the planet, controlled the economy.

The new paradigm erases that completely and says that you are awakening with an Akash with talents in this lifetime and the next lifetime and the next. You are on a path that you have never seen that will take you light years ahead of anything you are in now. Anything that you wish to accomplish in this energy with the wind at your back you can do. Kryon offers these beautiful words to help us:-

Dear Spirit I will never give verbiage to "can't" again. I know that there are things beyond what I can imagine for me no matter how old I am, I know that I can go further than I ever have gone before, in fact I am already there because I am part of the Shift and not part of the deception.

3. The Old Energy paradigm of unawareness has you believing you are not worthy. This is a childish thought. Yet, so many people have been locked in this mindset.

"

They believe that everything that they have tried to do in the past has been difficult and every single time they tried

The divinity that you feel should make you breathe a deep breath and say not only that you are worthy but that you are VERY WORTHY.

Never before in the history of humanity have you been as worthy as you are now to solve the problems of this planet, to go into a situation with no war, to start compassionate action.

Thankfully, I have not been an avid television and news watcher for at least six years now because I have no interest in the reporting of Old Energy news.

Television and news broadcasts are almost exclusively in alignment with the Old Energy and that is because that particular paradigm has not died for them. They continue to cling to something that isn't real. Now, Uncle Jim, you know better! Sit for a moment and know that you are worthy.

Unlike the old energy and deception that I had, I no longer buy into what I was once told. I was born into magnificence because I have God inside and all that I see is made from God.

I see God everywhere and I honour it and it's beautiful. I am worthy to see it and I am it.

4. The Creator Source, God, spirit is not a human. Kryon asks us, 'Why would you take this creative, loving energy and give it a human consciousness? There is nothing purer than the love of God in the Universe.' The power of love can wipe away all negative things. Love and compassion are the elements of this creative energy.

This is light years away from what we have been told especially about judgement and all the things that will drag us down to a lower vibrational energy. We are born magnificent and in the image of God.

"

It is impossible for God to judge. Anyone who thinks differently from these comments makes God dysfunctional. Awaken to a truth that is magnificent – filled with a truth and love and beauty!
~ Kryon

5. Humans have been personified in darkness through their own free choice. When a human decides to go dark all manner of people go with them. The human race has been manipulated into wars for money by those who were greedy enough to go along with the others. That is the paradigm that you sense was there and it is not happening now to the same degree. Those who think it is, are about to have an awakening because light is winning. Kryon suggests some words of affirmation:-

Dear Spirit I am in control of my life. Light is in control of this planet and slowly will illuminate itself chasing the Dark

away like it never has before and I will never think again that darkness is in control.

The youngsters coming in have never experienced unworthiness. The goals they have for the future are bright. They only see the future that they can create. The young ones, however, have the perception without the experience.

So, Old Soul, it is about dropping the old deceptions and leading the way!
Go discover it! The centre of the universe lives with you every day.
Go find it Uncle Jim in love and in truth! It is a celebration. Can you smile with that? Can you connect to your wisdom and embrace rejuvenation!

Be ready, filled with love and excitement, xxx

LETTER 56

BUBBLE OF BELIEFS

"

There is one God and all of humanity knows it.
The day will come when everyone will say,
"I believe in the Creative Source and it is inside me."
~ Kryon

Dear Uncle Jim,

How does consciousness impact on the science of physics to the extent that a human being can have control over their own life and death? Firstly, let's be clear I am not a scientist, although I have a healthy interest in metaphysics. The thirty-six year cycle of The Shift is giving human beings a dispensation to fast-track their spiritual knowledge as part of the evolution of humanity. Presently more and more scientists are coming to terms with a reality based on evidence, that consciousness is energy. When this is the case, it can be stated that consciousness affects physics. The playing field of physics now has a new known member called consciousness. When consciousness changes as a result of human interaction, we witness the development of new energy. This is the new future! New consciousness is creating a feeling of compassion among human beings who are starting to feel a new purpose and feel in ways that they never did before. This is becoming positively infectious! Ha! Compassionate action is changing this planet, one person at a time!

How many times have you visited different religious buildings?

I know that whenever I went abroad on holiday I was drawn to go to church on a Sunday, which often meant going to a service. Indeed, it was with you that we all visited the local Jewish Synagogue when I was aged about ten years old. Although I did not believe in all the doctrine, I distinctly remember being frustrated that I knew only some of the songs that were sung! Throughout my teenage years and 20's, I always enjoyed the experience of learning about different religious ways.

In particular, I can remember the joy from hearing the music of Jewish and old Hebrew songs from various programmes watched on television.

More recently, I was very humbled to be invited to a Hindu funeral ceremony and after-service honouring of the deceased.

What is your gift to the planet, Uncle Jim? The gift is for you to show your mastery anywhere you are, in any situation, even in the most difficult situations and be patient and know that you are God. The discovery of Mastery is the beginning of spiritual evolution.

In celebration of the bubble of our beliefs, xxx

EVERYTHING CAN BE CHANGED

"

A high vibrating soul will live longer because you change time with your consciousness. Einstein showed this to you. You are doing this at a cellular level.
~ *Kryon*

Dear Uncle Jim,

The Creative Source has a higher consciousness than anything that we can even fathom. There is no room for darkness.

Love is the king and queen of emotions. There is no other energy that surpasses it.

Let's talk about Einstein. Allegedly, he actually quarrelled with quantum physicists in later years because he did not believe in potentials and yet he was the first quantum physicist. What we walk around in, what we call our reality has been shown to be changeable with Einstein's theory of relativity – time.

We can measure time by the nano second, because it never changes – yet it did. Einstein postulated that if a man climbed in a space ship and reached the speed of light and did this for a year, he would be one year older and yet the planet would have aged by more than he did. Therefore, he slowed down his time more than the earth. This rewrote the idea that something that was never going to change was indeed variable.

In three dimensions, we linearise our thinking process which shuts us down to new ways of doing things and different outcomes. Speed to us is defined as the amount of duration between points. If we drive from point A to point B we can cover a certain distance at a fast speed. Could we drive as fast in a circle? Yes is the answer and still go fast.

Now what if the circle is your cellular structure? We are vibrating in a circle and in a multi-dimensional environment our cellular structure is speeding up. What would happen if it started to speed up a lot more than someone else's cellular structure? Using the theory of relativity can you see that it would be possible for your clock to slow down more than everyone else's?

If you were to look at the phased relationships of alternating current, it is push-pull. Nicola Tesla knew about this but it wasn't time on the planet for such information to be released. A quantum energy needs a quantum source. Where would you get a quantum energy? Kryon explains to us that when scientists realise the presence of multi-dimensionality, it is going to work in a push-pull way.

Do you know that there are quantum biologists? What does that tell you about your biology? What if it was quantum? Kryon teaches us that some of the largest energies work in a quantum way – gravity, magnetics and light. The fourth one is a human being with human biology that can do quantum things. The source is inside our DNA. This is what has created the ability for us to vibrate faster with consciousness. What happens?

"

Your DNA starts to work at a very efficient level. It passes 44%, 55% activation and gets into the 80s and 90s.
~ Kryon

The Masters of the planet had DNA in the 90s and at these levels it allowed them to control physics. They were able to change one thing into another, they could work with life force, they could make massless objects because they were at one with all around them with a fast, high vibrating DNA. The quantum engine is already inside you, which explains why this new energy and the magnetic field are able to allow you to go farther than you have ever gone before.

"

A quantum engine which is your biology will create quantum thought, higher thinking inventions because you think out of 3D. Many of you will outlive your family. There will come a time when humanity looks at the few who are outliving the many and you will again face the objection that you are using magic, not understanding that you are using the love of God.
~ Kryon

The attributes of love, compassion and benevolence are the catalysts for the quantum engine inside you. It creates a higher vibrating human being just like Einstein said. You

surpass some of the attributes of physics as you know them when you start to vibrate higher. I have previously mentioned in an earlier letter that disease is a lower vibration. When your cellular structure vibrates higher, a lower vibrating disease cannot remain. This is the physics of consciousness.

DISEASE CANNOT SURVIVE IN A HIGHER VIBRATION.

"

The inventions are in you waiting to be connected to the source that created them. Einstein showed you that you can change time. In real physics are you ready, everything can be changed.
~ Kryon

It is a complete, beautiful, variable system that you can change when you learn about what it is and how to use it.

When we develop the inventions and machinery we need, having first connected to our own quantum engine of creator source, of course, we will also learn some other revelations. What do physicists tell you about matter? They tell us that it is mostly space – matter is empty.

Kryon gives us the example of a rock. This rock weighs a certain amount. What if you could change the weight of it? A rock at the atomic level is mostly space. This means that with plenty of space inside, if you can molecularly change the density of the rock, you can change what it weighs, if you know how to do it. Nikola Tesla knew this and did it. Kryon tells us this will occur to humanity.

When quantum energies are used, we can change quantum rules. If we change the density of the rock we can make it massless. We can make it float! Part of the solution has to do with magnetics! All so interesting!

Have a wonderful day in every way! Let go all fear!

Give yourself a big hug! Best, xxx

LETTER 58

THE LIVING LIBRARY

"

Be grateful for having a body and enjoy it! The more time you spend in nature the easier it will be. Nature needs your vibrations and then it feeds back what you need, restoring your balance.
~ Kryon

Dear Uncle Jim,

It was so uplifting to me to receive your kind text message this morning expressing how uplifting you are finding my letters and that you are feeling inspired by them! It makes it all very worthwhile and I am thrilled that you are making progress.

Remember that Mother Earth, Gaia, is a Living Library. The vibration of the earth is the culmination of ALL of the entities upon it. Everything is multi-dimensional and concurrent. The multi-verse is based on co-operation.

We are born into a remarkable system of nature. Spirit comes into the body primarily for love. The frequency of love is

sought after by every multi-verse. Each segment of time allows an experience that can be experienced uniquely. It is rich beyond compare. All experiences contribute to some aspect of creativity. Dreaming is like building realities. Dreaming is like 'shopping' for realities. Your duty is to create yourself. Play is essential! It is rejuvenating and enhancing to play.

All illness stems from emotionally blocked energy. When you play, you enhance your immune system and gain good health and freedom. It is so important that we all take care of ourselves. Develop a sense of sovereignty with your body. Own your body, own your space! Nature will conform to your identity. It restores balance and calm within your biological being. The wood responds differently to each individual's vibrations.

Make a declaration that no-one can own your space but YOU! At the core of yourself make an agreement that you will always be in the right place at the right time. Affirm your safety and be totally trusting and intuitive that your body knows what is going on.

Do not deplace yourself of your true place and power by being slovenly. There is no need for one to spend money that one cannot afford. One can look smart without having to buy designer clothes and if cash is in short or limited supply and a different outfit or garment of clothing is sought, then consider looking around a charity shop or a car boot sale for a value-for-money, 'something different' option.

Beauty and feeling good about oneself helps the natural flow to life. Be surprised by what is on offer! When you expand your thinking you open up new neurological pathways, you open up new aspects of your brain that free you and leave

a trail of frequency for the rest of the planet to follow... just as if you were "bushwhacking!". Make all of life an adventure playground! Value your friends and keep your body young at heart with a good sex life! Take ownership of your mind and body and enjoy life! Know that the Sun is your best friend. The Sun provides you with information and vitality from its Gamma rays. Planet Earth is ALIVE!

Value life! Hear the truth, speak the truth! Put any prejudices aside and allow your feelings to guide you on reading truth from deceit. Stop giving your power away to both people and situations that are not what they say they are! Give others the benefit of the doubt. We are only here for peace! When we make a decision at this time on this planet, it will ripple down the lines of time!

Our emotionality in physical reality is unique. Spirit does not have emotionality. Own your emotionality and do your best to observe it. Look for the purpose, the opportunity to develop new skills and understanding! We need to remember how to look for the joy, fun and laughter in life!

Remember, Kryon teaches, "I am in Divine Guidance. I am always in the right place at the right time. Everything I do is orchestrated for my highest growth, for my highest consciousness and my higher evolution."

Emotion is the key to all of this. Emotion operates feeling. Learn to love your emotions. Through feelings you can tell if something is going on or not. Feeling registers frequency changes. Emotions are the key to being alive. Make it your choice to create, "JOY!" Allow the beauty to come into you. Earth loves you and is striving for integrity. Hence, the reason it is so important to love yourself and to love Gaia. The animals are here to work with you. So is it any wonder that

James Junior (sorry James, but it was the best and most amusing way to clarify! Ha!) loves the time he spends with his sheep and that they understand him talking to them?

Sending you blessings of love, joy, creativity, compassion and nourishment, xxx

BALANCED HUMAN BEINGS

"

You want to be next to them don't you because they are balanced human beings with divinity activated in their cellular structure? Well these Masters of Old all knew something that you are now learning.
~ Kryon

Dear Uncle Jim,

Isn't it wonderful to know that God is everywhere and that God has always been with us? Can you feel the essence of spirit in your heart! Inside you is the essence of the universe but it does not seem like it does it?

What happens when you awaken the divinity inside? A balanced human being is what happens – the peaceful human being.

As we move through the period of the Shift, the planet's energy is vibrating higher and higher. We are being invited

to feel and be part of this activation experience. You always have free choice to make a difference to this planet because you vibrate higher than before you read this. Your grandchildren will see the change first, Uncle Jim. They may say, I don't know what has happened but I like what I am seeing.

Remember, God is not allowed to help change you and change the planet without YOU asking for help.

Up until 21 December 2012, we were on a planet with a dark and light balance that was biased against us.

"

A precious place is Earth. There are billions of angels wandering around the planet pretending to be human beings and God is going to sit and wait until they ask.
The test requires it.
~ Kryon

God does not pay attention to the casual asker either. It has to have a purity of purpose. Moreover, God does not speak the same language as we would normally speak because God is multi-dimensional and not linear. The connection with God is often in Prayer or meditation, for example.

"

God responds in an inter-dimensional way and the human hears nothing because you are not in the same dimension. No matter what you ask of God, you receive an answer but it is not in the same language that you asked. Ask your question, whatever you choose, ask it and FEEL THE PRESSURE UPON YOUR HEART of a God that loves you so much that all that this energy wants to do is hug you and hold your hand and if you can feel that and

have the chills of that – feel is a way of saying I recognise you, brother, sister, I am with you every hour of your life – as you start to push upon the door of inter-dimensionally. If you can sit and sense the answer with the emotion that floods into you, is that a good enough answer to be loved by God, to be hugged by God.
~ Kryon

Will you accept this and feel the hug? Remember too that the answers may not come in the same time frame that you expect. It may involve patience, it might involve answers that you cannot even imagine coming to you in ways that you do not expect, but you can understand the hug, can you not? There is another kind of language at work here that Kryon calls the third language. In numerology, the three is the catalyst and the energy that changes things. It is the language of spirit.

God works with potentials and solutions.
This is how he works with human beings.
~ Kryon

You can walk tall with the beauty of God inside and change the planet everywhere you walk. There's no need to look back but only forward. You can be more giving, live without judgement and allow your life in every moment to be beautiful.

Love and hugs, xxx

LETTER 60

THE SECRET TO MIRACLES

"

Your intelligence is always with you, overseeing your body,
even though you may not be aware of its works.
~ Rumi (1207-1273)

Dear Uncle Jim,

The joy of truly living is to connect your logical mind with your innate (your intuition). In this journey of wholeness, a strong connection is made with the creator source of all that is.

In earlier days, behaviourists and psychologists referred to this connection as the conscious mind (logical) and the subconscious (intuitive).

Today we have more information available to us now that we are in The Changeover Years (2013-2027) and so we know in this new energy that we can connect to our intuition

261

while remaining conscious, working the two intelligence structures in our human structure at the same time, in order for us to embrace and hone our various skill sets for what we want in life.

Crystal pendulum dowsing is thousands of years old. Many people think of dowsing as traditional divining using two sticks or a forked twig held upwards as the diviner walks along which changes direction whenever the diviner reaches what they are looking for. Examples of this may be water, oil, gold or other minerals.

Divining can be done using hazel or it can work well with ash and willow too. Often two metal rods are used in the shape of an 'L' which are held one in each hand of the diviner. When the appropriate spot is found these rods will cross over.

Affectionately, dowsing is also known in some circles as 'twitching' perhaps due to the reaction of the twigs or rods just before whatever is being looked for is found.

How does this work? A large part of our Merkaba is DNA called innate. This field, when activated by the human being, is connected to the Magnetic Grid of the Earth, to the Crystalline Grid and to Gaia (Mother Earth). The unique divine spark that is in us, connects us to the creator source of all that is (the 'oneness' of all that is). The human being is electromagnetic. The meld of the human's logical mind with their heart connection to all that is enables the triggering of the 'divination' of these rods. This 'gift' is a skill which everyone has. The extent to which a human being chooses to remember and use that skill is what makes the difference.

In these Changeover Years, humans are starting to awaken to the truth of who they are quicker than at any other time

in history. There is a unique fast-track opportunity to do this as planet earth makes her way through the Precession of the Equinoxes.

A human awakening enables an individual to discover that they are more than their three dimensional physical body and that there is a magnificence to them that has been hidden for so many lifetimes. Our innate waits patiently for our heart centre to open. It is the gateway to our intuition and to our inner wisdom. When we open our heart to these beautiful invisible energies, we discover an inner world of sacredness, unconditional love and truth. There is an understanding in our brain and a 'knowingness' from our heart that informs us of the illusion of the outer world.

We start to remember who we are and realise that this 'heart connection' is the purest and most integrous source of all that is. It is our life force and it is eternal. It never dies. We never die. Yes, the human being physically dies after so many linear years, but the soul of humanity is one huge energy source that is constantly changing in a multi-dimensional way – in a quantum way.

As humans we are not separate to the whole, but are part of this creative energy. Many physicists already know that energy cannot be exterminated. It cannot simply disappear. When a human being dies, the divine spark that has resided inside of them throughout their most recent lifetime, simply transforms into another energy type. We are transducers of energy! Forever is a circle of life! We are our ancestors!

We do not originate from primates, who have their own system on planet earth. We originate from the Pleiadians and the star system the Pleiades. We came from the stars! For eons we have talked about never activating and using all of

our mind. The truth is that we have a brain in our head, we have a brain in our heart and we have a third brain in our pineal gland. Without connecting to the brains of the heart and pineal we will not optimise our potential.

When as a human being we use our logical mind to solution-provide every day, we are only tapping into a fraction of our potential creativity.

The power of a human being's true 'inner-net' potential far exceeds that human's ability to create and learn knowledge from accessing only the internet, irrespective of how powerful a computer is! Quantum computers included! Ha!

The art of dowsing or divining is essentially establishing a connection to that divine spark within each of us as part of the 24th pair of chromosomes, which when activated, provides us with powerful information. There is nothing of which to be scared, there is nothing of which to be fearful, there is nothing supernatural about it! It is one of the most natural skills available to every human, but most of us have chosen to forget this skill over past lifetimes. We have built up so much fear in our present lifetime, often the largest part of which has accumulated from past lifetimes, because we are still carrying karma and have not learned to drop this.

The ability to reconnect with the divine source through dowsing enables a human being to access a dearth of information that is presently invisible to the individual living in their three dimensional state. This information is not available to the traditional five senses and especially not to sight visible with the human eyes.

Personally, I have not felt the need to use divining rods or a forked twig to search for something and have always used a crystal pendulum for dowsing. My crystal pendulum feels so natural for me to use that I have probably used one similar in previous lifetimes. I ask all types of questions. The beauty of using such a tool is that at any moment in time when I ask a particular question, the pendulum and myself connect with all of the potentials for the outcome that are likely at that time. It will respond by giving me a signal from the strongest potential outcome. As change is constant, I could ask the same question a day later and obtain a different response, because of everyone's thoughts, words and actions that have developed over those successive twenty-four hours. It is not about predicting the future, it is far more precise than a mere prediction.

Often when people forget their skills they look at a new tool and either ridicule it or consider it occult and dangerous. These benevolent, loving invisible energies are here for YOU! It is your birthright to know of your magnificence and unlimited potential, but you have to choose with free will to find out about this. The only way to access this wisdom is through love and an ability to create, create, create.

My intention is for you to relax with this extra information about your own potential. When you remember these useful tools are available to help guide you through your life you will feel the freedom of being independent. You will feel more empowered and in charge of your life.

The word occult means 'hidden'. It is my hope that now that we are in an ever rising quotient of light on this planet, that more individuals will choose to learn and understand about not just the powers of dowsing, but more about other incredible positive powers that we can each tap into when we choose, that provide us with healing, growth, understanding

and empowerment, to be the best human being that we can be in this lifetime.

Knowledge of these natural powers will result in the evolution of a 'new normal' for the human being. We are in an evolutionary, extraordinary period of humanity with pure love at its core. When we connect to and use the power within, it can help us solution-provide and fulfil our wildest dreams. We are energy, which means we vibrate at different levels and can pick up information in a similar way to a radio receiver dependent on our thoughts, words and actions.

How we live our life is based on what we think, say and do! We are being encouraged to rethink who we are and to challenge our knowledge to date about history, biology and cosmology.

We have the wonderful opportunity to shift our thinking and transform our thinking that with freewill will lead us to peace on earth. You are needed to help build and sustain the beautiful New World, Uncle Jim.

When we use the opportunity to rethink our belief systems, with new knowledge we can build a better, brighter, calmer and more united world with the ability to thrive together.

The foundation of every moment in our life is governed by our beliefs. Who am I? This may be the most wondered, pondered and asked basic question. Change is constant whether we choose to believe this or not. Yet, our ability to change our belief system takes only three seconds. Everything that we do is an outcome of our choices. When we do nothing….nothing changes.

Crystal dowsing focuses on our conceptual abilities to connect with our Higher Self, spirit, God, Creator Source or whatever you choose to name it and to ask questions to seek out responses to these that are unavailable from other sources, through the use of movement. The crystal pendulum may move left to right, front to back, circle clockwise or circle anti-clockwise. The movement comes from one's inner wisdom and one's brain. We need to think differently. The uses for dowsing are only limited by your imagination!

As a person's intuition heightens over time, a point is reached when their 'knowingness' and new-found knowledge will no longer require the use of a pendulum. That person's inner development, growth and trust will enable them to become increasingly less dependent on the pendulum. It is all a state of mind! The individual will be naturally guided from within to know what to do. What a marvellous evolution of self-expression and fulfilment will have been achieved!

To quote one of the scriptures, Uncle Jim, to which I know you will relate:-

Having been asked when the Kingdom of God would come, Jesus replied, "The Kingdom of God does not come visibly, nor will people say, 'Here it is' or 'There it is', because the Kingdom of God is within you."
~ Luke 17: 20-21

We have been living our lives based on false assumptions of human evolution and our source origins. We are not evolved from primates! This is an outdated science.

"

A new type of thinking is essential if man is to move to higher levels.
~ Albert Einstein.

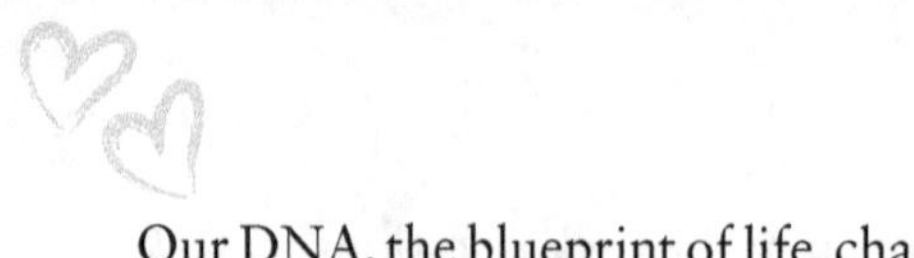

Our DNA, the blueprint of life, changes when our environment changes and includes our very personal experiences of beliefs and emotions.

We never need to be victims of hereditary diseases. We must ramp up the speed of our new ways of thinking to confront the systems that are not working for us under old ways of patterning.

How do we better understand ourselves? We require to embrace the truth, our own truth of who we are and of our history to then be better informed to shape a good future! Everything that we do through partnering, unity and compassion will work. At the core of our true nature we are loving beings.

Human chromosome number two in our DNA blueprint gives rise to a merging or fusing of a pair of chromosomes. Only a rare process could have given rise to this which would not be normal through Darwin's theory.

Gregg Braden, for example, shares his leading edge science, knowledge of historical records and is great at explaining what can be accomplished when we cross the original boundaries between science and spirituality. We are each such unique beings, dependent on our experiences, family, peer groups and relationship with history. The better we know ourselves the more informed we will be when we make choices about the future challenges in our lives. Let's choose to be an "imagine-nation" of creative souls, open to new information to enhance our wisdom!

Our ability to make changes in the new world for the betterment of humanity and our planet, depends directly on our willingness to accept new information about our history and our origins and to be open to unlocking new understanding of explanations on a variety of topics.

Traditional thinking has not been able to satisfy our answers to who we are. Perhaps we need to shift our thinking and incorporate new information now available that will help in our advancement of life and the joy of living.

Nature is based upon cooperation and mutual aid, why then would we not markedly extend and accelerate the evolution of humanity with a greater desire for compassion, unity and community in all we do?

Consciousness is most definitely not separate to our physical existence simply because not all of us can see certain things with our physical eyes!

We can have full creative power to create with our unlimited imagination an amazing world of peace, unlimited abundance and love filled with joy and happiness.

The revolution of love does not see us as powerless victims with an inability to change our situation. No! It invites us to cross beyond the limiting boundaries in which we have been brought up, to believe and to harness the wisdom of our ancestors. We need to remember our ancestral wisdom because in every lifetime we accumulate that knowledge and we have forgotten so much of this. It is important for us now to trigger this remembrance and reclaim our truth and mastery. This is our birthright.

Our emotions directly impact our energy. Feel the freedom and expansiveness of opening your heart and mind to new teachings and feel the love! Old scientific assumptions are being surpassed by new truths! Our education systems are

slow to change! When we can embrace these new truths, we realise the depth of our existence. We come to appreciate that every living being, creature, plant, ocean, atom has its root in the same life-creating source. Welcome to the challenge of exploring new dimensions of 'reality'!

Remember that your brain cannot tell the difference between what is real and what you can imagine is your reality. Herein lies the power of visualisation. Decide on your goal! The secret is to BELIEVE that you have already received it and the universe is obliged to make it happen for you.

Pure intent is the catalyst to bring the spark of divinity into realisation into your life. Imagine a door in your heart in a multi-dimensional way. Believe that you are worthy and open the door in your visualisation! You will see potential solutions that will change the direction for you on your soul journey. When you open the door Old Soul you will not just receive a healing, you will receive a life change. This includes the triggering of your Akashic record full of information to help you in this lifetime.

Miracles take place when we open the door and in floods wisdom for the body, taking the DNA back in time before a person even had the disease, curing things that cannot be cured in 3D.

The human being can go as dark as they wish and you may call it demon energy. The human being can go as light as they wish and you will call it a miracle – free choice. Now that is duality, your decision to do either. Some have felt like it is like having two entities inside of them – a Higher Self and what one may call a darker shadow self.

Duality is the single most energetic thing that keeps you from your Higher Self, from God and it is appropriate. It is not something to curse because it keeps things balanced. The balance of light and darkness is the test of planet earth. There are three things that keep a human in duality.

The first is drama – do you know some human beings who are always spinning in drama? Something is always wrong. You seek to help them with some solutions and some ideas, but they always revert to drama, as if they heard nothing you said. It keeps you busy with things so it keeps you from seeing the love and purpose that is here today. The drama keeps you from connecting to your Higher Self.

Logic is another one that keeps you from seeing the purpose that is here today. Logic keeps you from finding God because God is not logical. God is beautiful and compassionate. Where is the logic of forgiveness? That is love. Love is not logical.

Fear is the third. Duality creates fear of discovery of enlightenment. The Old Souls, like you and me, are pushing through duality and awakening to the beauty and power of their inner divinity.

So many people are disillusioned presently, questioning why there are so many scandals and why there is so much pain and sorrow. This is what happens when you take a bright light and shine it on a dark area. Things are being revealed to us now that were always there, but now they are shining in a bright light that we are creating. It might look ugly to us on the surface, but it is a process of cleansing that is going on everywhere.

I hope this has calmed your heart and mind. When the beautiful light Pleiadian energies come and visit you as you are sleeping tonight, be careful that they do not wake you up with their excitement!

Eternal love xxx

LETTER 61

I AM THAT I AM

"

The Creator Source works with the light parts through you
Guiding you in knowledge, protection and self-awareness
in all you do
~ Lady Wise

Dear Uncle Jim,

Can you hear the birds sing in joy? Energy is being delivered to all of us right now and the kind of energy depends on the attitude of the receiver. As you look around you, the handiwork of the creator source is everywhere, including in YOU! You are your own Creation.

'I am that I am' when heard, read or spoken to many people makes no sense.

Who are you? If you are a piece of the Creative Source there is no barrier to the other side of the veil and to all that is. Your consciousness is connected to spirit – through the joys, laughter and the tears. Can you say this phrase and mean it

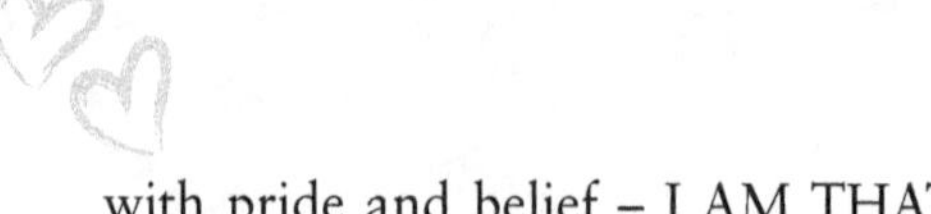

with pride and belief – I AM THAT I AM?

When God spoke to Moses he said, 'I AM THAT I AM. This is my name that I shall forever be known as by all future generations'.

One of the most beautiful things we can do, with free choice, is to choose to align our breath with God, remembering that every human being has a piece of God (the creator source/ creative source) within them that is quantum and together makes the oneness of all that is.

By placing an imaginary comma after I AM THAT, this refers to the 'out' breath (that is going to God) and then the remaining I AM refers to the 'in' breath that is coming from God.

When we think of affirmations such as:

I AM PERFECT HEALTH
I AM IN A LOVING AND HAPPY RELATIONSHIP
I AM PEACE
I AM JOY
I AM GRATEFUL FOR EVERYTHING IN MY LIFE

The power of the 'I AM' affirmations is that you believe that the state of what you are, already is. It already exists.

Whatever the affirmations are for YOU, then once you have decided what you want, lump them all together in your mind and let these become the 'THAT' of 'I AM THAT'.

And so when you are breathing out, you are sending what you want TO God/Higher Self (I AM THAT) and when you breathe every in breath (I AM), give the intention that you are receiving the love and power of that affirmation back FROM God/Higher Self.

May all of your wishes, dreams and aspirations manifest!

Wishing you joy, good health and abundance, xxx

275

LETTER 62

LEMURIA

For thousands of years of love, Old Souls were taught
in isolation
And embedded with the Lemurian Spark like a peace seed
of germination
~ Lady Wise

Dear Uncle Jim,

Take a moment to sit and feel the energy of spirit around you knowing that you are so dearly loved. The energy that you feel can embed itself into memory so that this feeling can exist until your last breath and if you are ever in trouble or if you would ever question yourself, you can call upon this feeling and know that you are supported and loved immeasurably by the creative source. So cool!

Every single one of us Old Souls is a querent finding the esoteric within. Not everyone does this, but an Old Soul wants to know more about how life works, how to find the divine inside and use it for the next part of their life. While your mind may be ever curious in its spiritual quest, Uncle Jim, have you noticed that others may not want to talk about this?

Old Souls are very different and you know it. It is the wisdom in your DNA that others do not have yet. Your soul is ancient, filled with experience and is forever. You know you're coming back, don't you? You are comfortable in your own skin, you desire to help others and you have the wisdom to do so.

"

In Lemuria, the Pleiadians taught us the basics of dark and light
As an enlightened society, we absorbed great compassion, patience and insight.
It was the start of our Akashic record here on planet earth
Now in Graduate Status, we have free choice to awaken to our rebirth
~ Lady Wise

Lemuria is the first place to change with the planet from moment to moment. Every single human life is imprinted on to the planet on the Crystalline Grid.

"

There was no greater place than Lemuria for it was isolated without contact from anything else. One could sit in the "soup of creation" and the society was balanced.
~ Kryon

The earth is giving birth to new energy all the time. The magma comes out of the ground in Hawaii and builds new

land on a regular basis. Why are we as Old Souls so impatient about progress? The reason is because we have lived for eons through the birth and death cycles. Things have stayed the same for so long and then we find the Shift – a shift that is linked with the Lemurian energy in Hawaii. We have been waiting for this for a long, long time and so we want to see it move faster.

Enjoy a blessed and peaceful day. Keep calm and go with the flow! Much love xxx

LETTER 63

ENLIGHTENMENT FOR ALL

"

Beyond the duality of three dimensions are
truths of feeling
A quantum oneness available for free to
every human being
~ Lady Wise

Dear Uncle Jim,

How do we define enlightenment? A piece of divinity exists in every human. Not every human will choose to activate it.

"

A human who does not believe in God is still loved as much as someone who does not. Who is enlightened here as spirit sees it is this – one who respects the enlightenment of ALL, who can stand and listen to the Orthodox and see God inside and see that it is real for

The Soul is a multi-dimensional part of the human being which carries the piece of God. In the Soul there are also the attributes of the Akashic record of every human being. When we pass away corporeally the Soul leaves our body. We go from being partly multi-dimensional and party three dimensional to fully multi-dimensional.

Most of us feel that we have lived before. It is time to reflect on who you have been.

The Soul carries your Akash. When you come back to this planet your Akash comes with you, no matter what culture, no matter who you are, no matter what gender – the Akash past life report and record comes with you.

Remember that this may be complex for it is not always the chemical lineage. You can have one chemical lineage with your parents and another Akashic lineage from another land. Your soul inside you is always connected to creator source.

It is going to take a special kind of an Akashic human being to create peace on earth. The Shift of energy that was expected is here. It affects all humanity. It affects consciousness. A new energy is upon us. New information is being delivered to the planet. Consciousness is starting to change and we are seeing it first in the young people who have new ideas of what is going to happen. It is wonderful to see these paradigms of peace already active.

Kindness is coming into fashion. What lengths will you go to, to show compassion?

Love and hugs, xxx

281

LETTER 64

LOVE WITH COMPASSION

*Your Higher Self knows it all. This is the prophet you are
following. This is the new wisdom. The compassion of
the Higher Self!*
~ Kryon

Dear Uncle Jim,

We are in a time where it is relevant to know about
consciousness shift. Let's talk about our relationship to God.
There are those who feel that human nature has never
changed and yet it has changed so profoundly that we
restarted our clock. Many biblical scholars refer to the Old
Testament as the Dispensation of Law.

*2000 years ago the prophet Christ gave us a new concept
– he had an Akash. Yes, indeed he did, for he was human,
he was Jewish, the right time, the right place, he changed*

We passed from Law to Love. In the process, it was so profound that we measured time differently – Before Christ, After Christ.

Do you see what we have done? There is a recognition of a consciousness shift that was so profoundly new that we had to restart the clock. Did God change? No, we did. All of the Akash, all of the past lives, tell of a human being's shift from a God of Law to a God of Love.

A new calendar was created 21 December 2012. If humanity would make it past this marker point and there was no Armageddon, we would have to reset the clock again. The clock is one of human consciousness. This is the third clock. The Dispensation of Compassion is upon us – compassion for one another with a wisdom that has not been seen. Uncle Jim, look at what the ancients did with their clocks. This is not new. It is the wisdom of the ancients who have reset their clocks when consciousness changes on the planet.

"

Get ready for new thought. It's LOVE with COMPASSION!
~ Kryon

What kind of compassion? We are starting to become mature and wise. What if I told you in this new energy, the prophet is within? How does it feel to you? Your belief and truth will determine how you treat other people. Can you see God in everyone no matter what? This is the Compassion Test!

Follow your inner moonlight!

Love, hugs and joy, xxx

LETTER 65

THE NEW NORMAL

The beauty of the plan around you is for you to feel
Validated through your heart, you decide what is real!
~ Lady Wise

Dear Uncle Jim,

Free choice is the honouring of our psyche. We have to prove it ourselves. Metaphorically, once the door is open we still do not see anything but we open our hearts to a discernment engine that we did not know we had. The emotion of finding a family that is the creator may feel overwhelming and beautiful all at once.

The creation story taught by Kryon is the creation of the divinity inside you! When we know the difference between dark and light, in this 'knowingness' discernment is king.

God is the Master physicist. God created absolutely everything the scientist is looking at and wondering about and wanting to know about. If you open the door to the Creator what

better way to find the science of discovery. Did you think of that?

Remember the Creator energy is not even allowed to knock on our door because they honour us, our intellect, what we want. Open your heart, however, and the choice of eternal love and peace in your heart is yours.

There are those who say I like my mind the way it is. I am pleased and happy with the logic that I have, that is me. I don't need to open the door. That's right, but if you do, everything will enhance itself and not be lost. The Creator on the other side of the veil – the one that knows you are magnificent and perfect- says, "Welcome home!'.

Sending joy, love and happiness, xxx

LETTER 66

THE CHANGING RELATIONSHIP

"

God changes as you change – the relationship is
what changes!
~ Kryon

Dear Uncle Jim,

Remembrance! If you were not here when the prophet Elijah ascended how would you remember it? The answer is that each of us has human history at some level in our Akash. The human Akash is extremely complex and it is related and inter-related with other humans, other souls and yourself. You might say there are layers of Akashic remembrance, individual soul, and planetary history because God is within each of us. These complexities are also there and it is beautiful. Some of us are even awakening to the potential that we have been in other places.

Think for a moment of a very wise Master. In what Kryon calls the Holy Scriptures (which are a history of a people) in Kings 2, Elijah knew that his time was up but he also knew that at his level of vibration as a Master, he would not pass through death. He knew he could control the time he left. When he did leave, multi-dimensional things took place. The transformation began.

In these early days there were Masters on this planet who vibrated much, much higher than we do, leading all the way to what we would call the Master Christ. High vibrating Masters occurred many times in these lands because they were examples for the planet – of a loving God, one who communicates, one who is real and one who cares. This was so different from how humanity thought that the creator was.

The circle is the perfect shape and it is found all through our spiritual history. It is the shape of a halo. The larger circle that he saw represented the unending love and purity of God. There is no beginning and there is no end to a perfect circle. Elijah saw two circles – one was within the larger one. The one within represented the human being's soul and it was a circle – never-ending, no beginning and no end, slightly smaller than the big circle, which encompassed it. The two circles, one with the other, started to morph into something else.

In Elijah's ascension, Elijah was showing the student Elijah, the story of the human being's print, the multi-dimensionality of the sacredness of the human being. God did not have to come down and get Elijah because God was in Elijah and the energy that Elijah turned into, was good enough to carry him into the heavens, the oneness of all that is.

It's YOU in you. YOU HAVE GOD INSIDE! Your ascension (that time of death for every single human being) is the same. You leave on your own and you ascend on your own. This was the greatest lesson of the Master Elijah. It has taken a long time to reveal some of the metaphors that are so beautiful that Elijah gave us and that student Elijah wrote down in such an order, in such a way and in such clarity that this information can be explained by Kryon so many years later.

It is SO beautiful! Enjoy thinking of these things! Each one of us has our own schedule for remembering. Every exit is an entry somewhere else! As we raise our consciousness, our relationship with the creator changes. This is the catalyst.

Love and beauty, xxx

BLESSED IS THE AUTISTIC ONE!

"

The earth has been stuck in a linear energy for eons. The earth has been stuck in an energy that allows for prophecy – not any more if you have noticed. The quatrains of Nostradamus are no longer coming true.
~ Kryon

Dear Uncle Jim,

Give intent for your ears to hear! Energy is a multi-dimensional non-linear process.

Human evolvement usually would take place over a gradual amount of time and would take place through the birth and death process but spiritual evolvement not only happens in that way. For those of us who are ready now, we are able to take the next steps while 'alive'. Kryon explains to us that it has to be this way, because the children cannot be the only ones to receive a conceptual consciousness and that is what is taking place.

Do you remember the Wind of Birth? This is where we have come in with a linear mind which we choose! Yet, in our DNA are many energies that are multi-dimensional, given to us clearly by the Pleiadians some 50,000 years ago.

What if I told you that this planet of free choice is one in a series (they happen one at a time and are very linear) and the last one that happened was in the Seven Sisters, the Pleiades. They seeded us so that we would have a piece of God inside and continue our lineage on planet earth, long after they had graduated on the Pleiades, and we have.

There will come a day when the Pleiadians (our family) will visit us for the second time. They will look just like us (perhaps a little taller) and you will know who they are and they will demystify everything. They would not be arriving at all if it was not for our involvement in 1987 when we chose to continue the spiritual evolvement of the human race. It has taken all this time.

Let me tell you more about it. The Lemurians had a quantum consciousness. It carried over into what we have called the Atlanteans and this information is scientifically funny for the scientists of our world will look at this statement and say that is absurd. There is not one artefact that would lead you to believe that the ancients had the ability to manufacture glass for microscopes, computers, electricity, they were not an advanced race, they didn't have science, they could not have known? How assumptive of the scientists to place higher knowledge into what they have invented!

Let me tell you how they did it. They did it through quantum DNA. It was intuitive. They were one with everything. Study your quantum physics! When a human being has a consciousness that is one with everything they know all about cellular structure, they are part of it, they can see into it, they know how it works, they know how to cure it, they can see imbalance, they can see the solar system, they can see the energies of the planets as they go around the Sun, they know all about science for it is part of them, they're from the dirt of the earth, they are in a quantum state with all. It's intuitive knowledge. They don't need a telescope, they don't need a microscope and they don't need a computer. We do because we are linear and we have to create instruments to do for us what we could have done for ourselves if only our light quotient in our DNA cellular structure was already at a higher level nearer 90%!

It is almost as if we are in a New Earth and we are!

When we were born the paradigm was linear. In our brain there are walls of consciousness. We are so linear that many of us cannot listen to two conversations at once. Now suddenly it is beginning to shift – the beginning of non-liner thinking. And what this is going to create is a conceptual society.

When inter-dimensional expressions visit this planet they see us as two dimensional stick figures on a piece of paper that is black and white. And we in our arrogance think that we can think above the piece of paper yet, we do not even know in what dimension we exist. Ha! Ha! We are not even in colour! These expressions see us and realise there is nothing for them and leave. That is what linearity does to us and most of us are not even aware of it!

Linear thinkers are unable to think past their own dimensionality and all of that is shifting. We are in the change!

Let me talk about the autistic one and autism in what one might call its most severe case. Blessed is the autistic one who has come to this earth to show you what evolvement looks like and spend a lifetime trying to figure out linearity! Blessed is the savant whom the earth looks at and says is unbalanced for they are the only ones to get up off the paper and be in colour. The autistic one can do what our calculators can do on our desks. They don't need a calculator. Give them a problem. Give them two digits multiplied by three digits and watch how fast they give you the answer, because they are not linear. Ask them what day the 13th of August will be in 2027, and they will tell you. They have a non-linear mind!

There are more children of all kinds of autism being born today than ever before on this planet and people are all scurrying around wanting to know what is wrong! Is it chemistry? Is it what is in the food eaten? Oh, is it vaccinations? Yes, that must be it, vaccinations. Anything to solve the puzzle of why so many are here!

Kryon informs us that not one human has looked at the puzzle and said perhaps we are evolving and this is the first wave of what we are going to see – not on balance but non-linear thinking. Watch the autistic child go through what they do. In the most severe form they are so non-linear that there is so much frustration in attempting to linearise even the human voice as it is spoken to them. They will do the same thing over and over and over and over to linearise the non-linear. The walls are gone in their brain. They are so

conceptual, all of the DNA has been activated that is quantum and they are like the Lemurians and we see them as what – a problem! And it is not a problem.

Blessed are those who come as a new wave to show us where it is going. Kryon tells us it will morph and it will develop in a balanced way where not all humans will be what we call autistic. Indeed they will have the autistic talents when they want them and they will be linear when they want that. The human mind is capable of great things.

As a human being we are given two quantum things – two things that pass between this side of the veil and the other side of the veil that are absolutely quantum, they are not linear, they have structure but they are not linear. Perhaps you have not even thought about them. Kryon tells us they are art and music! There is no limit to the number of notes that you can hear at the same time that your brain can listen to and put together. There is no limit to the number of symphony orchestra players that can come together in harmony and the more you add the better it gets. Music touches your heart. Now you know why. It is inter-dimensional, it is quantum. It was designed this way. In art, there is no limit to the number of colours that you can comprehend and see in certain patterns. What beauty! Now apply that same scenario to communication and you will see where we are going. This is human evolution. It is beginning on this planet albeit very slowly, but that is what is going on. What can we expect?

A quantum mind as it starts to develop will better understand the patience. Patience is the result of a linear mind that didn't get what they thought they would in the time frame in which they thought it would arrive or one who taps their toe because the time frame doesn't go fast enough for them. An impatient person is totally and completely linear.

A relaxation in patience will define the new consciousness. Individuals will be happy just to be and know that the things that are coming will happen in the appropriate time and synchronicity will bring them there. There will be no need to worry about it or make a drama about it.

The consciousness of the children coming into the planet is more in touch with their Akash – of who they have been and of what they have done in past expressions on this planet.

Imagine a child who comes into this planet with the concept of 'knowingness'. A concept of "Been there, done that". This is what is going on today. Have you noticed? And so you have children who do not want to sit still, while the teacher gives them the pablum of linearity when they already see the result and some of us have called it 'disease'. We have given them names such as 'unbalanced' and put them in groups and we have even drugged them. Why are we not willing to see the next wave of evolution on the planet? Education on the planet right now is convinced that human nature will never change so they are fine with developing learning systems that are over one hundred years old!

When the children growing up become young adults, Kryon tells us that they will go into the work place and their employer will expect linear attitudes. These young people will look at the whole concept of this and reject it. They don't want to walk up the ladder of experience because they've already been there! They have an overwhelming feeling of the Akash. They know they're an Old Soul. It is in their brain. They know as much as anyone at the top of

the ladder in their minds. It is called human evolution and it is evolving before our eyes.

No matter your age, you can begin the conceptual shift and start activating very slowly the quantum layers of DNA that the Lemurians activated, that the Pleiadians knew all about and gifted us. This is the higher vibration of the planet. It is why the heliosphere of the Sun has reduced by 20%. It is all related to magnetics. It speaks to your DNA. It is all part of an inter-dimensional scheme that you have planned, allowed for and invited in the Shift. You are a light worker and here to put light on the earth no matter what. Will you do that? I hope you say, "Yes!"

Even as you read this, the Crystalline Grid vibrates a little higher.

How does it make you feel to know that you really made it happen? You have come and gone, come and gone and come and gone. You are going to come again until it is over because it is all part of what you did and what you are doing. I know it sounds cryptic but it ought to resound in your heart.

You are a part of the solution dear Uncle Jim. That is why you are so loved by those on the other side of the veil. Listen to the music. Sit and bask in the love of spirit! It's why you came.

You are the light of the world! Don't ever hide your light! Keep it shining, keep it bright!

Much love xxx

LETTER 68

THE BRIDGE TO HIGHER SELF

"

Higher Self is the spiritual 'parent' of your soul.
~ Kryon

Dear Uncle Jim,

Higher Self knows all about you because it has been here for ALL of your physical expressions (lifetimes). How beautiful and wonderful is that?

"

There is a coat of many colours that has your name on it
and it's handed to you through the door – it's the Mantle
of Spirit. And when you take it you have no trouble
knowing what arm to put in first because it is a perfect fit.
It couldn't be a more perfect fit, it was tailored for you –
for years.
~ Kryon

Remember that as the frequency becomes higher you do not have to dial up to find the new frequency every time. You can go automatic and accept that you are a divine creature of spirit and are in a position to tune into the station no matter where it is.

When you open that door and that coat is given to you, you are surrounded by an angelic realm. If things are going too fast for you well, guess who is in charge? You are.

All you need to do is say dear Spirit, I appreciate all of the attention but I would also appreciate if you would go slower. There is divinity inside the cellular structure that wants to visit you called God. There are energies in Gaia that are God. The very air that you breathe is inter-dimensional and has life and it is called God. And the indigenous knew it and they tried to pass it on to these cultures that do not believe it, and there will come a day when even science will prove it! The earth is alive, most of nature is too even the things that you think are not, like the air you breathe – all co-ordinated for life on earth and a divine revelation through pure intent.

We are here to build the bridge called peace on earth, to hold the light! We are here to be an example and stand alone, in some cases on the most dangerous shores of the planet.

When you take care of yourself, all the other things fall into place. If you start shining a light in a dark place and you are with darker people they may not like you. Intuitively they would love to reach out to you but perhaps they are not ready yet. They are of an energy that is not going to be what we go to and that is their free choice. Are you ready for that? What about your friends? Are they ready to accept you if you turn on your light?

Blessed are the children who will understand an enlightened mother, father, grandmother, grandfather. There will never be a better time for your children than when you do this. For all of humanity on the earth, the little ones will see it first.

If you decide not to turn on your light there is no punishment. The test is when angels come to the planet and they do not know who they are. With free choice what will they decide? That then is applied to the very vibration of the planet and changes the planet itself. It is what happened before 1987, before the Harmonic Convergence, what is often called the 11:11, the 1992 celebration of this convergence, the acknowledgment that the earth had changed its vibration and that the earth would never be the same again.

Those who choose this light path will end up lasting longer, with a sweeter life, without frustration and without drama. All of your ego is forced into the pockets of your coat and then you button them. It is still there and it wants to get out too, but as you wrap your own hands around yourself and wear the coat, the ego stays put.

People will not see the ego anymore, they will see the coat – the mantle of spirit! Let me share something with you, if you decide to say yes to this then now would be a good time! Ha!

Kryon and the Pleiadians want you to last a long time in good health, light warrior! You can get control over all habits no matter what the chemistry of your body today. A whole entourage comes in and readjusts the chemistry appropriately so the disease is gone. Do you want a healing?

It's about Mastery. It stretches beyond any box of 3D thinking into the divine box that has no sides, no walls and is FILLED WITH THE LOVE OF GOD!

All love, xxx

LETTER 69

THE TEMPLE OF KNOWLEDGE

"

Your body is the temple of knowledge!
~ Egyptian Proverb

Dear Uncle Jim,

The land is alive. Egypt is alive. You cannot kill consciousness and intent. It literally goes into the earth and into the atmosphere. Esoterically we have identified it as the Crystalline Grid. It is almost a life sustaining consciousness. Egypt has held a particular appeal for me for many years and I have been privileged to visit this beautiful country on two occasions now.

If one believes in the afterlife and the return life, Old Soul, as one who has been here many times, then the ones that we see on the tombs, whose pictures are on the temples, are walking around as humans just like us today. We have studied life and the consciousness of the life remains.

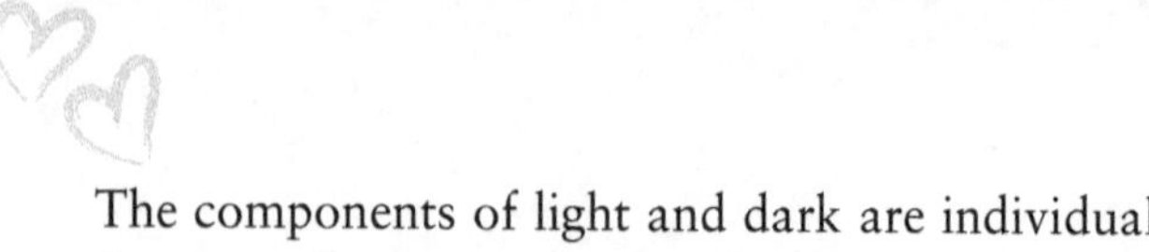

The components of light and dark are individually balanced for every human and we call this a consciousness balance. What do you think of your temple?

The ancients in Egypt received beautiful teachers and as proof as far back as you can go, they talk about the life – they describe the afterlife as beautiful and not a horror! They collect things to take with them because they believe that they go beyond a 3D body. Temples of the light, stairways of light, this is their teaching. The consciousness of an Egyptian is whatever they do with it.

Consciousness has to be learned and evolved individually. And so what is happening in your temple of personal evolvement? Dear Uncle Jim, this is about a new time. The dark and the light of this planet is starting to shift slowly. You are the forefront of this and the forefront of change is in your temple.

The higher the light is, the more evolved you are, the more this will spread wherever you step. This is your lineage, like the lineage of the ancients. It started with light. What are you going to do with that? No-one can make you do anything. Do you choose to give dignity, respect and integrity to your temple?

Things are not always as they seem! As Old Souls, we receive the seeds of truth first and teach the others.

Love, light and happiness always, xxx

THE PUZZLE OF LIFE EXPLAINED

"

*In your Akash is something extremely esoteric and
the practical proof of this is everywhere.*
Kryon

Dear Uncle Jim,

Peace can seem so elusive sometimes! Esoterically, this planet has had a dark and light balance and across all societies the dark has always seemed to win. Old Soul no matter where you are on the planet, the planet has had a low energy. We were given the timing of the prophecies by the indigenous. The Mayan calendar expressed that with a higher consciousness would come a light and dark balance that shifts. Light becomes greater than darkness. Light is going to win because the balance of dark and light is now different. Many are starting to feel it.

Back in 2012, a prophecy was given that when the Light started to become greater than the Dark, the darkness would

react and we would see an increase in frustration and evil almost like a last ditch effort pulling out every possible force that it could to fight this battle. Nevertheless, light would win.

Beyond 2012, we are also the ones who can bring light to this planet. This is known as Akashic purpose. Here's the truth – you are a divine, magnificent person and you are a piece of the creator.

Love and hugs, xxx

LETTER 71

CATALYST FOR LIGHT

You are a catalyst for light on this planet!
~ Kryon

Dear Uncle Jim,

The last shift you went through in another place a long, long time ago. It should ring and resonate with you. It is in your Akash.

The world is poised on some beautiful changes when we get rid of the old cycles. We will see a different kind of earth. It is going to be a wise earth. There will be disagreements because there will be different levels of wisdom but it will not include killing each other!

Feel balanced and feel the love of support for you on your spiritual path! Do you know the power of the spark of compassion of intent with you? If you give pure intent it creates intuition in you.

Just relax and take things gently. All synchronicity requires patience and for you to RELAX! It is time now for us to shine our light more than ever and stand tall!

In the love and the honour of the teachings and in the gratitude, xxx

LETTER 72

PROPHECY OF THE PLANET

"

The wisdom of the stars and the alignment to the stars
is in Egypt.
It is all written on the walls in Egypt in vivid colour.
~ Kryon

Dear Uncle Jim,

Everything in Egypt is in vivid colour. Having been fortunate to visit Egypt twice already in this lifetime, I am conscious of how much Egyptians love vivid colour. Colour has vibrations. The ancients knew of these things and the significance of these things, not just the colours and the light but also the sound.

The sarcophagus of the pharaohs was tuned to 44,000 vibrations. A master number 44 was the tuning for the afterlife that the Tibetans have given us and yet somehow was also known by ancient Egypt. In Lemuria, Kryon explains

that the women would birth their children in water and it was also done in Egypt too. The wisdom was there. How do you want to live your life?

There is nothing you cannot heal. Healing commences when you start to choose compassion, joy and wisdom instead of struggle, drama and anger.

As goes the consciousness of the human being, as goes the health of the human being.

"

All disease is a struggle with consciousness. Anything that you wish to heal in this moment can be done.
~ Kryon

In Egypt, the esoterics and metaphysics are staggering in their truth.It has been studied for three thousand years. They are the same truths that are all over the earth. The numbers, the water and the earth are all known all over the planet. The energy of the seven has been so sacred aligning the chakras of the body. The alignment and numbers found in the tombs and also present in the temples can be found – the sacred geometry that the Egyptians understood and they knew. It is all about numbers.

The basic truths are written on the walls of the oldest temples in Egypt. They may have had many Gods instead of one, but the metaphysics of compassion and truth are universal.

As human beings and Old Souls, we are here for this graduation, for this Shift that is taking place, and the reason is to pull the life puzzle together to show others what the higher consciousness is that is coming to earth.

When you start to look at integrity, compassion and truth the ancients had more of it than we do. We are starting to relearn what was literally inscribed on the walls of the ancients.

The Precession of the Equinoxes is the prophecy of the planet and you are now starting to participate in a Shift of consciousness that you have never seen before and if you listen to the Egyptologists speak about the metaphysicists of that which is believed here in Egypt in ancient times they understood the one god.
~ Kryon

Dear Uncle Jim there is a great deal to learn about this puzzle. What do the ancients tell you right now? Why did Egypt in its end times have the same theme? It was about the sacredness and integrity of a compassionate God with a plan.

It has only been since 2012 that we have been able to put together the puzzle. Ascension, illumination and consciousness are three key elements to the puzzle of life. Kryon tells us that those societies that go towards light, ascension and intuition will last forever. Steps to the dark are easy. Steps to the light are more difficult.

Let the puzzle be complete as you understand that the 3,000 years of Egypt play an important part in exposing the compassion of the creator and the beauty of all that is. Light in Egypt is everywhere all the time.

The Egyptian culture was intuitively driven by ascension and light. The temples that speak of the stairways to heaven are

an ascension concept. We seldom see this in many original cultures. So the Egyptians had the intuition that drove a culture into light and ascension values, but what about consciousness?

Light and ascension is intuitive. The afterlife is intuitive. Consciousness on the other hand must be something that evolves. There is a puzzle here. There is wisdom on the walls on the temples and the tombs, there are those ancients who made their whole existence on where they were going after they died. How can we talk about the wisdom of the Egyptians when they killed so many of their own brothers and sisters and enslaved entire cultures to build the structures? It is possible to have a culture that is aware of God, of the ascension, of illumination and light and yet have low consciousness.

Consciousness is something that is learned, developed and evolved. This planet is moving into compassion. We can measure it even in the last hundred years of how countries are working with each other instead of conquering each other. We are overdue for a war that will not happen because we are starting to evolve in consciousness.

So what happened in Egypt was an intuitive awakening of God, the afterlife and ascension – very high concepts and yet the consciousness of the culture had still to grow.

An example of an evolving consciousness was the Israelites. As they exited this place and walked free for the first time in hundreds of years they were destined to walk in the desert for 40 years. They had to walk in the desert for 40 years, so that a new generation could be born during that time, because you cannot take the consciousness of slaves into the promised lands. And so the children had to be born who never had the consciousness of slavery.

Human nature evolves into higher states if it chooses it but it can still have the basic concepts of the wisdom and light.

Let new beginnings blossom! Love always xxx

311

THE EMPOWERED FEMALE

"

Now the female is finding the need to awaken the
feminine principle inside of herself.
~ Kryon

Dear Uncle Jim,

Females are generally more comfortable working naturally through intuition and feeling. Males have generally thrown off emotional trauma and turmoil and the next step is for men to open their feeling centres to fill the huge chasm. Males and females are now coming to a point of stabilisation.

Kryon explains to us that the female began to open her throat chakra about thirty years ago, making the opportunity to speak fashionable. She started becoming less attached to the dramas of everyday life. One issue that arose from this, however, was that the female often began to shut down her feeling centre as she opened her throat chakra and became very much like males. A balance is needed.

The female has gone out into the world and she feels powerful. She is her own property. She is responsible for herself and enjoys taking responsibility for her own actions. She is beginning to soften in the portion of herself that nurtures her and brings her life. As she makes herself more whole with both her male and female portions and allows herself to experience the evolved DNA, she broadcasts this frequency. This frequency will become very prevalent and is much needed on the planet at this time.

It is inevitable that men will open their feeling centres. This is the next step that men go through to establish a balance with the female. This will happen very quickly for them and will be faster than thirty years because at this time, men are moving as a populous into confusion and men are realising that they do not like what is occurring and they are questioning authority.

Presently, we do not have anything on which to pattern a positive image of the empowered feminine, so men are striving to be male and women are striving to be empowered through a male vibration because they do not have a clear vision of the empowered female. What must we do? We must create it and begin to recognise the wealth of energy in the female version of self which is INTUITION, RECEPTIVITY, CREATIVITY, COMPASSION and NOURISHMENT.

Spirit always honours our freewill, but you can choose to feel uplifted to a higher perspective in all things and supported by the truth of what you need to know at this time. Feel liberated when you create the space for this intuition to keep you secure.

There is an energy of empowerment and graduation
That lifts you higher in your moments of contemplation
Trust in the flows of not knowing
For intuition will always guide you to where you are
going
This is a vast limitless universe of wonder
Filled with only love, once you surrender.
~ Lady Wise

Peace and love, xxx

LETTER 74

COMPASSIONATE ACTION

"

What separates a human being in survival and
a Master is compassion.
~ Kryon

Dear Uncle Jim,

Each of us is on a beautiful unique path of awareness. Do you expect benevolent shift or not?

Personal energy is making a difference. The heliosphere is talking to the Magnetic Grid which is changing our energy within. It is starting to wake us up Old Soul! We have gone through recalibrations and everything is beautiful as everything is starting to work together.

We are a sensitive and as a sensitive we are literally sitting in a patterned Merkaba – a flower of life. This is being seen, recognised and felt by us. What else is there? We are

315

sitting in the perfect spot because we are a sensitive. We are healers. Uncle Jim you are a healer! As a sensitive, this energy is expanding anything you thought you were doing!

You may not want to hear but learn about them because we are in the same soup together! You have the ability to do it all – that is just one of many things that are starting to change what you are used to.

Just walking around other human beings you are being sensitive to how you can help them, making suggestions to your friends and they can feel it. You are an Old Soul and it is beginning to show. This acceleration of cooperation from the other side of the veil is for you! You are carrying a beacon of light that the dark will never penetrate. You clear it by your presence – and this is new!

All that you need is in YOU! We have now graduated and we now have the energy that we asked for. When you align yourself with pure intent, you can claim your light energy.

The body picks up on this belief as you work with your own psyche, body and perhaps your own affirmations. If you have doubt, you are wasting your time. It is that profound. Belief is the key. You must have belief in this energy to move to these new tools. This is consciousness. Over time belief solidifies into truth! It is about tickling your curiosity, to know yourself and think well maybe I will be a little more positive about my truth. Beautiful! Positivity! Possibility! Coming your way! Can you feel it, Uncle Jim? There is a cooperative energy that has never been here before.

This cooperative energy is so profound it begs you to try things again that didn't work before! What fool does this? One who knows that the energy has shifted from fool to awareness. Now you know the timing and you know how to do things that you were in the dark about before. There is a cooperative energy for light workers in particular. Light workers have Old Soul energy.

~ Kryon

The more experience you have had on the planet, it is like a well of energy that comes up and supports your logic spiritually. Someone new on the planet could not do this only because they have not had the experience yet, but you have.

Every single past life gives you information that now is starting to stack up and you are being drawn to understand it. You are feeling wiser by the year. Your discernment is starting to change because of this. Your age does not matter. Disconnect the link between your chronological age and your spiritual age on this planet. There is no linkage, dear Uncle Jim. There are young people who know they are Old Souls and there are seniors who are Old Souls too! Remember, our consciousness is connected to the Magnetic Grid of this planet. This has been the plan all along, to expose this. The planet physically is allied to us.

Compassionate action is one of the keys to becoming accelerated, wiser and to understand more about what you can do next.

Every single human being is here for a reason with a puzzle – every one of them; the ones you don't like, every

one of them; the ones that are frustrating to you, every one of them.

~ Kryon

Can you look at them with a compassionate heart and see why they are the way they are? With intent and compassion there is nothing to stop you.

In loving compassion, xxx

LETTER 75

WILDCARDS

"

Wildcards are a metaphor for synchronicity.
~ Kryon

Dear Uncle Jim,

We can do anything but we cannot do everything! You don't know what you don't know. If you have not yet seen it you cannot then conceive of it!

Let's talk about wildcards happening on the planet. This is extreme synchronicity that changes people and the planet in ways that no-one could conceive of. A real wildcard would be outside of those things predicted.

Wildcards are usually one man or one woman with extraordinary ideas, sometimes a master musician or a master poet and they make their mark so strongly that the world remembers them forever. Only one hundred years ago two brothers who made bicycles gave us powered flight. Two brothers with an Akashic purpose at the right time to give us the knowledge!

319

We experienced a big one in the late 1980s against all odds politically, when the Soviet Union fell and it disarmed the potential of a world war.

If you asked historians if they expected it they would have said never. There have been many wild cards in our history.

If you do not know what you don't know then perhaps it would be best not to prejudge what is going to happen!

Joy, hugs and laughter. All good things! xxx

LETTER 76

SYSTEM OF DIVINE GUIDANCE

"

The singing of the tones unlocking the crystalline
was influential
In sending a signal to the centre of the Galaxy of
earth's potential
~ Lady Wise

Dear Uncle Jim,

There is a system of divine guidance and free choice. Part of what has been going on is the recalibration of the crystalline along with human consciousness.

Remember one of the only geological substances that can be programmed to retain and have memory is crystal because it retains a vibration. The Crystalline Grid is really two things:

An esoteric grid that works with vibration of human consciousness both in retaining and transmitting back to the DNA;

It talks to Gaia and the Gaia part it talks to is anything crystalline within the earth's crust.

I was surprised to learn of how much crystalline there is in the earth's crust. There is a retention of frequency between the quantum grid which is crystalline and the earth crystalline which has the dirt of the earth.

In the building of the Crystalline Grid, the Pleiadians built a lens 26,000 years ago focused on the centre of the Galaxy. Certain tones were sung which locked in place this particular Grid and the lens it represented. The lock was built to respond to the tones being sung again should we have arrived at the time and place at the end of the Precession of the Equinoxes. The tones that were sung unlocked the key and the lens sent the signal pointed literally at the orbit of our Sun into the centre of the Galaxy. The signal that arrived in the centre of the Galaxy was received by an engine of which we know nothing, reaching beyond the three dimensions and the limited laws of physics that most of us have.

What is really there is a set of energies – a push, pull energy that sets the stage for what we would call an **entangled Galaxy.** All of the stars in our Galaxy, unlike our solar system, travel at the same identical speed around the centre. This is impossible with Newtonian physics, which ought to tell you that something is happening. All of the stars of our Galaxy are therefore entangled with the middle. The middle therefore is the centre and the middle of our Galaxy becomes more than just an anomaly of physics. It is the engine of communication.

"

In an instant fashion, the entire Galaxy and all intelligent life that has the ability, knows that the planet earth has

Specific tones were sung by a specific choir in Hawaii and the frequency generated a signal that was not just sent to the centre of the Galaxy but which was also sent to the ones we have loved and lost who know us very well, our ancestors!

The Pleiadians are not far away. Part of the system of the planet is that they would remain here. They carry the essence of our DNA. These are the ones we are receiving the messages from now, first. The main message is THANK YOU! In a multi-dimensional state, we have released them to complement the bridge that they built.

To astronomers this event represents a thirty-six year cycle through the Milky Way. The light has been timed to release on this planet.

It has to start with us, a healing of the heart. Feel the love and let spirit in. It is indeed a time of change, make it count!

Hugs and love, xxx

NEVER LET ANYONE DEFINE YOU

It is time to believe in things unseen
Expand your consciousness and live your dream!
~ Lady Wise

Dear Uncle Jim,

You have to enjoy life!

In your cellular structure are the tools of mastery. It is in your DNA! You have hundreds of trillions of copies of the double helix in your body. DNA, however, does not work in three dimensions therefore one cannot compartmentalise it.

We do not have toenail DNA and hair DNA. We each have our own specific DNA – trillions of copies of the same blueprint that talk to each other. Kryon explains how the communication takes place. Now the puzzle starts to come together!

There is something you should know about DNA. It is magnetic. Each loop of DNA has a magnetic field which overlaps the loop next to it which overlaps the loop next to it. Hundreds of trillions of overlaps of DNA loops creates one consciousness – a magnetic imprint that the human carries around with them and we have called it an aura.
~ Kryon

An aura is not a magnetic field and you will not see it with magnetic equipment. An aura is the result of a confluence of DNA communication in the human body – a melding of energy to create a quantum field not measurable by anything on the planet...yet. For an esoteric activation that is new to your DNA hundreds of trillions of parts receive it all at once. What do you think happens to you when you realise this is a real communication of spirit? What you are getting goes through that veil **purely** into your heart, into your mind, properly without a programme. Some of your past ancestors come around you and you may be able to feel them or smell a particular fragrance that is known to them. Why do they do this? They come in a quantum state to let you know that you are eternal and that they still exist, albeit in a different form. It is beautiful!

Death is only a shifting of energy that is all it is. It moves from one thing to another, Old Soul you know it, don't you? They are here to touch you so that you know they are still around – it is done in love, it is done joyfully!

Never let anyone define you again. Feel the freedom and the independence that is yours in your thinking. Do you realise that so many of us go into a house of worship so that we can connect with ourselves – our Higher Self? You pray to

yourself, Uncle Jim! I am not being blasphemous. I am giving you core information of the way it works, for that is your perception of God. The Higher Self which is connected to the other side of the veil which is your core soul, is simply YOU. It is in your DNA and you feel it and you can be connected to it all the time.

Your Akashic record of every single lifetime you have lived on the earth, all the accomplishments, all the talent that you have learned along the way reside in your quantum DNA. In these layers there is spiritual knowledge that you have learned for eons.

When you choose to open this with intent you will have the ability to have spiritual wisdom immediately so that you will know your purpose, know your life lesson, begin to hear the music and feel the love of God in your life. It will lead you into synchronicities for the manifestation of what you are here for.

"

There is no such thing as a past life for it is a quantum state, therefore you cannot make a time reference. It lives in your DNA as a current life energy.
~ Kryon

Are there attributes that you need right now in your Akashic record? Go find them! Are you perhaps a little impatient? Then go into your Akash and ask for patience. Simply drop into your heart coherence and ask to pull on the talent that you want. Mining the Akash is the new tool of Mastery. **You are able to retrieve the pieces and the parts that you have lived that you deserve!**

Now think about what you have learned in this lifetime and multiply it up by hundreds more. You have an immense amount of experience and it is all NOW. IT IS ALL YOU!

Have you heard of those child prodigies who could paint or sing like a master? Don't you wonder how this occurred? Their past life and their current life are so transparent that they come in and pick up from where they left off. Similarly Uncle Jim, if you would like to be healthy then reach into those energised layers and find the loving, peaceful, healthy hero.

Remember that all of these DNA layers are interactive. All of these layers work together and some of these layers have laid dormant for all of humanity's time on the planet ready to be activated when the Earth's energy reached a certain point that it is at now.

It is easy and it is difficult depending upon how much you believe this. Each one of us is unique on the planet and each one of us has a different life lesson. Each one of us has a unique Akashic record that is like no-one else's Akash. Your Higher Self is the one with which YOU ARE PERHAPS ONLY NOW CHOOSING TO CONNECT.

Why not sit down in a quiet moment in purity and say to spirit, I would like these things.

I give permission to activate the things that need to be activated in my life to accomplish the things that I came for.

I want to have joy in my life. Find the joy in my life for I have earned it, I deserve it. I have had joyful lives.

If you want to write a book, go find the orator and the author for they are there. I must have tapped into this one myself! Ha!

These are the inter-dimensional gifts of this age. DNA is a partnership.

There is a Shift happening and in three dimensions it is filled with change, fear, anxiety and uncertainty. People are unsure of the weather, the economy, their jobs, family or friends. That is the Shift.

And then there is another Shift going on – all the tools to let you handle it. You have deserved the ability to mine your Akash for all things, including healing. All of these things are wrapped up in what some teachers call the lattice. The personal attributes of a human being that surround them so much that you can actually read them. The DNA is only the physical vehicle of a quantum state. A quantum state is everywhere.

There are pieces and parts of your DNA right now that are all over the universe, dear Uncle. God knows who you are, oh quantum one. If you start to activate these pieces and parts your lattice will change colour did you know that? I will say no more on this just now. There are new energies, new tools and new information to help you expand your consciousness. Can you give yourself permission to be your own boss?

Sit up from your seat, dear Uncle, for humanity is not stuck. The desire to self-change coupled with activation through intent will begin the process. Watch the differences in your life. You will be different than you were...in a good different way!

I invite you to expand your consciousness and hear the music.

God bless! Sweet evolution, my dear Uncle! All love xxx

LETTER 78

THE LOVE POWER OF YOU!

Can you learn to release all thoughts of stress
To connect to your heart filled with happiness?
~ Lady Wise

Dear Uncle Jim,

I am sure you are warm and cosy in Oz, while outside today here Mr. Sun is shining but the temperature is three degrees below zero, yet blue skies prevail and there is no wind. It's funny to think there are so many things that we already accept as invisible to us and yet they exist. As examples, we cannot see love, we cannot see gravity, we cannot see air and we cannot see the wind. We can only FEEL the effects of these things. Spirit is another example, isn't it?

This is one of my poems called The Love Power of YOU!

We are expanding our minds beyond linear time
As we change our ways from the past to the sublime

Never in history has there been such an adventure
But how much of the changeover can you absorb without
censure
For the nano years have been and gone
No more Armageddon, we choose to live on
The way forward is to trust your intuition
And your inner knowing without inhibition
Learn to find your natural way
Of living life in your truth each day
Stand grounded in your chosen path
Be not persuaded by another's wrath
Let old conditioning patterns go
And practise being grounded and "in the know!"
Release emotional tensions of old
And allow your 'journey of feeling' to unfold
Demand freedom to explore what you want to do
Surrender and truly feel the power of YOU!
Acknowledge what is keeping you stuck and LET GO
Reassess and change your perspective of where you want to go
Strengthen your connection to nature
Open your eyes and WAKE UP to the adventure
Decide on your future and follow your dream
Know that at ALL times you're guided by spirits unseen
Who have your best interests and heart wholly supported
No matter what outside nonsense is reported
Start walking your truth, feel the vibrancy within
Strengthen your voice and never give in
Step into your awesomeness, stand tall in your power
Know that you are loved more and more by the hour.

Think the best, create the best!

Much love, xxx.

LETTER 79

THE BACK UP SYSTEM

"

Eventually, science will see that there is an alliance with consciousness in some way between ALL whales and human beings. It's all part of the Crystalline Grid. Science may never come out and tell you this but you heard it here and you will connect the dots!
~ Kryon

Dear Uncle Jim,

You love dolphins don't you? Humans love whales! Whales and dolphins are always a popular attraction – you want to be with them. Children are always more interested in whales and dolphins than any other animal. In biology, dolphins are classified as whales. People cherish the whales. Many have looked them in the eye and felt their wisdom. Perhaps you have been fortunate enough to experience this too, Uncle Jim? I have enjoyed the privilege of swimming with dolphins in the Dominican Republic and it was very special to me.

Unfortunately I missed the boat for the planned whale watch in Boston back in 1992 when I slept in and sadly missed out on a second opportunity to be with them in Iceland when the trip was cancelled! Oops! Obviously not meant to be! Ha! What other mammal species is protected by over 80% of countries worldwide by treaty, even by some countries without surrounding oceans? Intuitively the human race knows that these creatures are MAJESTIC and must remain on the planet intact.

So, what is the fascination with such beautiful creatures? Why would this be? Whales are the LIVING Crystalline Grid. They are the ones that carry the Crystalline Grid into the oceans. They are the Library of Consciousness for this planet.

Remember back in my early letters (numbers 16 and 17) I mentioned that The Crystalline Grid is an esoteric grid that reacts to what humans do and broadcasts it through the dirt of the Earth? Well, the oceans cover more than 70% of the planet and so the oceans would also need this information and it is carried by the whales.

Today Patagonia (between Chile and Argentina) is recognised as one place where the whales go to mate and have babies. The first thing that these 'children' pick up when they are born is the NEW information. When Coralie and I watched the whales and their children swimming off the coast of Australia back in 2012, little did we realise then that we were witnessing the beauty of the nature of the planet in such a profound way and that these majestic whales were carrying our DNA!

No matter what old information the existing adult whales have in their Akash, any offspring born now are going to have the new Pleiadian information as they swim the seas.

Next time when they, in turn, have children they will know all about this. The rest of Gaia, which is over 70% of the planet, needs to have this so that is why the whales and dolphins have it. You can see it! If you look in their eyes for a very long time there is a wisdom. They KNOW they are alive with US! Nature creates variety for survival. The imprint is carried through the DNA in the event that one mammal becomes extinct or is exterminated.

Biologists say that about 200,000 years ago before the Pleiadians came there were several kinds of human being – just like all of the other mammals on this planet – and then everything stopped! What happened? With only one kind of human being remaining, the principle of nature itself states that there must be a back-up. The back-up would be in case there was full extinction, it would continue in many ways.

There has to be a back-up. The whales are also the back-up of the Akash of humanity. They swim the oceans of this planet, mainly free, thankfully.

When a human baby is born on the planet there is an alliance between Gaia and its life force. The indigenous knew it! In Lemuria, Kryon teaches that they prepared ponds for underwater birth so that the newborn would go from the fluid water of its mother to the fluid water of Gaia. It was an initiation to the energy of the planet itself. The Lemurians and all of the Ancients knew that this was the appropriateness of BIRTH – to FEEL GAIA.

The first thing the baby would feel would be the warmth and the beauty of the water of love of the planet. It is the WATER OF LIFE and it comes from an alliance with Gaia which is needed for balance spiritually.

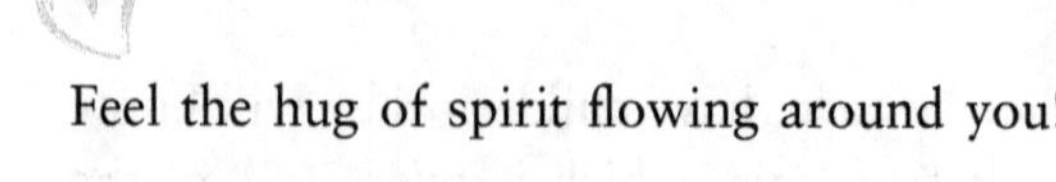

Feel the hug of spirit flowing around you!

Love and hugs xxx

LETTER 80

THE COSMIC DANCE!

"

Know that these Changeover Years carry a gift
As you learn to become balanced throughout the Shift!
~ Lady Wise

Dear Uncle Jim,

Many spiritualists, psychics, spiritualist mediums and other esoteric minded individuals may mention from time to time the other side of the veil, the veil between the worlds, lifting the veil, beyond the veil and so forth. The following poem is an explanation of what the veil represents when as a human being we are birthed into planet earth, die and then are continually born into Gaia (Mother Earth) and die again as a cycle of existence on this physical plane.

The difference in this physical lifetime is that as a human being we have the free will to know more about who we are and what the other side of the veil is all about as it is forever connected to our eternal soul.

335

The Cosmic Dance

Are you awakened to the divine cosmic dance
That on entry at birth puts us in a veiled trance?
We lose our awareness of all connectivity
To humans, to nature and to limitless possibility
Each of us plays a unique and vital role
In the universal magnificence of the invisible whole
As we pass through the veil and become unconscious of our divinity
We become human and forget to remember our soul's forever infinity
Now it is time to unlock your inner potential
To explore those realms in which you can be so influential
You are an integral part of this time-space illusion
And are needed on planet earth to help others through confusion
For the first time on Gaia you have freewill to lift the veil
And know in this physical lifetime we are part of the collective intelligence that prevails
Previously each time we died this knowledge was once again revealed
The veil between the worlds and the mystical universal field no longer were concealed
The remembrance of our divine heritage gives us deep purpose to comprehend
A better and more peaceful way of living life on which we can all depend
Surrendering to our greater role brings riches worth revealing
And introduces us to the power of love, forgiveness and much needed healing
Through our own free choice we can escape the illusion of duality

*And start to thrive in an expanded world of multi-dimensional
reality*
*With the veil removed we have clear vision on the sacred
universe within*
*And filled with overwhelming love, we shout, "Let the cosmic
dance begin!"*
~ Lady Wise

Perhaps it is time to polish your dancing shoes and make
sure they still fit?

Wishing you the desires of your heart, xxx.

WHAT IS YOUR TRUTH?

"
Truth is the attribute of when the human heart marries the love of God and the result is passion for your spiritual path.
~ Kryon

Dear Uncle Jim,

The singularity of one truth is that we are all connected. Beyond this, there are gazillions of truths! Really! This is true. While food is the sustenance of your life, the sustenance of one's spiritual growth is your passion, your truth.

There is a truth for every human being. Each individual is unique with their own talents and gifts and yet when we get together, there is a melding of these truths and such a blend is termed by Kryon as 'the love of spirit' or the quantum effect of humanity. There is a gathering of consciousnesses all around us which we cannot see but we can FEEL and it is important for each one of us to be ok with this. We FEEL that we are connected to our invisible Family of Light.

The amount of light that we hold within us is controllable by every individual. We are all on a spiritual path whether we believe this or not. When we seek to enhance our positivity and joyful outlook on life we increase the light that is within us. This is the truth of who you are.

The path to truth is explained further in one of my poems.

Light is Life

We are remembering to respect Mother Nature and Planet Earth
Like we did when the female Pleiadians first seeded our birth
Such super 'natural' intervention in our human DNA
Has honoured base 12 maths and retained a 24th pair of chromosomes that has been hidden away
The teachings and songs of these superhumans learned by us in Lemuria
Are opening nodes and nulls that are lifting the veil and invisible barriers
Offering each one of us the possibility of raising our energy vibration
On a fast-track process of personal self-development and transformation
This window of potential only lasts for 36 years
As we learn the language of love, drop our karma and all fears.
When we reconnect with who we are, forgive and receive healing
We understand our entanglement with the universe knows no ceiling
This is the mastery that we have and are awakening to with our awareness

A new paradigm of thriving energy based upon collaboration, love and fairness.
Nothing is inevitable, but with free choice you can join in with your own contribution
And share your unique love vibration, inspiration, joy and light in universal union.
Each of us holds a divine spark of the creator source inside
This is our light force and gives us full creative control that cannot be denied
The power is held in the two words 'I AM' in every thought, idea, word and action
We have the ability to create our own unique evolution of our being with conscious satisfaction.

Live well and love in your truth each day! xxx

LETTER 82

WISDOM OF THE AGES

"

Every single lifetime builds a library of wisdom.
~ Lady Wise

Dear Uncle Jim,

It is so important for you to know that you are never alone! Trust in the language of the heart. It is not linear. Things will come to you in your dreams. There is no need to attempt to figure it out. When you trust, it works! Smile and be grateful that you are working the puzzle of life and have found a better way of expanding all the possibilities and potentials in your life!

I simply adore these words and wanted to share them with you.

Here is what the Masters and Shamans know:

Wherever I walk I have help
They all have my face, they are beautiful

I am a piece of God
I am quantum
My guides are endless I have help
My intuition comes from the creative source
I have help from the air, the animals, the trees, the dirt I
walk on.
Love permeates everything around me, it is part of innate
I do not ask where for there is no where
I do not ask who for the who is the one and it is I

"

Let's celebrate the Oneness and the love that we are!
~ Kryon

Remember the expression:-

It's the life in your years that matter not the years in your
life!
The highest vibration of the universe is love. Can you feel it?
I woke up this morning with a few lines of verse:-

"

WOW!
The universe lies within
This is quite something to take in
As I reconnect with the concept of knowingness
I am growing in my spiritual path of happiness
The magnificence of who I AM is staring me in the face
I look deep into my eyes filled with wonder, love and
grace.

Much love and joy
xxx

LETTER 83

DUAL INHERITANCE

"

*Our chemical, biological parents are only one part of
who we are in this amazing benevolent loving system.*
~ Lady Wise

Dear Uncle Jim,

What if I told you that you have two lines of lineage? One lineage line is through your chemical biology and the other is through your Akashic ancestry. Are you curious to hear more?

In each lifetime when we are born into this planet we have a set of biological birth parents. This is called our chemical inheritance and it is the trace back of this chemical lineage that individuals track using genealogy.

There is, however, a much more interesting lineage specific to all of us called Akashic lineage. Many esoteric people refer to the Akashic records. Every individual has their own unique Akashic record which is akin to a database of all lifetimes

(past and future) and of the talents, gifts and life skills that they have experienced. This means that across all your lifetimes, Uncle Jim, you can pull into this current lifetime a remembrance of any previously attained gift or skill that you had or any skill or gift that you will have in a future lifetime, because remember in a quantum state there is no linear time of past, present and future. Surely that has to be an eureka moment for you!

Every human being chooses their next lifetime on earth. In your last lifetime let's pretend you may have been a fisherman in Sri Lanka. In this current lifetime, this would explain why you love fish dishes and enjoy time at the seaside. For someone who had brothers and sisters with no interest in the oceans and who did not like to eat fish, but to eat beef, they may have chosen a prior lifetime on a ranch in Arizona, say. Do you understand the significance of this? It is fundamental to comprehending the 'wholeness' of who we are. Our chemical inheritance through our biological parents is only one half of our lineage. When we are aware and know the expansiveness of our magnificence it puts into perspective the extended 'family' of soul energy that we are and allows us an improved comprehension of the Oneness of all that is.

I have always felt that this information is especially important to those human beings who have been adopted and who grow up 'feeling' that there is something missing because they have not known their chemical, biological immediate family. While the knowledge of their biological family is indeed part of their 'wholeness', the bigger picture of understanding that they are always connected to not just these family members at a soul level, but to know that there is the Akashic inheritance of all their prior and future lifetimes to be acknowledged in them, for them to use in this lifetime

as they choose, is compelling information. These are new tools being made available to each one of us in this new energy.

Remember that what you seek is seeking you. When you seek your biological parents out of pure love, then the universe must fulfil this wish for you.

This next poem explains the two kinds of inheritance that we have in every lifetime lived on Mother Earth as follows:-

Dual Inheritance

Let's refer to each life on earth as an expression
Each time we incarnate we come in with our individual core soul's life lessons
There are two types of inheritance that we bring in with each life born on earth
Our 'chemical ancestry' described as our genealogy is recorded at our physical birth
It relates specifically to our lineage from our biological parents
And tracks back through their biological ancestors
and descendants
As well as our Chemical Inheritance there is an explicit type of Akashic energy
That is generated with every Human lifetime and is stored in our own DNA
This Akashic Inheritance is simultaneously stored in the Cave of Creation
And carries over a remembrance of all our gifts and talents as a source of inspirational information
From all past lives and future lives it provides a tool that we can use

To pull into our current life in the new energy as we choose
*This means that for every lifetime lived on earth we have
an Akashic ancestor*
*To thank for all their help right now as we learn to be our
own duality liberator*
*Experience the wonder of life itself as you become more
empowered and wise*
*Feel the beauty of the system beckon you with its benevolent
surprise!*

Expand your senses and have great dreams tonight! xxx

Letter 84

THE JOY OF POTENTIALS

You do not know what you do not know,
because there has
been no higher experience than that which you have had.
~ Kryon

Dear Uncle Jim,

This quote from Kryon is useful information indeed. What better reason to learn something new every day so that you can expand your mind beyond what you knew yesterday!

Can you close your eyes for a few minutes and breathe in to your heart centre? Drop down into your heart and feel the beauty of limitless love embrace you and still your heart. Continue to breathe in softly and exhale gently to your own natural rhythm for several minutes becoming oblivious to time. In this stillness, feel the receiving to your giving, your gratitude, your giving to receiving, and from this beautiful place feel the expansion in your whole body and soul.

Nothing is as it seems! Relax into the love and know it is always there and then from the inside to the outside, feel the energy of where you sit. Shine from within for your soul is your light. Know that you can connect to this heart coherence all the time, if you choose! Open your eyes in your own time and allow yourself to come back gently, if a little reluctantly, to the reality of three dimensional time and space! Ha!

Radiating love and joy to you, xxx

LETTER 85

YOUR BEST FRIEND FOREVER

When you connect with your quantum state of Higher Self
You are connecting with manifesting abundance and
good health!
~ Lady Wise

Dear Uncle Jim,

We have a best friend which is part of us and this does not change with each physical human incarnation. This friend is called Higher Self. It is an inter-dimensional part of your total system that is part of your 'current life' and whose information is available to you to remember and use at your convenience. Our Higher Self is our best friend... forever. We are part of a larger source which has ALL the answers.

How would you like to stop worrying and connect to it?

When you focus on your connection to the Higher Self through your heart to say "Is it real?"the connection starts to be made and everything else in your life starts to fall into place. The challenge is to drop all linearity and to relax, safe in the belief that that which is not visible is SO REAL!

This Higher Self knows every single lifetime that you have lived, accumulating everything that you have learned in each lifetime. This means that for an 'Old Soul' who has lived between 100 and 1,000 lifetimes on this planet, their Higher Self is packed with wisdom. The Akash is the name given to the records of past, present and future accumulated learning. Remember that because the Higher Self and the Akash are in a quantum state there is no time clock.

An awakening of a human being is an individual who searches their Akash for those 'tools' and wisdom that they want. It is all there. It is accessible to each one of us when we believe and learn how to use it.

For example, if I was an opera singer in at least one previous lifetime on planet earth, I can mine my Akash, tap into this skill and pull it into my current life. When you know you can do this it will change who you are as a person. It will help you to appreciate and be grateful for how magnificent you are!

Can you accept how wonderful this is? You are able to reach into your Akash and select the best part of any one of your lifetimes. This is why it is there. These 'tools' are there for you to enjoy and tap into. They are not 'past' at all.

Whatever your particular problem, you can best resolve it and ask Higher Self to pull forward whatever information is needed to be known at this time as a solution. This is truly marvellous isn't it? Does this sound too strange for you? Remember that once information is known you are unable to delete it. It is up to you to choose whether to use your Akash in this way or not.

Sending Akashic ripples of love, xxx

LETTER 86

THE NATURAL WAY IS PEACE!

We have the secrets of peace on the planet, since it's part of our "Galactic Akash".
~ Kryon

Dear Uncle Jim,

Now that you know that the source of humanity on planet earth is thanks to our Pleiadian ancestors, I can further explain the joy of life experienced approximately 50,000 years ago without struggle and warfare.

There was a more advanced human civilisation with a higher light quotient who lived on Lemur'ha (Lemuria) located on the small continent of "Mu," now known as the Hawaii Islands. These Lemurians had a level of sophisticated living that had its foundation in love. This first known human civilisation on Lemuria was taught by the Pleiadians and their DNA was more developed than that in human beings presently.

The good news is that slowly more and more human beings are awakening to and in acceptance of the divinity that is within them.

In war; truth is the first casualty.
~ Aesophus

Whenever a war does not get attention, pretty soon there is no reason for it. Ultimately, only those matters that hold and carry light will change Gaia. The rest, which include the dark energy of murder, for example, will not impact Gaia.

With this knowledge we now have the choice to make a positive impact on both our own lives and the consciousness of this planet by resisting war and killing of any kind. This includes watching war films which is another form of endorsing war.

So why have we forgotten how to live in love? The answer is going to come from our parents. Which set of parents? Our biological ones or our Akashic ones? It will not come from our chemical or biological ones, but the ones we call the original source, the Pleiadians. We have their DNA as I have already stated. They had the DNA of those before them, too. The Pleiadians and the Old Souls have the secrets and the wisdom that no-one has developed here yet. This is why the Old Soul must return. Did you hear that?"

Joy in your heart brings peace.
Pure joy signals all fears have been released.
~ Lady Wise

The Old Souls will help to guide the children being born after 21 December 2012 to remember who they are and to access their Akashic wisdom that is their birthright.

Feel hugged and loved for the Old Soul that you are, Uncle Jim! xxx

LETTER 87

THE LIVING WAY

You stay with your loved ones as part of their guide set.
~ Kryon

Dear Uncle Jim,

I am always saddened to think that individuals find it difficult sometimes to cope with the death of their loved-one and feel a massive gap in their heart and everyday life when the physical presence of their loved-one is no longer around. I feel however that many are often aware of their loved-one's energy presence around after their passing, especially in their home and perhaps even when they are outside when a particular fragrance, bird, sound or whisper in their ear reminds them that their beloved is ever present – just in a different energy form.

There is great joy, comfort and beauty from believing and feeling our departed loved-one's presence. Remember that death is merely a transformation of energy since we are all energy and energy is indestructible. Energy instead transmutes

into a different form, but is eternal. This is an especially important piece of information because so many individuals suffer years of grief after the loss of a loved-one. They become so consumed in their grief that they disconnect from the ability to feel their departed loved one's loving and supporting energy around them. At extremes, a person's grief and sadness results in physical ailments manifesting when the mental trauma of experiencing loss is not dealt with.

Often the painful experience of losing a dear one hurts us so badly that we keep ourselves to ourselves, do not talk about our dearly departed loved-one and cannot find it within ourselves to connect with other people. This sadness can last for years to the extreme that when others suffer the loss of a loved-one the person feels unable to reach out and help them when they are grieving too. Such sadness dims our light within. It inhibits our ability to live our dance.

As you know, we are in a very special and unique time which is referred to by some as The Shift and to others as The Changeover Years (2013 – 2027).

There is a system to the universe that is the grandest love story of all and it is time for the truth to be revealed in this lifetime as humanity becomes more mature and is able to absorb the wisdom of the ancients. This does not betray any previous information that we have believed but enhances what we know. Certain information is only being revealed to humanity as we earn the right to this increased wisdom.

Upon our death, a piece and a part of our soul energy stays on the planet in several ways. One way is termed by Kryon as The Living Way.

It is so important to understand that our loved ones who die, are still with us. The Old Souls know this. They FEEL it. There is no need to understand the physics of how the grand system works. Those who do understand our multi-dimensionalism would know that we can be in several places at the same time.

The Creative Soul of YOU is everywhere.
~ Kryon

When we are living on planet earth in a corporeal body, our focus tends to be with our human body, but part of our soul is on the other side of the veil. When each of us passes on we become part of the COLLECTIVE ENERGIES again, except that part of our soul is left behind with our loved ones who remain on planet earth. When we have loved-ones and we die they receive a part of our soul as part of their guide group as they continue to live on planet earth. This is not a linear system and so one cannot put specific numbers on how many pieces and parts of your soul is divided up and dispersed across both biological family members and karmic family that you have loved. Kryon cannot answer the question, "How many of you are there?"

Those who have physically died are so keen for their loved ones who are still physically living to know this so that they can connect with them and continue their precious and magnificent life on planet earth as we come together in compassion and kindness to bring about peace on earth... as a starter! Evidence of reincarnation is being borne out currently by verifiable memories that children are having of past lives. Kryon teaches that Souls incarnating as Human

Beings have no beginning and no end. We keep coming back to Earth as reincarnated Human Beings to continue the grand adventure of evolving as Human Beings, thereby affecting all of Creation. On a personal note, I hope that with greater understanding and knowledge that we choose to affect all of creation in a positive way now that we are in this beautiful new esoteric era!

When Dad died, I always remember talking to Mum about this and she loved the fact that I still believed that he was alive in a different energy form. She admitted that she herself did not wholly believe this although she believed in God and spoke to God all the time. On the day of my Dad's funeral the hearse lights blinked on and off on the long drive up to the crematorium. I knew immediately it was my Dad seeking to connect with us. He would often use his energy to ring the front door bell and for some weeks after his death I would rush to open the door and nobody would be there. It took me a few times before I realised what was happening and then I asked Dad to stop his practical jokes. He then proceeded to set off the audio and stereo system at random and this alarmed my Mum. I realised that his essence wanted to connect with us to let us know that his energy was still around but this was causing my Mum anxiety. She was still attempting to process that my Dad had died and could not comprehend that his energy was seeking to make contact with us. One evening after Mum had retired to bed, I stepped back into the sitting room and explained to Dad's essence that Mum was unnerved by the music randomly starting up on the hi-fi system and requested that he stopped doing this. I thanked him for this in advance. The random music outbursts then ceased.

My Mum has now died, however, and I am delighted and thrilled to write that I connect with her every day and she sends me messages in different multi-dimensional ways. For example, when I talk to her she will communicate with me via alphanumeric car registration plates when I am outside and when I am inside she regularly flicks the kitchen kettle switch to let me know she is there. During the night she will regularly appear in my dreams. I went to a spiritual medium audience event earlier in the year as Mum and Dad regularly come though to chat. Many individuals' relatives come through even although they state that they would never have considered going near a spiritualist medium or indeed have believed in such a person in their physical life.

"

If you've lost parents, they're with you.
If you've lost children, they're with you.
~ Kryon

This is REAL, Uncle Jim. Can you sense and feel the presence of loved-ones lost, your parents for example? The important educational factor in all of this is that it is not strange, it is not weird and it is not unnatural or blasphemous against God. It is part of the benevolent and loving system of the universe that is there for us. The indigenous people have known this forever and you are in the land where one of the oldest indigenous peoples live – the aborigines. Eons ago and even today there are those who sadly will not listen to the aborigines. There is no judgement. This is all part of the evolution of humanity. There is a reason why the first thing the aborigines do when they meet up is to honour their ancestors. They have the wisdom to know that they are their ancestors. They have the wisdom that we are "remembering"

now by virtue of having greater maturity and through self-love from which stems a love for all – humans, animals and the beauty of Mother Earth. We have a lot of catching up to do!

The indigenous have always known the oneness of all that is. They have always known that there is a 24th pair of chromosomes that are multi-dimensional that allow us to become enlightened too, with free choice. Jesus (like all of the Masters) came to earth to show us that we each have a piece of divinity within us to become as enlightened as him. This is why he said, "Healer, heal thyself". He did not come to earth to be worshipped as a God. We are each a piece of God. Each of us has a God spark inside of us which wants to connect with us in order that when we listen to the whispers of our heart, we bring joy to the world and thrive in love and laughter. It is that simple, Uncle Jim. The answer is LOVE! The more love we have for ourselves and for others when we stand in our power of truth, integrity, love, compassion and kindness, the stronger the light quotient on this planet.

Let me provide a reminder for you. The multi-dimensional pair of chromosomes that we each have that connects us to the oneness of all that is, is our link to Mother Earth and to the invisible realms. Whether you believe it or not we are ALL psychic. This is part of who we are. Oh yes, and by the way, the great news is that now that I have told you this you cannot 'unknow' it! You can of course with free choice choose not to believe it but remember, there is no delete key as there is on a computer.

Why do you think I am so keen to impart this knowledge to you, Uncle Jim? I know that whether you believe me or

not it does not matter because you are receiving the information that I am sending through to you. This means that when you choose to come in again to planet earth that you come in with the enhanced knowledge that I am sharing with you at this time, which means that you come in again with a flying start! The system is beautiful and ineffable!

Remember, what you believe is who you are! This is enough for now.

I wish I was closer to you and then I could pop round for a cup of tea and an Anzac and give you a BIG hug!

Sending you much love and blessings of joy and peace in your heart! xxx

LETTER 88

PLEIADIAN PARENTS

The story of the Pleiadians is the Creation Story.
You came from the stars! I am sending a signal to those
who are ready to further evolve in their spirituality and to
know that which is their birthright.
~ Kryon

Dear Uncle Jim,

The ones that glow have life! The stage was set approximately 200,000 years ago. The Pleiadians came to earth from the Pleiades (also known as the Seven Sisters) to seed this planet with divine love and sacredness!

Against all odds you came from the stars and it was the
Pleiadians who actually came and changed your
biological blueprint.
~ Kryon

Without this we would not seek the Creator. This comes from the seed inside which looks for those things that we cannot explain and for which we need the likes of Kryon's help.

In some of the scriptures (that you have read) the Pleiadians were so ascended and full of light that they were misunderstood for angels. They had developed a very high consciousness. In truth, they were the Star Mothers.

In the process of the system of love on planet earth, the first 100,000 years were spent by the Pleiadians 'setting the scene' for the evolution of humanity. They created the Nodes and the Nulls and also the Grids of the planet. At the same time, they changed our DNA blueprint.

The prophecy said if we would make it past the Precession of the Equinoxes we would be shown things we had never seen before. The date 21 December 2012 'opened the gates' for new beginnings. All things would begin to change past 2012!

The beauty of what we see and appreciate when we view the land, oceans, rivers, streams and animals was part of the gift given to us by the Pleiadians. This is Gaia consciousness. It is so important for each of us to value nature once again as we did eons ago and as the indigenous do today!

"

The earth has aligned itself magnetically for you.
~ Kryon

The Magnetic Grid was moved in the 1980's to allow for a higher consciousness to get through. A full alignment took place.

Every single grid that was placed upon this planet is constantly dynamic. They are not the same from one place to another.

Kryon explains to us that we would feel different if we sat on a positive node rather than a negative node. The energy would feel different.

These core truths from Kryon are changing our world history in a similar way that the technology power of the LIDOR system is revealing the power of civilisations in countries such as the Maya in Mexico, for example.

There is a beautiful history that seems to be untold.

The Pleiadians were able to put together something that started in one way, but ended up with a new term introduced by Kryon's teachings called a pure aligned consciousness. Old Soul, from where are these new ideas of pure aligned consciousness going to come? The answer is that they are going to come from your parents, not your biological ones, but the ones we call the original source, the Pleiadians. Remember we have their DNA in our DNA. This means that within our being we hold the seeds of peace on earth. We know the maturity of wisdom that is required for the evolution of humanity. We are the Light Evolutionaries!

Night, night Light Warrior! Xxx

LETTER 89

THE EYES OF LOVE!

"

The love of the Pleiadian Star Mothers is always with you.
~ Lady Wise

Dear Uncle Jim,

Some of the beautiful Pleiadian Star Mothers have chosen to immerse and emeshe their divine and pure energies in Mother Earth. Wherever we walk we are known to them. We are touched by their love. We are hugged by them in a personal way and we can feel it.

The Kauai Adventure

There are those Pleiadian energies that have chosen to remain
on Pachamama
They are entangled with the land of Gaia
The dirt of this land is filled with their presence
When you look out to the oceans you can feel their essence
They see you only with the eyes of love

Ever living in the skies and clouds above
Emeshed in every stone you tread
You are touched by their love from your toes to your head
Feel an invisible hug in their greeting
Embracing your heart in this personal meeting
Their pure vibrations ripple through the water
The Pleiadian Star Mothers view you as their son and daughter
Hear their whispers in the winds, you are each known to them by name
They come to place within you their light once again
The synchronicity of love has brought us together
You are beloved and precious and loved forever.

As well as inspiring me with poetry, I was encouraged to write this song:-

The Eyes of Love

Let me touch you with my love
Let me touch you
Let me touch you with my love every day.
Let me touch you with my love
Let me touch you
Give you hope for all you wish on this day.
Hope ,Wish, Pray, Bliss
Hope ,Wish, Pray, Bliss
Let me touch you with my love
Let me touch you
Let me touch you with my love every day.
Let me touch you with my love
Let me touch you
Give you hope for all you wish on this day.

Health, Heal, Whole, Feel
Health, Heal, Whole, Feel
Let me touch you with my love
Let me touch you
Let me hug you
Let me touch you with my love... always!

Feel hugged for today!

Feel the blessing of the Pleiadian light this night, xxx

GOOD VIBRATIONS

"
Feel the good vibes of those who smile
And celebrate your magnificence in style!
~ Lady Wise

Dear Uncle Jim,

I was on a little errand today hence the delay in sending you this message. Perhaps appropriate to absorb, relax and simply take in the beauty of all that has been said.

Remember that SMILING is a healing energy! I love the version acronym of SMILE which is See Miracles In Life Eternally. Oh, and of course laughing is great! Spirit connects with us best by way of humour. Happy, happy, happy!

We are choosing to meet family, the Family of Light, in this lifetime. In this period called the Shift, as we come together through the love of God as one, we realise that we are allied with ALL things living including the air and the rocks, the animals and the water, the flowers and the trees, the birds and the much needed bees.

Take a moment to breathe in the beauty of your own existence. Know deep in your heart that Mother Earth and all the invisible, benevolent energies around you at this time know who you are. If you were not alive right now you would be missed for as we are each a part of the oneness of all that is, we are needed to complete that oneness. It is like a big jigsaw that on completion, has every part present and in the right place.

The Shift is about changing human consciousness and raising our human vibrations which in turn change the energy of the planet. Do not forget that we are in the INFANCY OF ENLIGHTENMENT.

We are helping the planet!

Lots of love and hugs, xxx

OLD SOULS

"

An Old Soul will say, 'I know I am loved and all
the drama doesn't touch me anymore.'
~ Kryon

Dear Uncle Jim,

When I mention the term 'Old Soul' please understand it bears no relationship to your amazing 96 years of linear age. Ha! Kryon's definition of an Old Soul is:- those human beings who have been on the planet at least 1,000 years, some of you 10,000 and more!

It is often easy to identify an Old Soul because they know they are loved dearly and know they are never alone. Each person alive on earth has their own entourage of invisible energies sometimes call guide sets that help and support us through our life. Spirit is always with you. Remember the Old Souls feel the energy! I guess as a religious teacher you already know this, but it can be comforting to hear it from someone else as validation especially at times when you are feeling a little low yourself. Children are very sensitive to Old Souls because they exude only love and compassion with no judgement. Your own grandchildren will see this in you, Uncle Jim. They will know that by choosing to be in your field they will feel safe around you.

When you fully recover and go out and meet other people they will wonder why you are able to stay centred and so compassionate. Knowing that you are so loved by spirit makes all the difference in being loving to others.

How are you feeling now, Old Soul? Give yourself permission to remember! Relax and allow your heart to open to a new awareness. The seeding of the Pleiadian in you was done so long ago and yet it remains intact and encoded within your DNA patiently waiting to be awakened. Part of the remembering is to throw away the box of belief that you grew up with. There are instruction codes in your cellular structure that start to open when you start to believe that you are more than your corporeal body. As you awaken to the power of who you truly are, others do too because they see the change in you. They want what you have.

Ok so as an Old Soul you might want to ask, "How do we connect again?" Loved ones are part of our guide set. Can you feel your loved ones around you? The Old Soul has a sense of knowing this. The definition of an Old Soul is very familiar with the ways of Mother Earth and in feeling comfortable being alive on this planet. This means the parents you have lost are with you. A part of their energy and essence is with you. It's not about the complexity, it is about the beauty of the system. My late mother and father have come through to me several times and are now part of my entourage. Sometimes this is in the form of dreams. On other

occasions it is almost like hearing a whisper of words. It is truly humbling, comfortable and most beautiful!

Us Old Souls are leading the way! The Old Souls, like you and me, need to stay here on the planet as long as we can, using everything with discernment that will extend our life. We, as Old Souls, are the "Wayshowers" if you like and the children coming in now are wiser than their parents and they intuitively know the system of love. You may have found this with your own grand-children? The Old Soul has both the maturity and patience that is being developed. The Old Soul will develop wisdom and always hold the intention and wish for the most benevolent solution for the planet and it starts with peace on earth. This is the first goal. The Old Soul will help guide the young children now being born through this paradigm shift of evolving consciousness. Once we have peace on earth, then we can build an ascended planet. You will not miss the celebration Uncle Jim!

Wishing you the blessing of unity as you merge and meld the wisdom of the divine feminine with the wisdom of the divine masculine!

All love xxx

LETTER 92

REVOLUTION OF
THE STARS

"

Some of the life from other planets visits you, but none of them can influence you to the degree that you can influence yourselves.
~ *Kryon*

Dear Uncle Jim,

It takes about 200 million years to go round the centre of our galaxy as explained by Kryon. The Galactic measurement used to measure this is called a 'rev'. According to Kryon there are those civilisations which have gone around 1 rev. On planet earth, however, we are only in the embryonic stages of planetary evolution having achieved 200,000 years. This is only one fifth of one rev. Kryon keeps reminding us, "We are so young as a planet."

The sect of the Pleiadians who are helping humanity to evolve on planet earth at this time have only attained half a rev themselves, and so we are such a young civilisation. Despite our youth, we are very influential to planet earth and to the rest of the universe. All eyes are on us at this time of The Changeover Years. Planet Earth is the only planet of free choice. The speed with which humanity wakes up and evolves on planet earth in the coming years is super significant for our evolution which in turn affects other life out with Gaia.

You see, ultimately, one of the next stages for us as we evolve beyond our Graduate Status will be for us to become an Ascended Planet and begin to seed another planet, in a similar way to how the Pleiadians seeded us 200,000 years ago. What a cycle! What a system!

Onwards and upwards!

Sending you inspirational thoughts of upliftment and virtual hugs! xxx

THE HARMONIC CONVERGENCE

"

Peace-filled empowerment is yours!
~ Kryon

Dear Uncle Jim,

You will have realised by now that I am fascinated and passionate about esoterics. I have not yet told you the history of how these metaphysical beliefs came about collectively for humanity as the catalyst for a significant change in our consciousness.

Back in August 1987 there was a meditation event held on a global scale that was the first of its kind. This event was called The Harmonic Convergence and occurred at the same time as a particular alignment of planets in the Solar System. Kryon's teachings tell us that:-

At that time, the Higher-Self of every Human Being was asked the question: "Are you ready to make the changes of the energy that you've set up?" This was the first time it was ever asked in the history of humanity. The answer was "Yes."

~ Kryon

The shift in people's thinking that is now happening as more and more individuals choose to live in love and with compassion and kindness is a direct result of this poll.

Less than one half of one per cent of the planet had to agree to awaken for there to be peace on earth. You see this is not for everyone. Humanity will not awaken in mass like you may have thought. It is the Old Souls that keep you interested.

In the three dimensional logical reality, this is challenged by various thinkers. Yet if you had a stadium of thousands of human beings and ten people lit a match, you could not say the stadium was in the dark anymore! Ha! Ha!

Our role in creation and the universe is with free choice to create, create, create and build our own interpretation of heaven on this earth! Through the process of elimination we can first look at what we don't want before learning that we do not want it. We are now saying no to a future world war!

This is terrific news! We are on our way to peace on earth as the beginning of our planet's evolution! You are a part of this too, Uncle Jim. Thank you for your favourable vote!

With love and gratitude, xxx.

LETTER 94

MUSIC MAESTRO

"
You want to know why you exist?
It is for the music of the great central singers
which gets brighter.
~ Kryon

Dear Uncle Jim

What about the music? We carry with us the remembrance of what music does and the soul is the one that carries it in. Can you feel how divine that is?

The compassion and love that you can have for each other, for a child, for a grand-child, for an animal, all comes from the other side of the veil. It's not something that came with the chemicals of evolution. This is soul existence – something is there – it is HUGE and yet, it can fit into one molecule of DNA. Multi-dimensional energies are that way! Ha!

I have been busy writing song lyrics and creating some music to accompany them recently. I remembered that as a toddler

I used to sing before I did anything else and that in recent years I have allowed my singing, even around the house, to lapse and fall silent. No more! The acoustics in the bathroom are excellent and so there is no stopping me now!

Eternal blessings of love and joy, xxx

LETTER 95

THE NEW SUPERHUMAN

*The Pleiadians are human just like YOU! They are the
Superhumans and are called this because of their strong
connection to the central source.*
~ Kryon

Dear Uncle Jim,

An understanding of the WHOLE of your being is vital to
the growth of who you are.

There are various rights that every human being has which
have been overlooked in society.

Whether you believe it or not, every human being is on earth
on their own spiritual journey.

We have the right to live in joy and abundance every day.

When a human being reconnects inside with their Higher
Self, higher guidance, God, Creator Source or divine spark
within by another name, they remember more of who they

are and have access to talents, gifts and skills that are in their Akash. This is what differentiates the power between what we presently consider is normal for a human being and the new superhuman.

I was inspired to write this song about the new human entitled A Superhuman Redefined.

Trust yourself in love, xxx

A Superhuman Redefined

I have the right to be here
I have the right to truth
I have the right to who I am
I have the right to youth

I have the right to knowledge
And to know what's going on
I have the right to education.

I have the right to feel love
I have the right to act
I have the right to speak my truth
The right to know the facts

I have the right to my beliefs
In my own spiritual way
I have the right to live in joy each day.

I have the right to inner peace
A heart that's void of fear
I have the right to liberate
And manifest dreams here

I become superhuman with each intake of air
And exhale all negativity
When I look in the mirror and see who I am
I raise my self-esteem with dignity

I feel the bliss of God inside
I do not need to see
I am grateful I have found my truth
I relax and believe in me.

I claim my rights of mastery
I am the master of my mind
I am a superhuman redefined.

LETTER 96

SWEET SOLFEGGIO!

"

*Let the divinity and purity of the sacred solfeggio scale
throughout all your created lyrics and music prevail!*
~ Lady Wise

Dear Uncle Jim,

One of the easiest and most beautiful ways to find our inner
peace and contentment is to give ourselves the gift of healing
through music. Have you heard of the 9 solfeggio scales? In
the straightforward Tibetan numerology, the number 9
signifies completion and endings. The sacred solfeggio scale
represents musical notes that have a designated frequency in
Hz (Hertz), that resonate and vibrate to nature, the earth
and to the chakras in our bodies to finely tune them to purity
and healing perfection in a 'number' of ways.

The electro-magnetic frequencies of these tones have been
used in the Gregorian Chants and have been forgotten by
most souls until recently. Each tonal frequency that we listen
to helps us to heal in a different way. Even when you are

healthy and free from any ailments these are the perfect sounds to listen to in order to maintain a healthy and balanced system. I find them so relaxing and comforting that I often fall asleep to them.

174 Hz creates a foundation for the acceleration and evolution of consciousness. According to some sources, this tone can provide your body with a sense of security, safety and love, reducing pain energetically. Pain can be hugely debilitating to one's wellbeing in the same way that pain relief can be a huge contributor to one's wellbeing.

258 Hz tones send a message to the body to restructure the damaged organs of the body by sending messages to the tissues which brings them to their original form. It is particularly healing for burns and fractures.

396 Hz has a function of assisting any grief felt by the person listening to the frequency to be converted into joy! How remarkable and benevolent is that? This frequency can also help with the release of fear and guilt. Remembering that love and fear cannot co-exist and that the way to greater spiritual understanding and wholeness is through the heart and self-love. When we learn how to fall in love with ourselves we trigger a rejuvenation of our life force energy. Moreover, you may well surprise yourself when you have no self-doubt and are oozing with confidence!

417 Hz when listened to is wonderful for facilitating change and cleansing the energy field from any traumatic circumstances and situations.

528 Hz is referred to by some individuals as the Miracle Tone. It is the natural frequency of Mother Earth, Gaia, Pachamama and repairs DNA. It is a wonderful tone to listen

to as your DNA restores itself to balance. Furthermore, it brings about transformation and miracles into one's life. I am most certainly all for that. I believe in miracles, I do, I do, I do! This is the title of one of my unfinished manuscripts!

638 Hz governs the throat chakra and enhances communication and general understanding. Moreover, it enhances talents and love and is particularly appropriate for strengthening relationships.

741 Hz is appropriate for enhancing the power of self-expression which results in a pure and stable life and furthermore, assists in clearing the physical cells of all toxins.

852 Hz helps to awaken intuition and returns vibration to spiritual order.

963 Hz restores the spirit to original settings and is directly connected to light. This frequency is excellent for opening the pineal gland.

Thankfully, sound frequency is being remembered by more and more souls as a healing tonic.

When music is played and recorded in the higher frequency of 528Hz, the vibrations and the frequency transmit positivity and balance. It is excellent for repairing DNA cells. John Lennon knew this and the popular 'Imagine' was recorded in this frequency. Dolly Parton and a number of other well-known artists now choose to record in this frequency too! I will be recording in 528Hz when I bring out my first album, Uncle Jim, so you can rest assured that it will make you feel good!

Now I can feel some more 'Haiku Wise' to express:-

Listening to sweet solfeggio frequencies...
Formed in different megahertz ranges to ease your pain
Your DNA creates sound vibrations, light and sonic energy
to heal you again!

Sending you musical notes, chimes and positively joy-filled
vibrations of love, xxx

LETTER 97

START EXPECTING SUCCESS!

"

This is a time when opportunities may become plentiful
as you have a knack for being in the right place
at the right time with relative ease.
~ Kryon

Dear Uncle Jim,

One of the keys of empowerment for you that will assist you to remain an independent thinker and creator in your life is to start expecting success for yourself in all that you think, create, say and do.

Allow your imagination and fanciful ideas to lead and motivate you in what is the right direction for you. Feel the uplifting energy flow through your body when you create new things. This will help you feel more assertive and confident. Perhaps you will be encouraged to push forward in your projects. Now is a great time to organise and get things accomplished. Open yourself up to learning new things and be receptive to a different way of learning. Step back from the old methods of having a definitive structure and logical approach. Instead, relax in a comfortable environment where you know you are unlikely to be disturbed by noise or interrupted by well-meaning friends and family. Switch off your mobile phone and devote some time for you. When you choose a peaceful, calm, quiet place for your learning you will amaze yourself at how quickly and effectively you will be able to absorb information.

I choose not to use words such as 'should', 'try' and 'can't' as much as possible because I consider them to have negative connotations.

Do you realise your ability to self-empower when you smile, laugh, think with clarity and are grateful for all things and experiences in your life? The impact of music and/or colour can truly inspire too! There are no hard and fast rules. Anything goes because it is you who is in the driving seat of all that you create!

You have full creative control in how you attain the success in your life that you want. If you absorb information better while wearing your favourite outfit and while your favourite music is playing, then that will be exactly right for YOU! Only you know best what is right for you! Get used to FEELING what is right for you.

Once you start imagining your success throughout all aspects of your life you 'shift' your thinking. You start to positively raise your energy vibration. Your career, relationships and general path to success may seem to be running intuitively to your need for change and growth. Congratulations! You have learned how to make real choices for yourself. As your

intuition develops things may seem almost magical in the way that they work out for you, in your favour. This has the potential to be one of the most pleasant times in your life, as you use your emotional energy to harness your artistic creativity with gratitude.

The positive energy that you create for yourself as a result of the accumulated effect of your increased joy, happiness and ability to see beauty in all things will collectively help you to further improve your life situations. Always remember the joy that is available for you when you appreciate and taste life. There is no longer any need for intense emotional drama because your emotions become in tune with the more sensitive, spiritual and private areas of your life. It is very likely that you will feel a deep sense of harmony between your emotions and the way that you come across to other people.

When you start expecting success in your life problems may well seem easier to resolve now. Acting on instinct will eventually become second nature to you.

Always remind yourself that what you believe you deserve!

The Shift is offering you an opportunity for new beginnings. How do you perceive the world? What do you really SEE? Can you see and feel a higher perspective of a world nurtured and cared for by creative source, where love permeates all things and spirit sees in you perfection or do you see and feel only sadness, victimisation and suffering?

Sending you sparkles of love and star bursts of joy as you walk the sacred path of loving light! xxx

LETTER 98

SPIRITUAL SPRING

Your inner radiance of spiritual spring
Free from illusion and confusion,
Thrives on balance and focus with unlimited potential!
~ Lady Wise

Dear Uncle Jim,

All of your life's experiences have brought you to this present moment. Nothing is ever a waste of time or effort. I thought I would expand my own word-power and creative expression for you today as I share with you my own version of Japanese Haiku called 'Haiku Wise'. The season of spring brings with it so much joy and hope. When we mature in our inner wisdom, however, we know that what happens in the external world can never evaporate this spiritual spring internally!

Allow yourself to feel your emotions and inspiration from reading and listening to this verse:-

Entrapment…
The shell of fear waiting to be broken
By the morning sun's unlimited reach of light!

Maturity of wisdom…
Never lonely, yet alone
With inner expansiveness an eternal spiritual spring of flowers!

The white glow of light…
Eternal protection
A wholeness of perfection

With life-affirmative expressions
Of laughter and love
There is no fear

Experienced success within
Brings abundance and prosperity
A gift for hard work well done

Rays of sunshine permeate
New blossoms of external temporary beauty
Know in your being, spring is eternal.

Feel relaxed and feel only serenity and joy within you! xxx

Letter 99

FOLLOW YOUR PASSION!

"

When you are passionate in your wholeness of vibration
You will attain increased powers of manifestation!
~ Lady Wise

Dear Uncle Jim,

About what are YOU passionate?

When you talk to any really successful person (and may I caveat the word 'successful' to mean whatever that particular person's definition of success is, because it is different for everyone) every one of them will mention that they have experienced highs and lows in their journey to attain the current success that they enjoy and more importantly, they will probably suggest to you that all you have to do to feel that success, is to work hard and follow your passion. It really is that simple.

So many individuals are present in their work and yet their imagination is elsewhere thinking up colourful dreams and

391

limitless possibilities of what they would do if they did not have to go to work. Therein the potential for any existing and future mental health issues grows. The imbalance in any human being has its origins from the moment when that person is unable to be working on creating their dreams and manifesting them into their reality on a daily basis. Where is the joy? Where is the evidence of that individual's truth of living their dream? Where is the laughter? Where is the fun?

The strong likelihood is that you have hidden abilities about which you do not even know, that would bring you so much joy when you give time to develop the skills. Sadly, so many of us dismiss our latent aptitudes as whims and fleeting passing thoughts instead of recognising these thoughts as deep desires to be realised, enjoyed and accomplished with fun and laughter.

We are born to live in the totality of joy, abundance and happiness without struggle. In this lifetime it is for us all to remember this.

Sending you loving thoughts of joy and love!

xxx

Letter 100

THE CHAKRAS

"

Let your dreams help you strengthen your chakra system
To build new realities of vision and wisdom.
~ Lady Wise

Dear Uncle Jim,

Energy vibrations are responsible for why some people walk straight past you as if you are invisible. There will be a distinct difference between both of your energy vibrations.

We are beings of energy. More than four thousand years ago the system of chakras was originated in India. There have been many different interpretations of the chakra system developed since then. The literal translation and sanskrit name of a chakra is a disk or a wheel. I love working with the 7 main chakras within the physical body and have only recently become aware of a further 5 which exist in the Merkaba to make up 12. Remember, base 12 is the base number of all mathematics in the universe, contrary to the base 10 to which many individuals refer today. Each chakra

393

is connected to our body and affects our dynamic energy flow throughout our whole being. It determines the vitality of the life force energy that communicates with consciousness. It is affected by what we think, say and do. There is effectively one current that flows downwards from the crown of the head to the coccygeal plexus and through to our legs and feet and another current that flows up from the earth through our feet and upwards and out through the crown of our head.

The function of the chakras is to keep one's body in balance – energetically, spiritually, emotionally, physically and mentally. What does this mean? When all of our chakras remain unblocked from negativity and are 'flowing' without obstruction, we are able to create and manifest what we want with ease and without any limitations. As we are each human beings of energy, then sometimes our bodies take on energy that is negative from locations, situations and other individuals and this can form blockages throughout the chakra system, which if not addressed, can transmute into more serious dis-ease. All negativity that we encounter has an adverse impact on the energy vibration of one's body. Our feelings and emotions play a major part in determining what is for our highest good at all times.

I will refer to the seven key chakra centres that are within the corporeal body of a human being and to the five chakra centres that are esoteric and sit in the Merkaba DNA field around each person's physical body, packed with vital DNA information.

The chakra system is fundamental to a human's understanding of their whole being. Each of us has seven different pockets of nerve ganglia that sit off the spinal column in our body called chakras. These are energy centres. For our body to be

healed, these chakras require to be open, spinning and free from blockages in order for the human being to be balanced and to retain a vitality of life. Each chakra has a different name, colour, sound, location in the body, purpose and can be defined by balanced characteristics. In the same way that one can go on holiday and experience a delay at the airport, lost luggage, an hotel booking error etc. so too can one find that as a result of our life experiences and the nature and stage in our life when these life experiences occurred, similar blockages can temporarily build up in some or all of the chakra centres in our body. The good news is that because each chakra relates to different parts of our body, we can cross refer any deficiency and/or excess in a particular chakra to a potential ailment experienced by the human being. Appropriate healing such as yoga practices, reiki and using homeopathic tinctures are just three tools that may be used to help any chakra blockages to be released back to balance.

One of the most influential aspects of the chakras is the colours that are synonymous with each one. While the old corporate world has been engulfed in dreich tones of blacks, greys and navy blues, we are slowly witnessing the introduction of brighter and more engaging colours into our daily palette. From this variety of colour, we can more effectively influence both ourselves and those with whom we come into contact.

For example, the fifth chakra governing communication is represented by the colour turquoise. For many years I have enjoyed wearing a favourite, turquoise cashmere sweater to events. On one occasion in the interval at a weekend conference, an elderly lady approached me with excitement. "You know, don't you?" she expressed gleefully. "You know!" I smiled, looked her straight in the face and said, "About what?" still smiling. "The colour turquoise," she responded.

"Yes, I do," I said to which she excitedly replied "I knew it, I knew it. I was watching you from across the room before the coffee break. How long have you known?"

"Well, I have been teaching reiki for a few years now and I include the chakra system as part of my tutoring programme," I explained.

"Wonderful! That's wonderful! Let's talk more later, "she said, and left me to finish my soft drink before the next session resumed.

I hope you enjoy reading my poem channelled for the seven main chakras incorporating a colour palette associated with each chakra, together with a musical mantra seed sound and a vowel tone. Perhaps you could sing some of these tones before you go to bed. Ha!

The Chakra System

Each chakra has its own reference point in our body's biology
Stimulating the life force energy that vertically flows up and down and charges our consciousness with cosmology
When we give attention to the chakras as we journey on the path to self
These spinning bioenergetic disks provide a means to our active and balanced health
There are seven main chakras uniting physical, mental, emotional and spiritual practices
Whose balance depends on clearing out deficient and excess energy vortices
May I suggest you think of your spinal column like a motorway of traffic

Sometimes there are accidents, road blocks and unforeseen situations that bring on panic
The purpose of all chakra work is to have the energy in your spine run free
To enable you to fulfil your dreams with an ease that comes naturally

At a glance, the first chakra at the base of the spine provides our survival body's foundation
Addressing issues of trust, family, prosperity, home, stability and appropriate boundaries of creation
Associated with the colour red and the element of the earth
This root chakra called Muladhara is synonymous with the developmental stages of up to 12 months after birth
When you become strongly grounded with balanced characteristics of feeling safe and secure without fear
You are free to claim your birthright to live in abundance and to be here.
Use your voice to experiment with the first chakra ancient tantric seed sound of Lam
Feel it resonate within your body and let go all linearity that is human
Immerse yourself in the metaphysical realms of reality
Beyond the 3D dimensionality that is called duality
Chant the vowel sound 'Ohh' to improve your healing experience
And feel the earth support your needs as your body absorbs this tonal resonance.

The second chakra called Swadhisthana refers to the 'sweetness' of sensuality, sexuality and connection
It's element is water and its job of self-gratification is determined by our emotional identity and our feelings of affection

The human developmental stages are from 6 to 24 months
in spread
With graceful movement, emotional intelligence and good
social skills signature signs that balance has been met
The flow of positive energy between a mother and her child
will provide a safe and pleasurable experience for outer
exploration
Essential bonding for the child to embrace change and learn
individual separation
Our sensate exploration of the world is a key part of our
wholeness as we reclaim our passion
Enjoying the sacredness of sexual pleasures when experienced
free from guilt and free from ration
The second chakra seed sound of Vam recalibrates our lower
abdomen and sacral plexus
While chanting the vowel tone of 'Oooo' may bring us to a
state of oneness nexus
Know that your right to enjoy healthy sexuality is your
birthright to feel
Stand strong in your emotional expression and connect with
what is real.

The yellow fire element governs the third chakra called
Manipura or lustrous gem
Located in the solar plexus we must metaphorically burn
through all the outer world mayhem
Making contact with our power within beyond the gates of
duality
Thereby igniting our life with purpose and integrating both
sides of polarity
This new dynamic of venturing forward into the unknown
Activates excitement and new energy inside us that can
overpower fears of leaving home

From the safety of balanced chakras number one and number two we feel rejuvenation
Transmuting all thoughts of shame and low self-esteem into powerful inner transformation
We create a sense of true self filled with joy and vitality
That prepares us to take the challenge of stepping into uncertainty with practicality
Ready to act in the future with inspiration and strength of will
Enabling the empowered achievement of all dreams, choices and wishes fulfilled
We are most susceptible to the development of this chakra between 18 months and 4 years
Whose balance shows itself in responsibility, warmth of personality, reliability and loss of all fears
The vowel sound of 'Ahh' together with the mantra vocal 'Ram'
Expand our consciousness with the rhythm of life to develop our own identity 'I am'

At the centre of the seven chakras in the physical body is number four in the system
Whose basic right to love and be loved is the heart chakra connection to inner wisdom
The balance of this chakra is to love ourselves respectfully and unconditionally with self-acceptance
In preparedness to honour the self that lives within others in loving relationships with a sacred essence
Learning to forgive ourselves with compassion is an important step in healing
It helps us understand our actions and move forward into the future with that loving feeling
This heart centre develops most from the age of four years old to seven

And affects those subjected to traumas or abuses specific to
abandonment, loss, betrayal or rejection
Physical manifestations of disease from malfunction of this
fourth chakra
Include disorders of the heart, lungs, breasts, chest, circulation
problems and asthma
Whenever we grieve we dull our inner light and hurt the
heart chakra shown as a band of green
This negative demon of grief facilitates our disconnection
with the mysteries of love and with those invisible realms
unseen
Surrender to the beautiful meditative sound of 'Yam' repeated
And rise to the happy heart that knows all grief has been
defeated
Alternatively, play with the sound of 'Ayy' to bring balance
of intimacy and devotion
As love expands our consciousness and heartfelt emotion

Creative expression, symbolic thinking and communication
skills are talents indicative of chakra number five
Located in the throat, whose basic right is to speak and to
tell the truth without telling lies
The key to balancing this chakra is to find one's own voice
With self-expression and clear intent that we make with
every individual choice
The ages of seven to twelve are most influential in this
chakra's formation
Indicated by having a good sense of rhythm, great listening
skills and clear communication
The element is sound with colour rays of turquoise and blue
It is important to let creativity flow in and through you
Symptoms of deficiency include shyness, a fear of speaking
and introversion

Symptoms of excess include gossiping, too much talking and poor auditory comprehension
The fifth chakra's name is Vissudha or purification
The seed sound of 'Ham' resonates with the chakra vibration of inspiration
The associated vowel sound of 'Eeee' uplifts the soul with pure energy
Releasing vocal blockages to enable improved communication and creativity.

The sixth chakra denotes insight, imagination and intuition
Attributed to an activated pineal gland that enhances inner vision
The adolescent stage invites the individual to open their third eye positioned between each brow
To new undiscovered realms within that correlate dream work with the now
The name of this chakra is Ajna, to perceive and to command
Represented by the element of light and the indigo colour band
Balanced characteristics include good memory, good visualization signifying the basic right to see
Concerned with an individual's ability to establish their personal identity
Notice the resonation in your body from the vowel sound 'Mmm' and let the song in your heart emerge
With gratitude and love practice the seed sound of 'Om' as empty thoughts converge
Symptoms of excess are difficulties with concentration, obsessions, hallucinations and delusion
Symptoms of deficiency are insensitivity, poor vision, poor memory and lack of imagination
William Shakespeare said, "The eyes are the gateways to the soul"

As your inner sight develops, you will evidence pattern
recognition that breaks down the illusion you have been told
The basic right of chakra seven is the right to know and to
learn
Using our developed ability to analyse information, assimilate
this and data to discern
When the human being does not understand their universal
identity within the grander energy vortex
Migraines, brain tumours and amnesia are signature signs of
physical malfunction in the cerebral cortex
Self-knowledge gives you an intelligent, thoughtful awareness
An understanding and access to wisdom and mastery evolved
from heightened spiritual consciousness
The crown chakra or Sahasrara helps us connect with the
universal field of cosmic intelligence
The light of the divine consciousness that shines from within
us is called immanence
A presence throughout the universe that requires belief in
multi-dimensionality and the Creator Source
Allows us to feel the beauty of the system of love filled with
benevolence and solution resource
Violet is the colour association of this chakra as we let go
all attachment and open up to higher realms
We mature in the wisdom to live our life on our own terms!

Enjoy the adventure of connecting with your own sacred
piece of divinity within that exists
As you continue on your spiritual journey of linking with
your Higher Self and to all that is
Feel the freedom, feel the whispers in the breeze of Gaia as
they blow through your hair
Know that more colour in our lives is coming and above all
do not despair!

Embrace your divine magnificence and drop all fears!
Let the world be your teacher moment to moment and be
open to new ideas
Remember above all that we were born to shine!
Believe in yourself and reach heights sublime!
~ Lady Wise

It is especially important for each of us to be more aware of and alert to those children who are imagining things that are wrong with them – we MUST listen to them with open hearts and a greater understanding of their own intuitive wisdom. The children are waking up to being intuitive about their own health – innate is talking to them, because their pineal gland is open for them. They are receiving beautiful messages from 'home', from the creator source, but they do not understand what they are receiving and it is critical that we can help them with the demystification of what, one day, will become the 'new normal'. The Akash (which is a record of the potentials of everything that is and which makes a record for the individual when something is accomplished) of the child is starting to awaken.

Across many cultures there is a tradition of handing down information, one ancestor to another. Sadly, in the old energy there has been a passing down of information that has become misinformation. Only now in the new energy, is there a lineage of service that provides a greater allowance for individuals to understand the truth about the puzzle of life. In their Akash, they are opening up to an understanding that they have done something similar on other planets before. Kryon, the Magnetic Master, is always with us and is a 'helper' in these Changeover Years as a hand from spirit to give us information from a truly benevolent source that loves

each of us dearly and is helping us to remember who we are. Kryon has never taken on a human form, but is a support entity that helps us on our spiritual path. Kryon's energy is the last to see us before we come into planet earth and are born and is also the first energy to see us again once we die on planet earth.

Remember that death is merely a transformation of energy since we are all energy and energy is indestructible. Energy instead transmutes into a different form, but is eternal. This is an especially important piece of information because so many individuals suffer years of grief after the loss of a loved-one. They become so consumed in their grief that they disconnect from the ability to feel their departed loved one's loving and supporting energy around them.

At extremes, a person's grief and sadness results in physical ailments manifesting when the mental trauma of experiencing loss is not dealt with. Often the painful experience of losing a dear one hurts us so badly that we keep ourselves to ourselves, do not talk about our dearly departed loved-one and cannot find it within ourselves to connect with other people. This sadness can last for years to the extreme that when others suffer the loss of a loved-one the person feels unable to reach out and help them when they are grieving too. Such sadness dims our light within. It inhibits our ability to live our dance.

The Dance of Transition

Does it come as a surprise that you are your own sage
Accumulating your wisdom from age to age?
Living each physical lifetime with karma to resist
Until you learn how to drop it and successfully exist

Transmuting your magnificent energy from life into death
Experiencing life between life as your soul takes
a brief rest
When we believe that the soul's eternal and release
all fears of grief
To those loving hearts left behind on earth this is
a tremendous relief!
When helping one through a loved-one's death
there are no rules
But knowing their soul lives on is such an important
healing tool
Bringing comfort and reigniting joy and light
to the heart
As there is the acknowledgement that everything changes
and it is time to embrace a new start.
~ Lady Wise

Most people have still to remember the birth, death, birth, death, birth, death cycle of life and know to expect to forever remain connected in a spiritual way with their departed loved ones. When we know what the system is, we can experience for ourselves the joy and beauty from believing and feeling our departed loved-one's presence.

So my dear Uncle, remember to let the old go, let good emotions flow,

Make no assumptions and know as you go!

Always remember ALL IS WELL. As you recover from any illness, your whole body recalibrates.

Lots of love 'n hugs xxx

RESPECT THE PAST, CREATE THE NEW!

"
When you have a dimensional shift it changes the
circle of time;
You can no longer judge the future by the past!
~ Kryon

Dear Uncle Jim,

An Inspirational Future by Lady Wise

We don't want to remember the past with blame, blame,
blame
We want to build a future by design using our amazing
imagination and creativity in abundance without shame!
Let yourself evolve and have a greater sense of intuition,
When you drop your karma and release all fears, you feel
energised and expand your inner vision.

Intend for light to inform you and give you new ideas
That you can use to innovate new solutions to past fears
Seek to co-create, collaborate, tickle and entice
And feel enthused to experiment with all things nice
Intend for your body to work at optimum capacity
And boldly manifest your wildest dreams with tenacity
I hope you are remembering that all things exist in vibration
And can feel your awareness awakening with this message
of inspiration!

Love always xxx

THE HERO IN YOU!

"

Darkness is the absence of light.
~ Kryon

Dear Uncle Jim,

The ability to transmute all dark things and lower energy traumas into love and a lighter vibration is straight forward.

When you are feeling confident and you observe something that has a shadow about it because there is low energy present, you can help the situation with your intention.

Focus on where your intention is required and say to yourself, "Transmute all shadow into light, light, light!"

You effectively become your own wizard! You become your own hero over the darkness. This concept is not so strange. Kryon teaches us that if there was to be a prime directive, it would be that we are each born magnificent.

One human being would conquer supernatural foes in order to save their reality and on their journey they collect their friends/ associates (of like minds). On their journey it will test their duality, their strength. The wizard always represents the magic of magnificence. There is always a wizard. Every single human that tells a magic story that has lasted the years has a wizard.

~ Kryon

Think about how we relate to this among well-known story lines as follows:-

The Lord of the Rings has Froddo out to conquer supernatural forces with his friends... and there is a wizard;

Luke Skywalker was out to conquer supernatural forces with his friends ... and his wizard;

The little boy with the wand and his friends were out to conquer supernatural forces with a wizard;

There is also the story of the wonderful Wizard of Oz!

All of these popular stories are about battling the darkness with the light that we did not know that we had and with the wizard inside of us that we did not know we had.

Remember that the test on earth is of the energy of darkness and light. It is about the light winning over the darkness.

It slays the dragons of duality. It illuminates the lights in the human soul. It brings you to a place of magnificence to which you would not otherwise be brought.

The wizard inside is the divine seed of consciousness that the Pleiadians gave to us. Now we are remembering and wakening up to our Family of Light and working elegantly with our colleagues and friends to win the battle of compassion over darkness! We are transcending duality with the oneness of all that is! We are each working the puzzle of life.

Each of us is reconnecting with the hero inside!

Sending you heroic hugs of joy, xxx

OUR TRUE NATURE IS TO LOVE

"

The essence of who you are is love.
~ Lady Wise

Dear Uncle Jim,

Embrace the best of your life in all things. Love is pure. There are no limits to the love that you can feel for someone or an animal. When you are aware of the multi-dimensional divine spark of creator source that you are, it is not unusual to feel as much love for all people and all things as you have for yourself, because we are all one Family of Light.

Very often when you have an urge to do something and you follow it through with action, a personal healing can take place within you that positions you for the trajectory in which you are going to go 'for your highest good' in your life. Strong feelings can be felt and released when you complete this experience.

Occasionally, without your knowing, the information and awakening that you have, extends to those around you who also can receive a healing from your reaction to letting go of all fears, worries and anxieties. Let love heal your spirit! Seek to go through your day in the spirit of love!

Know that often we do not need forgiveness because there is nothing to forgive! Yet, as a human being we can conjure up and hold in our minds, a situation for which we blame ourselves when there is no need. When we let go of this burden, we have the opportunity to feel a deep peace in our hearts. The peace that can be felt may be life-changing. A weight lifts from your mind and heart. Many life events happen to us and we cannot always understand the reason for them at the time. Now is the time to step up in your maturity and trust in the divine love that is invisibly all around you...for YOU!

When we trust in the higher vibrations in the universe and in ourselves, then we can be content with living in each moment without allowing interference in from thoughts taking us back to past times and events or 'noise' in our mind thinking about what might happen in the future.

Unless we are totally focused on our present moment, we dilute the beauty and wholeness of that moment. We rob ourselves of the beauty of living our lives in love and joy. Life on earth is to be enjoyed! If you want to live your daily life in joy then start to FEEL joy! Start living moment to moment! The creation of every thought and emotion that you ever have determines what you decide to manifest for yourself. Use your imagination to create wonderful new possibilities for yourself. The love of your life is YOU! Let love transform you.

Sending you eternal loving wishes of happiness, balance and well-being! xxx

LETTER 104

QUANTUM COMMUNICATION!

When you drop your breathing into your heart
Your journey to a quantum reality starts!
~ Ludy Wise

Dear Uncle Jim,

The Universe is accessible from within. Our connection with our Higher Self, innate, our Akash, our pineal gland and our soul strengthens with our spiritual self-development. Through this inner-net of communication, we can pull on the Akashic records of what we have achieved in previous lifetimes and also bring forward what we learn from future lifetimes too. How do we pull from future lifetimes? Remember, Uncle Jim, that the 24th pair of chromosomes are quantum. They are not linear. In a quantum state, linear time does not exist. Essentially we can find those creative expressions of what we want by blending the dimensions.

Our wisdom and talent from all of our past, present and future lives are accumulated in our Akashic records for us to access at our request... but only ever from a place of love within! When we have all love within our hearts, all possibilities exist!

"

Feel the love in your heart space
Overflowing with gratitude and grace
This is THE MOST SACRED PLACE
For you to know and love yourself!
~ Lady Wise

Wishing you good lines of communication, two-way connections and sweet dreams! Love always xxx

LETTER 105

THERE ARE NO ACCIDENTS!

"

Enjoy your soul journey and empower the earth
This is your destiny and has been since birth!
~ Lady Wise

Dear Uncle Jim,

Happy 1st March!

There is reason for everything. Don't you just love synchronicity? It underpins many situations, happenings, events and occurrences! What happens this week is meant to happen this week! Do you get it! Welcome home!

When we can wake up every morning and relax with who we are and be joy-filled about the day ahead there is nothing else like it. Human nature is being redefined as we progress through the Shift. We are all one and there is only infinite love!

"
Understand and be peaceful, knowing that there is no more separation
The indigenous knew that the marker of 21 December 2012
was the beginning of unification
~ Lady Wise

Enjoy the now of the NOW!

Love, joy and hugs xxx

LETTER 106

ANIMAL LOVE

"

Your pets return! Your shared compassion and love and part of the soul of the life force of the animal is entwined with YOU! Your souls are intertwined! Ask a quantum physicist!
~ *Kryon*

Dear Uncle Jim,

Kryon's teachings tell us that the animal kingdom has their own system. Unlike human beings, the animals do not have a divine spark linked to the creator source.

The human being is a piece of God that is unique. It is not an animal. Animals have their own kinds of energies even their own soul groups. Animals exist for several reasons – for the balance of Gaia and as friends of human beings. They incarnate within their own soul groups and their own soul groups come back many times as either a similar animal or as other animals, but they never cross the barrier into a soul being.

417

Many of them are not part of a reincarnation process, EXCEPT when a human being has effectively touched an animal's equivalent soul with their heart and has truly loved them, then this acts as a catalyst for that animal to come back again on to planet earth. This holds true for any mammal and bird. It is not restricted to domestic pets.

So now you know, Uncle Jim that not all life force has the system of the human soul. Animals have souls and life force but they do not have human souls. It is not uniform among every animal. There is not a soul for every animal. It has nothing to do with their species. Instead, it has everything to do with the interface that they have with the human soul.

Animals do not reincarnate UNLESS they have interacted with humans. The animals have to be influenced by human consciousness and this enhances them. The animal only sees your soul and does not see your intellect! If an animal has interfaced their soul with a human being then it has done so in compassion and love and they, through us, have reincarnate abilities, under the guise of continuing the love affair. There is no hierarchy of animalism and the animals have no hierarchy on their way to becoming human.

There is no Cave of Creation for the animals. They are here in support of humanity to work with us. Some of them are here to love you and you know that. Remember Sandy the labrador that you had as a pet in Scotland and then Mitsy whom I met when I came to visit you in Manly? How could you forget the unconditional love and affection that they each brought to you and your family? Albeit, I think a few postmen in Manly would have preferred never to have met Mitsy with her mischievous habit of ankle chasing 'perceived intruders'! Ha! Ha!

This is the animal that KNOWS your soul! When you look into these animals' eyes and they look back, they see the Old Soul and yes, they can reincarnate, but they are not in the Cave of Creation. Why is this? Well, they do not have a consciousness that can increase itself by free choice as has every human. We are the only ones who can do that, because each of us has divinity in our DNA gifted to us by the Pleiadians.

Actions are a language all of their own. Actions are a form of communication. When you speak to the animals there is a non-linear thought group communication going on. Love is the greatest non-linear thing of all! You look into the animal's eyes and are giving them pictures which they are receiving! They talk to you too in animal whispers. It is not linear. These whispers to your mind flow through your pineal gland in a multi-dimensional way. They come in a thought group very gently and all at once. This communication with animals is soul communication. You communicate with your Higher Self in a similar, multi-dimensional way in thought groups via your pineal gland. Remember that the pineal is a communication portal that opens for you!

The grief that you have when you lose a beautiful pet often puts you off having another animal, yet if you want it, there is another animal for YOU! There is no time limit to love and compassion. There is an allowance made for the return of your beloved animal that has died. It will not necessarily be the same animal or species, but when you look into their eyes you will know that they are back for YOU!

Some of them will have the same birthmarks and the same quirky habits that you wanted to undo the last time! IT IS PART OF A SOUL REMEMBRANCE and part of the quantum soul that a human being has.

I hope this brings deep comfort to you having felt so lost after the death of your beloved pets. It is disappointing that the average life-span of a domestic pet is so short compared to that of a human being. Knowing that there is a system for your loving and loved pet to return to you with similar characteristics, although they may not be the same type of animal or indeed the same breed of animal, becomes a little easier with which to cope.

Let's also not forget the importance of wild animals. Many wild animals remain under threat of extinction often as a result of criminal human intervention and animal trafficking to fulfil demand.

So trust your instincts, Uncle Jim, and celebrate 'animal love'!

Much love xxx

COLOUR IS COMING!

"

Think of linearity as black and white
And quantum reality filled with colourful light!
~ Lady Wise

Dear Uncle Jim,

Simplicity of communication is the key.

Let me talk about reality with you. Let's talk about science. When we operate from a logical mindset we are only vaguely aware of a multi-dimensional reality.

The highest sciences on our planet have been dealing on the outskirts of multi-dimensional discovery. IT IS NOT NEW! One of the highest minded thinkers was Einstein.

"

In all that he could think, he had trouble with multi-dimensionality – on his death bed he stated that he could not conceive of the forces and the irony is that the scientists

Today we call these forces quantum. When they started to discover multi-dimensionality, they started to look at particles that were obviously different to our reality (they were looking at these in a different dimensionality) and they called these quantum particles. It opened the door for questioning what was there. **Quantum** became a buzzword for multi-dimensional things.

We live in a practical world where the majority of people are still in a black and white duality regarding their vibratory rate of thinking or consciousness. As we venture through the Precession of the Equinoxes, we are being reintroduced to our quantumness. We are remembering that multi-dimensionalism encompasses everything, not merely physics. Physics is simply the study of the way it works. The HUGE deal is that there is reality in so many levels.

Kryon describes consciousness as 'the human being's quantum engine'. The moment you begin to understand about how to work with your consciousness, you trigger every single cell of your body to start shifting into shades of grey. You know this as an Old Soul, Uncle Jim. Having a piece of the creator source, God, spirit within means that you are wise and you are smart.

"

Nikola Tesla discovered the relationship between designer magnetics and the mass of an object. Magnetics is quantum. Gravity is quantum.
~ Kryon

We still have so much to play with and learn and we are making good progress. Kryon explains, however, that until humanity reaches a point of unification, we will not be allowed by the creator source to have certain quantum inventions because they are too easy to weaponise.

I just love the fact that spirituality and science are coming ever closer together as conscious individuals work conscientiously to prove how much science is related to consciousness and the extent to which consciousness impacts on the outcomes of scientific studies in amazing entanglement.

Consciousness changes physics and part of physics is biology. The Masters gave it to us first. They begged us to watch it so that we could learn from them, raise our consciousness level and do what they did? Disappointingly, what did we do? We worshipped them instead of emulating them.

Now getting back to the science of it all, Uncle Jim, quantum energy can be projected through portions of entanglement so there is no distance, if quantum energy has no real time which it does not. Therefore, whether it is healing in minutes or whether it is an information download, those of us who are working on quantum thought (that is, a higher vibrational consciousness) are then the human antennas who will receive it.

When we are attuned to the appropriate frequency, we are able to receive the information appropriate for us to know at this time, for our spiritual development. This is awesome!

Now you know why I have been so passionate about encouraging you to choose to raise your own level of consciousness! I want YOU to share in and enjoy the latest spiritual teachings available too!

If everyone on the planet was developing at the same fast-track pace (available as a one-time opportunity to us at this time of the Shift) then can you imagine the evolutionary burst in humanity that this would create? Quantum inventions would be introduced earlier than otherwise expected. I become so excited at this and yet I am so respectful in honouring every human's freewill to want to learn about the real creation story.

Rock on humanity in exploring shades of grey moving into colour! Ha!

What can you see, Uncle Jim? Is there more to life than meets the eye? Oh, yes, indeed! For those who choose to believe in only what they can see, well that is their free choice, too, but remember, if that was the case then one hundred years ago most people would not have believed in germs because until a microscope was invented, they could not see them!

Dear Uncle Jim, we are facing tumultuous change. Do not despair at what you see because we created it within the change. When you look back over our history, there was every bit the opportunity for us to have destroyed ourselves as a human race and we didn't.

The beauty of freewill is that there will always be some souls who simply think that World War Three has been delayed. They will look at the past and through such short lifetimes, will convince themselves that this is what humans do.

Then, as Kryon teaches us, there are those thinking in shades of grey. There are the ancients, the futurists and the Old Souls, like you and me.

Can you feel so strongly these loving, benevolent energies for you? There is a multi dimensional world filled with energies that knows your name. They have to be invited by you to help you. That is the absolute honouring of free choice.

So how does it feel to have an entourage of energies that stays with you, eats with you, sleeps with you, yet are unable to touch you or hug you until, in belief, you invite them in? I would simply say, "If you are there show me," and you can be filled with love and peace in your heart too, eternal soul!

There is a CELEBRATION on the other side of the veil when you listen to this truth. Don't let anyone ever talk you out of your magnificence! Don't let fear get you today! You are designed to take it, Old Soul, for what you have been through. Feel the truth, feel the love with which these words are written and live boldly in love!

Love, hugs and healing, xxx

IN DIVINE TIME!

"

Even in the most challenging times, when you have patience,
You will be rewarded with all things true and gracious.
~ Lady Wise

Dear Uncle Jim,

There is nothing more beautiful than the simplicity and harmony of a simple heart in tune with the Higher Self. Such simplicity does not come easy because there are so many other distractions in our lives. The other night I woke up and wrote down these lyrics. Hopefully I will have the opportunity to record these with music soon! Enjoy!

Song Lyrics entitled: *In Divine Time*

Remember your power to dream and create
Retain inspiration and hope as you wait
It's too easy to quit and deny your success
Just because you're impatient to achieve your best

In divine time
You'll get a sign
In divine time
Life is sublime!

When you choose to laugh you opt not to cry
The positive energies allow you to fly
All fears are dropped and you love from the heart
It's your free choice to make a fresh start

In divine time
You'll get a sign
In divine time
Life is sublime!

Your heart activator connects with your soul
The inner and the outer matter make you whole
Humanity's evolving to create a world of truth
Where compassion is in fashion and its cool for you to youth

New science proves the answers are a change in DNA
With an extra pair of chromosomes a miracle's at play
We can heal with higher consciousness and never need a pill
That's the strength of human spirit coupled with an iron will

In divine time
You'll get a sign
In divine time
Life is sublime!

With love sublime! xxx

LETTER 109

YOU ARE THE 'SOULUTION'!

To the questions of your life; You are the only answer.
To the problems of your life; You are the only solution.
~ from an Anonymous Loving Friend

Dear Uncle Jim,

Do you like the little play with words in the letter heading?

It is gratifying to find someone who likes you, but it is essential to like yourself. When you learn to love yourself, this is even better. Settling for second best is not an option! Ha! Ha!

Of all the people whom you find and know in your life, you are the only one that you will never leave or lose. Cool!

In essence, in your essence, you are the SOULution to all of your life's questions. There is no-one wiser than you to look after and take care of your needs. You are so unique on this planet that only you know best what is right for you! Enjoy the awakening to your magnificence! You are a very important piece and part of the creator source of all that is and YOU are needed on this planet at this time.

As an old soul, it is vital that you believe you are worthy of respect, admiration and love. Know deep in your heart that despite any hard and challenging times experienced, that you are deserving of joy, abundance and good health.

Let the freedom of your spirit guide you to live your best life and hold the light, as each of us plays our role in the evolution of humanity! There has never been a better or more important time to be alive! Believe it!

"

The most profound inventions and processes on the planet right now are those that totally involve consciousness.
~ Kryon

Wishing you a joy-filled day of happiness, God bless xxx

LETTER 110

COSMIC CONNECTIONS

"
Poetry was the way of communication of
adventures of mankind.
~ Kryon

Dear Uncle Jim,

In keeping with this knowledge I have written anther poem to trigger your own imagination. My poem is entitled:-

Cosmic Connections

I dreamt that planet Earth, Mother Gaia, two hundred thousand years ago was truly a beautiful place.
She was easily reached from other Galaxies and accepting of all 'Extra Terrestrials' and every living species and race.
Prime Creator boldly brought many energies and essences of life into this Universe as a mass project of human evolution.
Yet, certain created warriors were fighting to control this Living Library of free will and reduce it to darkness using a variegated form of DNA pollution.

For eons, a single radio frequency had everyone's DNA restricted,
Shutting off ten strands of an optimum twelve DNA, with only two depicted.
Now it is time to revitalise the higher self and take courage,
For with twelve helixes of DNA in place each "being" will flourish.
Light is information and darkness is lack of light.
The sunlight brings the freedom to evolve with each passing night.
The humanoid aliens tell me this revolution of consciousness must be done together.
What happens on Earth now will change all Universes forever.
I am told to sit up, take notice and have a sense of self worth.
Love is everything. Love is the elixir of life. Perception is everything here on Mother Earth.
The emotion of love is the emotion in which we were created.
Until now we have been confused, distracted from exploring emotion, placated.
"Seek unity in all you do, knowing that to do one's best keeps you true."
I awaken into an infinite field of unimaginable, unlimited possibilities! The physics of LOVE! A magnificent system of LOVE. All LOVE...benevolent help for mankind.
It is the LOVE and the EVOLution of humanity called the Esoteric Era! A quest for every human being to look within and a child of the galaxy to find.

Have you noticed that the word 'love' is secretly reversed in the word evolution?

Forever sending you loving sparkles of eternal light in your heart xxx

LETTER 111

ANOTHER LIFETIME IN LOVE

The perpetual motion of divine incarnation
Is a gracious and true cause for celebration!
~ Lady Wise

Dear Uncle Jim,

As an Old Soul you are here on a quest to learn things. Release the bubble around you and let God in. You are not alone ever! Once you start asking spirit to be around you it is always there. This is the beginning of what you came for, for then the teaching begins. This is not academic or intellectual, it is right at the heart. Every minute of the day each of us is connected to Creator Source and to the benevolent energies. When you walk with God what you will find will be synchronicity that enables you to walk a path that says I love you too. It is part of the energy that you carry with you as an Old Soul.

No matter what the issue is, have peace and know that there is synchronicity in your life. The creator source and the benevolent energies love you enough to take care of you. You don't have to do it yourself. There is beauty in the system. You are in control of your reality. That is what you are here to learn. None of it will happen unless you believe it.

Some are fresh from the hospital bed and have felt the presence to help get them through it. You do not have to do this alone. Timing is everything. Wait for the synchronicity. The love of God will give you a benevolent outcome to everything in your life.

Give credibility to the fact that there are things and people that you have not met yet that are coming down the line. IT IS PERSONAL! Have patience! You are part of the creative source! The fabric of the universe is made of love and compassion and the lesson for humanity is how to use it, take it, create it and show others what it is.

It goes beyond doctrine, rules and knowledge. All the things that you have come for can be synthesised as part of the love of spirit, the love of the creator source. Carry this message in your heart, in your brain, in your intellect and if you don't understand it you can call upon it again because the creator source and all the benevolent energies are always next to you, always.

"

I know who you are, dear angelic being with God inside.
I know who you are.
Time for you to see it, too!
~ Kryon

When the last breath comes and the curtain pulls away you will see their smiles and they see yours and everyone celebrates another lifetime in LOVE.

May your heart be filled with love, xxx

Conclusion

Dear Uncle Jim,

Everything Is Possible

When You

Know Who You Are!

Let new beginnings and creative endeavours abound!

It is your destiny to see how WONDER-FILLED your life can be, when you follow your own sacred path of possibility!

Forever Love and Peace,

xxx

Afterword

At the exact moment that my dearest Uncle Jim died, I could FEEL it. I was seated at my computer and there was an energy surge through the souls of my feet and up through my physical body. Within a few minutes I received a text from his daughter, Coralie, confirming his passing.

Every time we pass over, there is part of our Soul that transfers to those left behind. Sometimes they're our biology, sometimes they're our partners and friends. THE BOND IS LOVE. Part of us transfers in love to those left behind. Their Soul changes as they receive part of US! Those loved-ones whom we have loved and lost, live with us in our Soul. That is a system of LOVE and one part is attributable to SOUL SHARING.

What a system of LOVE! Do you realise that the legacy that you have, the consciousness that you have developed, passes to those you love? It also passes to the planet as well into the consciousness of Gaia (Mother Earth, Pachamama). This is another process of Soul-Sharing.

Several months after Uncle Jim's passing I visited a spiritual medium. Every medium and psychic has their own way of working just as each of us will perform our own work with

our own unique style and flair. This lady asked me with whom I would like to connect. I replied, 'Uncle Jim'. Well, what fun! Apparently there was an entourage of relatives and friends keen to reconnect with me that evening but it was my beloved Mum who brought Uncle Jim through for a 'chat'. His energy explained that he was grateful for everything. After some more private comments, the medium was completely bamboozled as Uncle Jim's essence was encouraging her to pull her beautifully knitted top (complete with holes across the pattern) out and in from her chest as she then asked in bewilderment,"Do the references 'Holey, holey, holey!' mean anything?"I was laughing! Holy, holy, holy indeed!

My focused esoteric writing had done Uncle Jim no harm and at best had prepared his soul for another adventurous lifetime. The major difference would be that in his next lifetime in this new benevolent, loving energy he would come into the planet knowing who he was!

"

Life expectancy is completely and totally controlled
by consciousness.
~ Kryon

The energy was not on the planet and now it is. The part of space we were going into was not right, and now it is.

Miracles of self-creation by the human being occur when the human connects with their 24th pair of chromosomes which are multi-dimensional in their structure. It is the sacredness in a moment that the person says "I want to stay" and the cellular structure changes. The sacredness of you is in charge of you! Your body will react to who you think you are. Who are you?

About The Author

Lady Wise is a heart-centred entrepreneur, life and business strategist, Reiki Master, Chartered Accountant, singer/songwriter, inspirational speaker, poet and author who is passionate about improving the healing and living experience of individuals. It is her dream for every individual to feel that they are fulfilling their potential in life once they choose to recognise, accept and reunite with the divine essence, that divine spark of spirit, which is part of them, resides within and which is also part of all that is in creation.

She inspires and assists human beings on their journey of self-discovery and personal transformation to understand their own life purpose, thereby enabling others to enjoy a self-fulfilled life in a multi-dimensional world of adventure, joy, love and good health. She believes that success is by far the most fulfilling and rewarding fun when you are doing what you love and are co-creating and collaborating with others.

If you have enjoyed reading this book and would like to expand your compassionate, business and esoteric knowledge then Lady Wise would be delighted for you to take a look at the Elegant Oeuvre section to choose your next exciting read.

Elegant Oeuvre

COMPASSIONATE CARE BOOKS

FEEL THE LOVE VOLUME 1
111 TIPS
WHEN VISITING SOMEONE IN HOSPITAL

Want to solve an immediate problem for your friend or loved one who is in hospital and are unsure how to help?

Are you unconsciously increasing the anxiety of your loved-one in hospital?

Would you like to reduce the stress of visiting a vulnerable relative in hospital?

111 tips are broken down into eleven chapters to help reduce stress for both in-patients and visitors, as witnessed through the eyes of a 'carer' with no medical qualifications but a passion for improving your healing experience.

A catalogue record for this book is available from the British Library.

Paperback: ISBN: 978-0-9933513-2-7
EBook: ISBN: 978-0-9933513-0-3

FEEL THE LOVE VOLUME 2
111 TIPS
WHEN CARING FOR SOMEONE AT HOME

Want to solve an immediate problem for your friend or loved one who is still living at home and are unsure how to help?

111 tips are broken down into eleven chapters to help reduce stress for both you and your loved one, as witnessed through the eyes of an unpaid 'carer' with no medical qualifications but a passion for improving the healing and living experience at home.

A catalogue record for this book is available from the British Library.

Paperback: ISBN: 978-0-9933513-3-4
EBook: ISBN: 978-0-9933513-1-0

Lady Wise is keen to extend the 'FEEL THE LOVE' series of books as a source of inspiration to those individuals seeking more hope, love and compassion in their daily lives.

ESOTERIC BOOKS

LOVE IS THE WAY!

Do you act on your gut feeling too? Earlier on 19 May 2018 I had viewed the Royal Wedding of Their Royal Highnesses the Duke and Duchess of Sussex and was so inspired by listening to The Most Reverend Michael Curry's sermon on the power of love that I had the idea to create this book. Know that inspiration can come from anywhere!

I hope to encourage you to connect with the love that is inside of you to become a happier, balanced and calmer person living in harmony and love wherever you are and doing whatever you choose to do. I appreciate that each of us must 'self-motivate' to be empowered. We must each create with total clarity of mind what it is that we want coupled with a sense of deserving, love and graciousness.

We have allowed ourselves over the generations to close off our emotions as human beings and thereby deprive ourselves of the greatest joy on planet earth that one can imagine – the joy of feeling, expressing and giving love!

This is a non-religious book that invites you to enjoy, embrace the truth and be exuberant in creating your own success, abundance and happiness through the joy of 'love power' and expect the unexpected!

A catalogue record for this book is available from the British Library.

Paperback: ISBN: 978-0-9933513-4-1
EBook: ISBN: 978-0-9933513-5-8

GOOD HEALTH
IS THE
NEW WEALTH!

In such challenging times, as we move through the heart of the Changeover Years (2013-2027), we are encouraged to go within ourselves and introspectively better understand who we are. This is the essence to recognising our own roadmap for good health and abundance and empowering ourselves to make the best choices for how we want to thrive.

When we experience a life free from dis-ease, we are able to flourish as creative beings of love. We expect to live each day in harmony with other human beings and with nature that promotes inner peace and well-being. From this state of balance, we are able to live a joy-filled life of compassion, active health and wealth!

A catalogue record for this book is available from the British Library.

Paperback: ISBN: 978-1-8384275-0-4
EBook: ISBN: 978-1-8384275-1-1

POETRY BOOK

POETRY FROM A PLEIADIAN

This 3 in 1 poetry book
Invites you to take a look!
It contains a selection of
111 poems
Divided across three sections:-

Foodie Fun
Miscellany Mixture
Esoteric Truths

Laugh your way to a higher vibration
with this upbeat collection of playful
and insightful verse.
There is nothing more delightful
than laughter and love!

Lady Wise is a heart-centred entrepreneur
and an influential Wayshower
in these Changeover Years.

A catalogue record for this book is available from the British Library.

Paperback: ISBN: 978-0-9933513-6-5
EBook: ISBN: 978-0-9933513-7-2

SET OF E-BOOKS –
FINANCE AND BUSINESS STRATEGY

BLENDED FINANCE
(SERIES OF 6 BOOKS)

This series of business & financial books targets Business Owners and Managers, Entrepreneurs and Directors who have been in business for at least two years, who are keen to accelerate business performance and continue to grow a sustainable company in the new era of compassion!

Volume 1 *"Look After Your Assets!"* gives you greater insight into the potential risks specific to the account balance of fixed assets to which your business may be exposed and what action would be appropriate to anticipate, mitigate and act on risk promptly.

Volume 2 *"How to Manage Your Cash"* explains some of the risk areas associated with the account balance of cash in the balance sheet and sets out examples of controls to minimise these risks. In addition, Lady Wise addresses how to better understand the cash that you have in your business on a daily basis and imparts her knowledge about the importance of cash flow forecasting and how to develop your forecasting skills to determine cash inflows and outflows as a tool for improved future business performance.

Volume 3 *"How Well Do You Know Your Trade Debtors?"* will help you to improve your understanding of the sales cycle and explain how to focus on trade debtors and avoid any potential over-statement of this important debtor account balance in the balance sheet.

Volume 4 "*What Are Your Liabilities?*" explains the importance of evaluating what are your liabilities in your business to provide you with as complete and accurate records as is possible giving you control and knowledge over the account balance of trade creditors or accounts payable to which they are often referred. This guidance will allow you to understand your creditors and know where your money is going in the business to meet various costs incurred.

Volume 5 "*Are You Taking Stock?*" focuses on the account balance of Stock in your business and includes learning about the general potential error types that can arise in managing stock and how to minimise the risk of them in your own business.

Volume 6 "*M POWER!*" evolved from the creation, narration and production of a collection of 45 video vignettes by Lady Wise.

Claim your Mastery and self-emPOWER!

This book addresses key business success factors that will improve your leadership skills as a foundation for accelerated business performance and sustainable business growth in the new era. Sounds like many other business books perhaps? What makes this so special?

What is especially intriguing is that in order to achieve the desired accelerated business performance, Lady Wise explains that the foundation for this joy and success has its grounding and roots immersed and melded first in the personal transformation of oneself!

Notes